DELECTABLE COOKING

CONTENTS

DELECTABLE COOKING

America's Best Hom... ...pes!

CONTENTS

OVER 600 FAMILY–PROVEN RECIPES!

EXCLUSIVELY DISTRIBUTED BY:

P.S.I. & ASSOCIATES, INC.

13322 S.W. 128TH ST.
MIAMI, FL 33186
(305) 255-7959

Address all correspondance to the address above.

© 1994

ISBN# 1-55993-326-7

© MAGAZINE PRINTERS, INC.

28933

Appetizers
APPEALING

DOUBLE SHRIMP MOLD

1 can cream of shrimp soup
1 envelope unflavored gelatin
2 (8-ounce) packages cream cheese, softened
1 cup mayonnaise
1½ tablespoons green onion, chopped
¾ cup celery, finely chopped
2 (6-ounce) cans small deveined shrimp
Dash salt and pepper, to taste

Heat undiluted soup to boiling point. Add gelatin to ½ cup cold water. Add to soup; mix well. Add cream cheese; blend well. Cool slightly. Add remaining ingredients; mix well. Spoon into mold or molds. Refrigerate for several hours. Unmold and serve with assorted crackers. May be frozen.

MUSHROOM TARTS
Makes 60

⅔ cup butter
2½ cups flour
½ teaspoon salt
⅓ cup sour cream
1 egg, slightly beaten

Cut butter into flour and salt. Add sour cream and egg. Cut with pastry blender until well-blended. Using 1 teaspoon dough, press into bottom and side of tart muffin pans. Bake at 400 degrees for 12–15 minutes, or until golden. Remove from tart pan and cool.

Filling:
2 tablespoons chopped green onions
½ pound chopped mushrooms
¼ cup butter
¼ cup flour
½ teaspoon salt
1 cup heavy cream

Sauté mushrooms and onions in butter. Stir in flour and salt. Add cream; stir until thick and smooth. Fill shells; garnish with parsley and serve. Can be frozen. To serve, heat 10 minutes at 400 degrees.

NUTTY WHOLE-GRAIN CRACKERS

1-1/2 cups quick-cooking oats, uncooked
1/2 cup all-purpose flour
1/2 cup whole-wheat flour
1/4 cup wheat germ
1/4 cup ground walnuts or pecans
1 tablespoon sugar
2/3 cup water
1/4 cup vegetable oil
2 teaspoons water, divided
1/4 teaspoon salt, divided

Combine first 6 ingredients in a large bowl; stir well. Add 2/3 cup water and oil, stirring just until dry ingredients are moistened. Divide dough in half. Roll half of dough to a 12x12-inch square on an ungreased baking sheet. Cut into 2-inch squares. Brush dough with 1 teaspoon water; sprinkle evenly with 1/8 teaspoon salt. Repeat procedure with remaining half of dough. Bake at 350 degrees for 25 minutes or until crisp and lightly browned.

Separate crackers; remove from baking sheets and cool on wire racks. Store in an airtight container.

HOT HAMBURGER DIP

1 pound ground beef
½ cup chopped onion
1 (8-ounce) can tomato sauce
¼ cup ketchup
1 (8-ounce) package cream cheese
1 cup grated Parmesan cheese
1 clove garlic, mashed
1 teaspoon oregano
1 tablespoon parsley
1 tablespoon sugar
1 (4-ounce) can mushrooms, chopped
Salt to taste
Pepper to taste

Sauté beef until brown. Add onion and garlic; cook until tender. Add all other ingredients and stir over low heat until cream cheese melts. Pour into Crockpot and keep warm. Serve with corn chips or taco chips.

SPICY STUFFED EGGS
Makes 8

- 6 large eggs, hard-cooked
- 1 green onion, including top, finely chopped
- 1 tablespoon reduced-calorie mayonnaise
- 1 tablespoon minced parsley
- 2 sweet gherkin pickles, finely chopped
- ½ teaspoon prepared mustard
- ⅛ teaspoon salt
- ⅛ teaspoon black pepper
- 8 sprigs parsley (optional)

Cook eggs; peel and halve lengthwise. Place 1 yolk in small bowl; discard remaining yolks. Mash the yolk with a fork, then add 4 of the white halves and mash. Mix in onion, mayonnaise, parsley, pickles, mustard, salt and pepper. Mound the mixture into remaining white halves, dividing it equally. Garnish each half, if desired, with a sprig of parsley. Cover loosely and refrigerate until ready to serve.

BARBECUED MEATBALLS
Makes 80

- 3 pounds ground beef
- 1 (12-ounce) can evaporated milk
- 1 cup oatmeal
- 1 cup cracker crumbs
- 2 eggs
- ½ cup chopped onion
- ½ teaspoon garlic powder
- 2 teaspoons salt
- ½ teaspoon pepper
- 2 teaspoons chili powder
- 2 cups ketchup
- 1 cup brown sugar
- ½ teaspoon liquid smoke
- ½ teaspoon garlic powder

¼ cup chopped onion

Combine beef, milk, oatmeal, crumbs, eggs, ½ cup onion, ½ teaspoon garlic powder, salt, pepper and chili powder (mixture will be soft). Shape into walnut-size balls. Place meatballs in a 13 x 9 x 2-inch baking pan.

To make sauce, combine ketchup, brown sugar, liquid smoke, garlic powder and ¼ cup onion. Pour this over the pan of meatballs. Bake in a 350-degree oven for 40–45 minutes.

To freeze for later use: Line cookie sheets with waxed paper; place meatballs in single layer; freeze until solid. Store frozen meatballs in freezer bags until ready to cook. Place frozen meatballs in baking pan; pour on sauce. Bake at 350 degrees for 1 hour.

PEANUT DEVILED-HAM BALL

- 1 (8-ounce) package cream cheese, softened
- 1 (4½-ounce) can deviled ham
- 2 tablespoons grated onion
- 1 teaspoon horseradish
- ¼ teaspoon liquid hot pepper seasoning
- ¼ teaspoon dry mustard
- ¼ cup chopped, salted peanuts
- 1 tablespoon dried parsley

Combine first 6 ingredients; beat until smooth and well-blended. Chill. Shape into a ball. Roll in peanuts and parsley to coat outside of cheese ball. Chill for 30 minutes before serving. Serve with party rye bread or assorted crackers.

OLD-FASHIONED SODA CRACKERS
Makes 8 dozen

4-1/2 cups all-purpose flour

1/2 teaspoon baking soda
1/2 teaspoon salt
1/2 cup margarine
1-1/2 cups water
Salt

Heat oven to 350 degrees. In large bowl combine flour, baking soda, and salt. Cut in margarine until crumbly. Add water; stir just until mixed. Turn dough onto lightly floured surface; knead until thoroughly mixed (about 3 minutes). Roll out dough, 1/4 at a time, on well-floured surface to 1/8-inch thickness. Cut into 2-inch squares; place 1 inch apart on ungreased cookie sheets. Prick two or three times with fork; sprinkle with salt. Bake for 20-25 minutes or until lightly browned.

BACON-WRAPPED CHESTNUTS

- 2 cans water chestnuts
- ½ cup soy sauce
- 18 slices bacon, cut in half

Marinate water chestnuts in soy sauce for 1 hour. Wrap each chestnut with bacon. Secure with toothpick. Place in pan and bake at 400 degrees for 30 minutes. Drain on paper toweling. Serve.

CHILI POPCORN

- 1 tablespoon margarine, melted
- ⅓ teaspoon chili powder
- ⅛ teaspoon salt
- ⅛ teaspoon garlic powder
- ⅛ teaspoon paprika
- 6 cups popped corn

Combine margarine, chili powder, salt, garlic powder and paprika; drizzle over warm popcorn. (41 calories per 1-cup serving)

PARTY MIX

2 cups Cheerios
2 cups Corn Chex
2 cups Rice Chex
2 cups thin pretzels
1-1/2 cups pecans
1 stick margarine
1 teaspoon salt
1 tablespoon Worcestershire sauce
3/4 teaspoon garlic powder

Heat oven to 250 degrees. Melt margarine; stir in salt, worcestershire, and garlic powder. Mix in cereals and nuts; mix well. Heat in 300-degree oven on cookie sheet about 45 minutes, stirring often, until nuts are brown.

CHOCOLATE PEANUT-BUTTER APPLES
Makes 6-8

6-8 medium-size apples
6-8 wooden skewers
1 cup semisweet chocolate mini chips
1 cup peanut-butter-flavored chips
1 tablespoon vegetable oil

Wash apples and dry thoroughly. Insert wooden skewer into each apple. Set aside. Melt mini chips and peanut-butter chips with oil in top of double boiler or in a heavy 1-1/2-quart saucepan over low heat; stir constantly until smooth. Remove from heat; dip apples in mixture (tilting pan as needed). Twirl to remove excess coating; place apples on waxed-paper-covered cookie sheet. Refrigerate until firm.

QUICK CRUSTY HAM BALLS
Makes 16

1 cup cooked ham, chopped
3/4 cup grated Cheddar cheese
2 tablespoons onion, grated
1 egg
1/4 cup dry cracker crumbs
1/2 cup sweet milk
1 cup cornflakes, crushed
Vegetable oil

Combine first 5 ingredients; mix well. Shape into 1-1/2-inch balls. Dip ham balls into milk; coat with cornflakes. Fry in vegetable oil until crusty and golden.

BUBBLING HOT CRAB WITH BEAN SPROUTS

1 (8-ounce) package cream cheese
6 ounces crab
1 tablespoon milk
2 tablespoons minced onion
2 tablespoons mayonnaise
1 teaspoon salt
Dash pepper
1/3 can bean sprouts, drained
2 tablespoons chopped chives
1/2 cup grated Parmesan cheese
1/3 cup sliced almonds

Mix all together, except cheese and almonds. Bake at 350 degrees for 20-25 minutes. Top with cheese and almonds. Serve with crackers.

CHEESY HASH BROWNS

1 (2-pound) package frozen hash browns, thawed
1 stick butter, melted
2 cups sour cream
2 cups Cheddar cheese, grated
1 can cream of chicken soup
1 cup chopped onions
1 teaspoon salt
1/2 teaspoon pepper
2 cups crushed corn flakes
1/2 stick margarine

Mix and combine all ingredients. Pour into a 13x9-inch dish. Top with 2 cups crushed corn flakes, mixed with 1/2 stick melted margarine. Bake in 350 degree oven 30-40 minutes.

VEGETABLE DIP

1 cup mayonnaise
1/2 teaspoon lemon juice
1/4 teaspoon salt
1/4 teaspoon paprika
1 teaspoon chopped onions
1 teaspoon salad herbs
1 teaspoon garlic salt
1 teaspoon dried chives
1/8 teaspoon curry powder
1/2 teaspoon Worcestershire sauce
1/2 cup sour cream

Mix ingredients together and serve with raw celery, carrots, cauliflower, and broccoli.

RADISH SPREAD

1 (8-ounce) package cream cheese, softened
1/2 cup butter, softened
1/2 teaspoon celery salt
1/8 teaspoon paprika
1/2 teaspoon Worcestershire sauce
1 cup finely chopped radishes
1/4 cup finely chopped green onions

Combine cheese and butter, and mix until thoroughly creamed. Add remaining ingredients and mix. Serve on party rye bread or crackers.

CREAMED ONIONS WITH NUTMEG
Serves 6

24 small white onions
3 tablespoons butter
3 tablespoons flour
1-1/2 cups milk
Salt and pepper to taste
1/4 teaspoon nutmeg
1/4 teaspoon garlic powder
Paprika

Peel onions and steam for about 20 minutes or until tender. Heat butter in saucepan; add flour; stir in milk. Stir constantly until mixture is smooth and thick. Add salt, pepper, nutmeg, and garlic powder. Blend well. Drain onions and pour cream sauce over them. Sprinkle with paprika. Keep in warm oven until ready to serve.

CREAMY CHEESE SPREAD

1/2 cup sour cream
6 ounces processed American
  cheese, cut in cubes
1 (3 ounce) package cream cheese,
  cut in cubes
2 tablespoons chopped onion
2 teaspoons Worcestershire sauce
2 teaspoons chopped dried chives
2 teaspoons parsley flakes
1/4 teaspoon dried minced garlic
1/4 teaspoon cracked black pepper

Put all ingredients in food processor or blender and process until smooth. Chill and serve with pretzels, crackers, chips, and/or raw vegetables.

SAUSAGE-CHEESE BALLS

Makes 75 appetizers

1-1/2 cups biscuit mix
1 pound grated Cheddar cheese
1 pound lean ground pork sausage
  or "hot" ground sausage

Preheat oven to 350 degrees. Combine ingredients until dough sticks together. Roll into 1-1/2 inch balls. Bake about 25 minutes. Drain on paper towels. Serve warm on toothpicks.

Note: Spray baking sheet with no stick coating before putting sausage balls on sheet.

HAM 'N CHEESE SNACKS

1-1/2 cups finely chopped, cooked
  ham
1 (8 ounce) carton plain yogurt
1/4 cup shredded Swiss cheese
1/4 cup finely chopped crackers
2 tablespoons butter or margarine
2 teaspoons caraway seed
6 eggs

Combine first six ingredients. Beat eggs until thick lemon-color. Fold eggs into yogurt mixture; blend well. Pour evenly into 8-inch square pan. Bake in preheated 375 degree oven for 15-17 minutes, until nicely browned. Cut into squares and serve hot.

FRIED CHEESE

4 slices Swiss cheese, cut 3/4 inch
  thick
Salt to taste
1/2 cup flour
1 egg, beaten
2/3 cup bread crumbs
1 cup shortening

Sprinkle cheese with salt. Dip slices first in flour, then in beaten egg, fry quickly in hot shortening until golden brown.

SODA CRACKERS

4 cups flour
3 tablespoons lard or shortening
1/2 teaspoon baking soda
1/8 cake yeast
1 teaspoon sugar
Pinch of salt
1/2 teaspoon malt extract
Water sufficient to make stiff dough

Roll out 1/4 inch thick on lightly floured board. Cut into desired shapes. Brush lightly with milk. Bake on ungreased baking sheet at 425 degrees for 15 to 18 minutes, or until lightly browned.

CROUTONS

Makes 2 cups

4 slices firm bread (stack slices and
  trim off crusts)
Cut bread into 1/2 inch cubes
1-1/2 ounces unsalted butter
1 teaspoon vegetable oil

Melt butter with oil in a heavy pan. Add bread cubes. Although white bread is most traditional for croutons, any good-quality bread will do. Experiment with whole wheat, rye, pumpernickel. Sauté bread cubes, about 2 minutes, turning to brown cubes evenly. Remove croutons with slotted spoon; drain on paper towels. Serve or keep warm in low oven until ready to serve.

CHICKEN HORS D'OEUVRES

Makes 38

1 (3 ounce) package cream cheese,
  softened
1 (5 ounce) can chicken spread
1/3 cup chopped apples
1/4 cup chopped walnuts
5 tablespoons chopped parsley
1/2 teaspoon Worcestershire sauce
Dash of cayenne pepper
Toasted wheat germ

Stir cream cheese in bowl until smooth; blend in remaining ingredients except wheat germ. Chill. Shape into thirty-eight (38) balls; roll in wheat germ. Place on serving platter.

PRETZELS

2 eggs, separated
1/4 cup butter, softened
2 cups flour
Salt & pepper
Milk
Coarse salt

Beat egg whites until stiff, but not dry. Beat egg yolks until lemony. Work (with hands or a spoon) the butter and egg yolks into the flour. Fold in beaten egg whites. Season with salt and pepper. Roll out; slice and shape as desired. Brush pretzels with milk and sprinkle with coarse salt. Bake on cookie sheets in preheated 350 degree oven for about 10 minutes, turning once.

CHEESE DIP
Makes 3-1/2 cups

2 cups sour cream
1-1/2 cups shredded Cheddar
  cheese
1/4 cup sliced pimiento-stuffed
  olives
1/2 teaspoon salt
1/4 teaspoon sage

Blend sour cream with remaining ingredients. Serve chilled. Especially good with saltine crackers!

DIPPETY DOO DIP

1 squeeze tube of hickory smoked
  cheese
1 cup sour cream
1 can bean with bacon soup (undiluted)
2 or 3 minced green onions (use all)

Combine all ingredients and warm over double boiler or in Microwave. Mix well. Serve with tortilla chips.
You can't eat just one!

BLUE CHEESE DIP

3 ounces blue cheese, crumbled
1/2 cup sour cream
1/2 cup mayonnaise
Dash of paprika
Dash of garlic powder
Assorted vegetables, cut in strips

Mix together all ingredients except vegetables and chill 2 hours to blend flavors. Serve with vegetables.

FRUIT DIP
Make 3 cups

2 cups sour cream
1/4 cup drained crushed pineapple
2/3 cup chopped red apples
1/2 teaspoon curry powder
1/2 teaspoon garlic salt
Apple slices for garnish

Blend sour cream with apple, pineapple, curry powder, and garlic salt. Place in bowl and chill. Garnish with sliced apples around outer edge of bowl.
Good with corn chips or shredded wheat wafers.

SNACKIN DIPS FOR CHIPS
Serves 4

1 can (6 1/2 ounce) chunk tuna
1 envelope instant onion soup mix
1 cup dairy sour cream
1 tablespoon prepared horseradish
Parsley for garnish
Potato chips - celery sticks - cherry
  tomatoes

Drain tuna. Combine tuna with soup mix, sour cream, and horseradish. Garnish with parsley. Arrange potato chips, celery sticks, and tomatoes on platter.

RAW VEGETABLE DIP
Yield - 2-1/2 cups

2 cups applesauce
1/2 pint dairy sour cream
2 tablespoons minced onion
1 teaspoon Worcestershire sauce
1/2 teaspoon salt

Slowly cook applesauce abut 5 minutes to evaporate some of the liquid; chill. Combine the applesauce, sour cream, onion, Worcestershire sauce and salt. Mix well. Use as a dip for fresh, raw vegetables of your choice.

FRESH MUSHROOM DIP

1-8 ounce package cream cheese,
  softened
2 tablespoons snipped ripe olives
2 tablespoons snipped parsley
3/4 teaspoon seasoned salt
4 drops bottled hot pepper sauce
1/2 cup sour cream
1/2 pound fresh mushrooms, finely
  chopped

Combine cream cheese and seasonings; fold in sour cream and chill. Stir in mushrooms just before serving.

LOW CAL CLAM DIP
Makes 2 cups

1-8 ounce can minced clams
1-1/2 cups cottage cheese
1/2 teaspoon seasoned salt
2 teaspoons lemon juice
1 teaspoon Worcestershire sauce
1 tablespoon minced green onions
Assorted crisp vegetable dippers

In blender container, combine clams with liquid, cottage cheese seasoned salt, lemon juice, and Worcestershire sauce. Cover and whirl around until smooth. Stir in green onions. Cover and chill at least two hours to blend flavors. Serve with cauliflower, broccoli, and strips of carrots, zucchini, and cucumbers.

CHEESE BALL

8 ounce cream cheese
6 ounce blue cheese, crumbled
6 ounce jar Old English cheese
2 tablespoons mayonnaise
Dash of garlic salt
2 tablespoons finely chopped onion
6 ounce chopped walnuts

Mix all three (3) cheeses together with an electric mixer. Add mayonnaise, garlic salt, onion, and walnuts to cheese mixture. Shape into a ball and wrap with plastic wrap. Refrigerate twenty-four (24) hours before serving. When ready to serve, sprinkle paprika.

7

RYE CRACKERS

2 cups rye flour
2 cups wheat flour
Salt to taste
1/4 teaspoon baking soda
1/2 cup vegetable oil
1 cup (or more) water
1 tablespoon caraway seeds

Mix together. Roll out thinly on floured surface. Cut into desired shapes. Bake on cookie sheets at 275 degrees for about 30 minutes.

DILL CRACKERS

2/3 cup Wesson oil
1 envelope ranch-style dry salad dressing
1 teaspoon dill
1/2 teaspoon lemon pepper
1/4 teaspoon garlic salt
10 ounce package oyster crackers

Mix all together, except crackers. Coat crackers with mixture, tossing until well coated, about 5 or 6 minutes.

NUT BALLS

1 stick butter
1 cup pecans
1 teaspoon vanilla
2 tablespoons sugar
1 cup flour

Mix all ingredients and roll into tiny balls and bake at 250 degrees for one hour. Cool slightly and roll in confectioners' sugar. Roll in sugar again about half-hour later.

TUNA SPREAD

1 can tuna (water packed), drained

1 (8-ounce) package cream cheese, softened
1 small onion, finely chopped
Salt and pepper to taste

Blend all ingredients until smooth. Serve with crackers. This can be rolled into a log and used for all types of festive entertaining.

NUTS, BOLTS AND SCREWS

1 pound pecans
1 large box Cheerios
1 medium box stick pretzels
1 tablespoon Worcestershire sauce
1 box Wheat Chex
2 tablespoons salt
1 tablespoon garlic salt
1 pound oleo or butter
8 8

Melt butter in large roaster. Pour in all cereals, nuts and pretzels and seasonings. set oven at 200 degrees. Stir every 15 minutes for 1 hour.

WHEAT GERM CRUNCHIES
Makes 3-1/2 dozen

1/2 cup all-purpose flour
1/2 teaspoon soda
2 teaspoons baking powder
1/4 teaspoon salt
1 cup brown sugar, firmly packed
1/2 cup shortening
1 egg, beaten
1/2 teaspoon vanilla
1/2 cup coconut
1/2 cup uncooked oatmeal
1 cup wheat germ
1-1/2 cups corn or wheat flakes

Sift flour, soda, baking powder and salt. Cream shortening and sugar. Add egg and vanilla. Add dry ingredients and wheat germ. Mix well. Stir in coconut, oatmeal and cornflakes just enough to mix. Drop by teaspoons on greased cookie sheet or roll into walnut-sized balls with fingers and place on greased cookie

sheet. Bake 15 minutes at 350 degrees.

TAFFY APPLES

1 large can crushed pineapple (save drained juice)
2-1/2 cups miniature marshmallows
1 egg
1 tablespoon flour
12 ounces Cool Whip
3/4 cup cocktail or Spanish peanuts
1-1/2 tablespoons vinegar
1/2 cup sugar
4-6 apples, unpeeled and chopped

Combine drained pineapple and marshmallows; refrigerate overnight. Beat pineapple juice, egg, flour, vinegar and sugar; heat until thick, stirring constantly. Cool and refrigerate overnight, separate from pineapple.

Next day: Mix sauce and Cool Whip; add peanuts, marshmallow mixture and apples; stir. Refrigerate at least 2 hours before serving.

CELERY PINWHEELS

1 medium stalk celery
1 (3-ounce) package cream cheese
2 tablespoons crumbled Roquefort cheese
Mayonnaise
Worcestershire sauce

Clean celery and separate branches. Blend together the softened cream cheese with the Roquefort cheese. Add mayonnaise to make the mixture of spreading consistency and season with a dash of Worcestershire sauce. Fill the branches of celery with cheese mixture. Press branches back into the original form of the stalk. Roll in waxed paper and chill overnight in refrigerator. Just before serving, slice celery crosswise forming pinwheels. Arrange pinwheels on crisp lettuce for serving.

FAVORITE SPOON BREAD

Serves 8

1 1/3 teaspoons sugar
1 1/2 teaspoons salt
1 cup cornmeal, sifted
1 1/3 cups water, boiling (cool 5 minutes)
1/4 cup butter *or* margarine
3 eggs, lightly beaten
1 1/4 cups milk
1 teaspoon baking powder

Preheat oven to 350 degrees. Mix together sugar, salt and cornmeal. Pour water over meal mixture, stirring constantly. Mix in butter; let stand until cooled; add eggs, milk and baking powder, blending well.

Pour into buttered pan (2-quart). Place in shallow pan of hot water. Bake in a 350-degree oven for 35 minutes, or until crusty. Spoon out; serve.

This spoon bread has a light texture, soft center, and crusty top. Most delicious!

NO–KNEAD ROLLS

Makes 2 dozen

1/2 cup scalded milk
3 tablespoons shortening
3 tablespoons sugar
2 teaspoons salt
1/2 cup water
1 cake yeast *or* 1 package active dry yeast
1 egg
3 cups all-purpose flour
Melted shortening

Blend together milk, 3 tablespoons shortening, sugar, and salt. Cool to lukewarm by adding water. Add yeast, and mix well. Add egg. Add flour, gradually, mixing until dough is well-blended. Place in greased bowl. Brush top with melted shortening and allow to rise until light. Knead dough a few times to make smooth ball. Form into desired shapes and bake in 400-degree oven for 15-25 minutes or until golden brown. Easy and very tasty.

POPPY SEED BREAD

1 package Duncan Hines Yellow Cake Mix
1 package toasted coconut instant pudding (Royal brand)
1/4 cup (scant) poppy seeds
4 eggs
1 cup hot water
1/2 cup Crisco oil

Mix well; pour into 2 well-greased loaf pans 9x5-1/2x2 1/2-inches. Bake at 350 degrees for 40-50 minutes. This is a very moist bread!

This is very delicious spread with Philadelphia Cream Cheese, plus makes a nice bread to serve along with fruit salad!

CHOCOLATE FUDGE MUFFINS

1 cup butter or margarine
4 squares semisweet chocolate
1-1/2 cups white sugar
1 cup flour
1/4 teaspoon salt
4 eggs, beaten
1 teaspoon vanilla

In a saucepan over low heat, combine margarine and chocolate. Melt, stirring frequently, so the chocolate does not burn or stick.

In a bowl, combine sugar, flour and salt. Stir in chocolate mixture. Beat eggs, then add them to batter with the vanilla. Stir until eggs are well-blended, but do not beat the mixture. Line muffin tins with paper liners. Fill each one about two-thirds full. Bake at 300 degrees for 30–40 minutes. Check to see if muffins are done by inserting a toothpick in one near the center of the muffin. If the toothpick does not come out clean, bake for another 5 minutes. Let muffins cool 5 minutes before removing them from the pan. These taste much like brownies. Keep any leftovers in a covered container, then rewarm them.

CRANBERRY BANANA NUT BREAD

2 cups flour
3 teaspoons baking powder
1/2 teaspoon salt
1/2 teaspoon cinnamon
1 cup fresh cranberries, ground
1 teaspoon grated orange rind
1 cup mashed very ripe bananas (3 large)
1/2 cup milk
4 tablespoons butter
1 cup sugar
1 egg
1 cup chopped pecans

Sift together flour, baking powder, salt and cinnamon. Blend orange rind with ground cranberries. In 2-quart bowl, blend bananas and milk. Cream butter and sugar together; blend in egg. Sift dry ingredients alternately with banana mixture, stirring until just blended. Stir in cranberry mixture and pecans. Bake in 9x5x3-inch pan at 350 degrees for 1 hour and 15 minutes. Store at least 24 hours before slicing.

BUTTERMILK CORN BREAD

3/4 cup Lysine cornmeal
1 cup white flour
3 tablespoons sugar
1 teaspoon soda
3/4 teaspoon salt
1 cup buttermilk
1 egg, beaten
2 tablespoons melted margarine

Preheat oven to 400 degrees. Stir together cornmeal, flour, sugar and salt. Set aside.

Dissolve soda in buttermilk. Add beaten egg and melted margarine; stir until mixed, then add to dry ingredients and mix well. Turn into greased 9x9-inch pan, or into greased muffin pan. Bake 20 minutes, or until golden and done.

These are delicious and healthful eating.

BRAUNSCHWEIGER BALL

1 (8-ounce) package cream cheese, softened
1 pound braunschweiger, at room temperature
1/4 cup mayonnaise
1/4 teaspoon garlic salt
2 tablespoons dill pickle juice
1/2-3/4 cup chopped dill pickle
1/4 cup (or more) chopped onion
3 drops Tabasco sauce
1 tablespoon Worcestershire sauce
1/2 cup salted peanuts, chopped

Combine half the cream cheese with the remaining ingredients, except peanuts; mix well. Spread in a mold. Chill for several hours. Unmold. Frost with remaining cream cheese. Garnish with chopped peanuts. Snack with assorted crackers or slices of party loaf bread.

DILL WEED DIP

2/3 cup real mayonnaise
2/3 cup sour cream
1 tablespoon dried onion
1 tablespoon dried parsley
2 teaspoons dill weed
1 teaspoon Lawry's seasoning salt
Dash pepper
2 drops Tabasco sauce
1/2 teaspoon Worcestershire sauce
1/2 teaspoon Accent

Mix together and let set at least 2 hours before serving. Fresh vegetables and bread cubes are great to serve with the dip.

SAVORY CHEESE BITES
Makes 7 dozen

1 cup water
1/8 teaspoon salt
4 eggs
1/2 cup butter
1 cup flour
1 cup shredded Swiss cheese

Combine water, butter, and salt in a pan; bring to a boil. Stir until butter melts. Add flour; stir vigorously until mixture leaves sides of pan to form a smooth ball. Remove from heat. Add eggs, one at a time; stir until well-blended. Return to heat and beat mixture until smooth. Remove from heat; stir in cheese. Drop batter by heaping teaspoonfuls onto a greased baking sheet. Bake 400 degrees for 20 minutes, or until puffed and golden brown.

SAUSAGE TEMPTERS IN APPLESAUCE
Makes 4 dozen

1   pound pork sausage
2   cups applesauce
1   ounce cinnamon red candies
2   drops red food coloring

Form sausage in ¾-inch balls. Brown and cook meatballs in a skillet. Turn them so they brown evenly. Place a toothpick in each ball. Heat applesauce, candies and food coloring until candies dissolve. Place sausage balls in sauce, toothpick side up. Serve hot.
Note: A chafing dish would be ideal in which to keep sausages hot while serving.

SALMON LOG

1 (1-pound) can salmon
1 (8-ounce) package cream cheese, softened
1 tablespoon lemon juice
2 tablespoons grated onion
1 teaspoon prepared horseradish
1/4 teaspoon salt
1 teaspoon liquid smoke seasoning
1/2 cup chopped walnuts
3 tablespoons snipped parsley

Drain and flake salmon, removing skin and bones. Combine salmon with the next 6 ingredients; mix well. Chill several hours. Combine walnuts and parsley. Shape salmon mixture into 8x2-inch log, or use a fish mold. Roll in nut mixture. Chill well. Serve with crisp crackers.

CRAB PUFFS

1   cup water
1   stick margarine
1   cup flour
4   eggs

Bring water to boil and add margarine, return to boil. Add flour all at once. Remove from heat and beat in 1 egg at a time. Then add all the following ingredients:

3   scallions, chopped
1   teaspoon dry mustard
1   (6½-ounce) can crabmeat
1   teaspoon Worcestershire sauce
½   cup sharp cheddar cheese, grated

Drop on cookie sheet by spoonfuls. Bake at 400 degrees for 15 minutes. Turn oven down to 350 degrees and bake 10 additional minutes.
These can also be frozen.

HAM BALLS

Makes approximately 48 appetizers

4 cups ground lean ham
1/2 cup finely chopped onion
1/4 teaspoon pepper
2 eggs
1 cup plain bread crumbs

Combine and mix all ingredients. Shape into 1-inch balls. Place in a shallow pan and bake at 400 degrees for 25 minutes.

Sour Cream Gravy:
2 tablespoons shortening
2 tablespoons flour
1/4 teaspoon dill seed
1/4 teaspoon marjoram
1/2 cup water
1 1/2 cups sour cream

Melt shortening; add flour and seasonings. Cook until it bubbles. Add water and sour cream, stirring constantly. Cook until thick. Makes 2 cups sauce.

Serve *Ham Balls* with *Sour Cream Gravy;* provide toothpicks for dipping.

DEVILED TURKEY BONBONS

1 cup cooked, finely chopped turkey
1 cup finely chopped nuts
1 tablespoon chopped onion
2 tablespoons chopped pimiento
1/4 teaspoon salt
Hot pepper sauce to taste
1/4 cup cream of mushroom soup

Combine turkey and 1/2 cup nuts. Add remaining ingredients except remaining nuts; mix well. Shape into small balls and roll in remaining chopped nuts. Chill until serving time.

SIMPLE HORS D'OEUVRES

It's true that these tempting tidbits have a French name, may be very elaborate, and are usually met in hotels, but that's no reason for not serving them simply, in the home, for a little variety.

Try a bit of pink, moist salmon on a piece of rye toast . . . some ripe olives . . . celery, stuffed with cream cheese flavored with mayonnaise, salt and paprika, or filled with a mixture of equal parts cream cheese and Roquefort cheese which has been seasoned with Worcestershire sauce . . . slices of salami. . . . All these are as truly and delightfully "hors d'oeuvres" as the most elaborate arrangement of caviar and egg.

CHEESE SURPRISE APPETIZERS

2 cups grated sharp cheddar cheese
1/2 cup softened butter
1 cup flour
1 small jar green, pimiento-stuffed olives

Mix cheese, butter and flour to form dough. Shape into small balls about 1 inch in diameter. Flatten ball with hands; place one olive in center, wrap dough around it, sealing edges completely. Freeze until just before ready to serve. (These *must* be frozen.)

When ready to serve, place frozen appetizers on baking sheet and immediately place in 375-degree oven. Bake about 10 minutes, or until golden. Cheese will puff up and melt.

ASPARAGUS ROLLS

Makes 20 appetizers

20 slices bread
1 package frozen asparagus
1 5-ounce jar processed pimiento cheese spread

Trim crusts from bread slices; spread each with cheese. Cook asparagus until just tender. Chill. Lay one piece asparagus diagonally across slice of bread. Turn opposite corners over asparagus, overlapping. Press firmly to seal. Wrap several sandwiches together in waxed paper. Place in covered container and chill for several hours.

MEATBALL APPETIZERS

Makes about 8 dozen tiny meatballs and 2 cups sauce

1 1/2 pounds ground beef
2 eggs
1/4 cup milk
1 cup plain bread crumbs
1/4 cup chopped onion
1 1/2 teaspoons chopped parsley
1 1/2 teaspoons salt
1/8 teaspoon pepper
3 tablespoons oil
10-ounce bottle chili sauce
1/2 cup grape jelly
1 tablespoon instant coffee

Combine meat, eggs, milk, crumbs, onion, parsley, salt and pepper and mix well. Shape into tiny meatballs and brown well on all sides in skillet in hot oil. Remove meatballs from pan. Drain excess drippings, leaving just 2-3 tablespoons. Add chili sauce, jelly and instant coffee to pan drippings and simmer, stirring occasionally, until jelly melts (about 4 minutes). Add meatballs and simmer 10 more minutes. Serve on toothpicks.

Meatballs can be browned, refrigerated, then cooked with sauce just before serving.

ANTIPASTO

2 cans tuna fish, undrained
1 can anchovies, undrained
1 small jar stuffed olives, drained
1 small bottle cocktail onions, drained
1 medium can mushrooms, cut up and drained
1 jar sweet pickled cauliflower, drained and cut in small pieces
1 small jar tiny sweet pickles, drained and cut in small pieces
1 No. 2 can green beans, drained
1 cup carrots, cooked crisp, cut in small rings
1 bottle chili sauce
1 bottle catsup

Mix all ingredients. Add a little salad oil if not moist enough. Marinate in refrigerator for at least one day. Eat with crackers. Makes a delicious hors d'oeuvre.

11

CHEESE-COCONUT BALLS
Makes about 30

2 packages (3 ounces each) Roquefort cheese
1 package (4 ounces) shredded cheddar cheese
1 package (8 ounces) cream cheese, softened
1 package (3 1/2 ounces) flaked coconut

Mash cheeses and combine them thoroughly with electric mixer. Chill for at least one hour. Shape into 1-inch balls and roll in coconut. Serve with fresh apple slices.

PINEAPPLE CHICKEN WINGS
Serves 4

12 chicken wings
3 tablespoons butter
1 small onion, sliced
8 1/2-ounce can pineapple chunks, drained, juice reserved
Orange juice
1/4 cup soy sauce
2 tablespoons brown sugar
1 tablespoon vinegar
1 teaspoon ground ginger
1/2 teaspoon salt
1/2 teaspoon ground mace
1/2 teaspoon hot pepper sauce
1/4 teaspoon dry mustard
1 1/2 tablespoons cornstarch

Fold chicken wing tips under to form triangles. Melt butter in large skillet; add wings and onion. Cook until wings are brown on both sides, about 10 minutes. Measure reserved pineapple syrup and add enough orange juice to make 1 1/4 cups liquid. Blend in soy sauce, sugar, vinegar, ginger, salt, mace, hot pepper sauce and mustard. Pour over chicken.

Cover and simmer 30 minutes, or until chicken is tender, basting top pieces once or twice. Remove chicken to hot plate. Add a small amount of water to cornstarch, blending to dissolve. Add slowly to the hot liquid in pan, stirring, and bring to boil to thicken. Return chicken to skillet, along with pineapple chunks.

Serve chicken wings and sauce with steamed rice.

BROILED CHICKEN LIVER ROLL-UPS

2 cans water chestnuts
1 pound chicken livers
1/2 pound bacon (cut each slice into thirds)
1 bottle soy sauce
1/2 cup brown sugar

Drain water chestnuts and slice each into 3 pieces. Wrap each water chestnut with a small piece of chicken liver and bacon piece. Secure with a toothpick and marinate in soy sauce for at least 4 hours.

Just before serving, remove roll-ups from soy sauce and roll each in brown sugar. Place on broiler rack and broil for about 10 minutes, or until crisp. Serve at once.

TASTY CHICKEN BASKETS
Makes 40-50 baskets

Baskets (directions follow)
Filling:
2 cups chopped cooked chicken meat
5 slices bacon, fried and crumbled
3 tablespoons diced, pared apple
1/2 teaspoon salt
1/8 teaspoon pepper
1/4 cup mayonnaise
1/4 cup finely chopped pecans
4-ounce can mushrooms, chopped

Combine and mix all filling ingredients. Cover and refrigerate for 2 hours. Makes 2 1/2 cups filling, enough for 40-50 baskets.
To make Baskets:
Cut 90-100 rounds from regular sliced bread using a 1 1/2-inch round cookie cutter. Spread half the rounds with softened butter.

Cut a small hole from the centers of remaining bread rounds, "doughnut" fashion. Place each "doughnut" atop a buttered round, and fill center with chicken filling, mounding high. Garnish with sprigs of parsley.

ROLLED SANDWICHES
Makes 25-30 sandwiches

1 loaf of bread, sliced into lengthwise slices
Filling:
1/4 pound (1 stick) butter, softened
4 ounces cream cheese
1/4 teaspoon paprika
1/4 teaspoon salt
1 tablespoon mayonnaise
3/4 cup minced nuts, raisins, dates and/or figs

Slice crusts from long pieces of bread. Combine *Filling* ingredients well. Spread on bread slices. Roll up from narrow ends. (Before rolling, strips of sweet pickles or olives may be placed over filling for colorful variations.) Press end of roll firmly and wrap each roll tightly in plastic wrap. Store in refrigerator overnight.

Before serving, slice each roll into 1/4-inch slices. Arrange on serving plate.

Note: Instead of the nuts-and-dried-fruit filling, you can use one of the following: 1 1/2 cups tuna salad, crab, shrimp, salmon, finely chopped raw vegetables, grated cheddar cheese, chicken, turkey or ham filling.

SHRIMP PUFFERS
Makes 60 appetizers

8 tablespoons softened butter or margarine
2 eggs, separated
3 cups shredded sharp cheddar cheese
15 slices white bread (thin-sliced)
60 cooked shrimp, shelled and deveined

Blend butter, cheese and egg yolk until smooth. Beat egg whites until stiff; fold into cheese mixture.

Trim crusts from thinly sliced bread; cut each piece in quarters diagonally. Top each slice with a shrimp and 1 teaspoon of the cheese mixture. Bake in a preheated 350-degree oven on lightly greased cookie sheets for about 15 minutes, or until puffy and golden.

CANAPE PUFFS
Makes about 25 puffs

1/2 cup water
1/4 cup (1/2 stick) butter
1/2 cup flour
2 eggs

Heat water and butter to boiling; reduce heat and stir in flour all at once. Stir about 1 minute until mixture forms ball around spoon. Remove from heat and beat in eggs, one at a time, until mixture is smooth.

Place by rounded teaspoonsful onto ungreased cookie sheets. Bake in a preheated 400-degree oven for about 25 minutes or until golden. Remove and cool on racks.

Slice off tops; remove any doughy insides. Fill with any sandwich filling; chill until serving time.

EGG & HAM HORS D'OEUVRES
Makes 20 appetizers

5 hard-cooked eggs
1 teaspoon minced chives
Salt and paprika
1-2 drops hot pepper sauce
Mayonnaise
1/2 pound boiled ham

Separate yolks and whites of eggs. Force yolks through a sieve; add chives, seasonings and mayonnaise to moisten. Beat to a smooth paste. Chop egg whites and ham together and mix with yolks. Form into 1-inch balls and garnish with additional mayonnaise.

BLUE CHEESE MUSHROOMS

1 pound mushrooms (1-1 1/2 inches in diameter)
1/4 cup green onion slices
2 tablespoons butter or margarine
1 cup (4 ounces) crumbled blue cheese
1 small package (3 ounces) cream cheese, softened

Remove stems from mushrooms; chop stems. Saute stems and green onion in margarine until soft. Combine with cheeses, mixing well. Stuff mixture into mushroom caps. Place on a broiler pan rack and broil for 2-3 minutes or until golden brown. Serve hot.

SWEET AND SOUR MEATBALLS

1 pound lean ground beef
1 envelope dry onion-soup mix
1 egg

Combine beef, soup mix and egg and form into tiny meatballs. Brown in skillet; discard all but 1 tablespoon fat.

Sauce:
8-ounce can tomato sauce
16-ounce can whole-berry cranberry sauce

Combine ingredients for sauce with reserved tablespoon of fat from meat in saucepan. Heat; add meatballs. Cover and simmer for about an hour. Serve with toothpicks.

PEPPERONI BALLS

1 package hot roll mix
1/4 pound mozzarella cheese, cut in cubes
1/4-1/2 lb.pepperoni, thinly sliced

Prepare roll mix according to package directions, but *omitting egg* and using *1 cup water*. Dough does *not* need to rise. Place one cheese cube on one pepperoni slice. Pinch off a piece of dough and shape carefully around cheese and pepperoni, forming a ball. Repeat until all ingredients are used.

Fry in deep hot oil for about 5 minutes, or until golden brown, turning once. Drain on paper towels and serve warm.

BLUE CHEESE BITES
Makes 40 appetizers

1 package (10-count) refrigerated biscuits

1/4 cup margarine
3 tablespoons crumbled blue cheese or grated Parmesan cheese

Cut each biscuit into four pieces. Arrange pieces on two greased 8x1 1/2-inch round baking pans. Melt margarine; add cheese and stir to blend. Drizzle cheese mixture over biscuits. Bake in 400-degree oven for 12-15 minutes.

CHICKEN WINGS

1 pound chicken wings
1/4 pound (1 stick) butter
1/4 teaspoon garlic powder
2 tablespoons parsley
1 cup fine, dry bread crumbs
1/2 cup Parmesan cheese
1 teaspoon salt
1/4 teaspoon pepper

Cut off tips from chicken wings and discard; split remaining portion of wing at joint to form two pieces. Melt butter, mixing in garlic powder. Combine bread crumbs, Parmesan cheese and seasonings. Dip chicken wing portions in seasoned butter, then roll in crumbs. Bake on a greased baking sheet (use one with edges) in a preheated 325-degree oven for about 50 minutes.

These can be frozen and baked later.

DEVILED EGGS

4 hard-cooked eggs
1/3 cup grated Parmesan cheese
1 teaspoon prepared mustard
Pepper
Skim milk
Paprika

Halve the eggs lengthwise; remove yolks and mash. Add the cheese, mustard, few grains pepper, and enough milk to moisten well. Beat until fluffy and refill the egg whites. May want to garnish with paprika for added color. (65 calories per egg half)

13

Beverages

REFRESHING

FRUIT-FLAVORED MILK
Makes 2 quarts

1 envelope powdered fruit drink (any flavor)
1 cup sugar
1 cup water
7 cups milk

Combine powdered drink mix, sugar and water. Stir until dissolved. Add mixture to milk and pour into pitcher to serve.

ORANGE APPLE CIDER

Mix the following ingredients together:
1 gallon apple cider
1 cup sugar
1 small can frozen orange juice, diluted
1 small can frozen lemonade, undiluted

Take out 2 or 3 cups and add:
2 teaspoons whole cloves
2 sticks cinnamon

Bring to a boil for a few seconds; then turn off heat and let sit for a little while. Strain and return to other liquid.

Keep in refrigerator until needed and heat up as desired.

FIRECRACKER PUNCH
Serves 30

4 cups cranberry juice
1½ cups sugar
4 cups pineapple juice
1 tablespoon almond extract
2 quarts ginger ale

Combine first 4 ingredients; stir until sugar is dissolved. Chill. Add ginger ale just before serving.

WEDDING PUNCH
Makes 1 gallon

3 cups sugar
6 cups boiling water
¼ cup green tea leaves
3 cups fresh *or* prepared orange juice
1 cup fresh *or* frozen lemon juice
3 cups pineapple juice
Food coloring (optional)
1½ quarts ginger ale

Combine sugar and 3 cups of boiling water; stir until sugar is dissolved. Boil about 7 minutes; do not stir. Pour remaining boiling water over tea leaves; cover and let steep about 5 minutes. Strain and cool. Combine fruit juices, sugar mixture, tea and food coloring. Add ginger ale and enough ice cubes to keep chilled.

SPICED PEACH PUNCH
Serves 12 (Hot drink)

1 (46 ounce) can peach nectar
1 (20 ounce) can orange juice
1/2 cup brown sugar, firmly packed
3 (3 inch) pieces stick cinnamon, broken
1/2 teaspoon whole cloves
2 tablespoons lime juice

Combine peach nectar, orange juice, and brown sugar in a large saucepan. Tie cinnamon sticks and cloves in a cheesecloth bag and drop into saucepan.

Heat slowly, stirring constantly, until sugar dissolves; simmer 10 minutes. Stir in lime juice; ladle into mugs. You may garnish with cinnamon sticks. Serve warm.

HIGH-CALCIUM BANANA SHAKE
Serves 6

2 cups non-fat milk
1/4 cup non-fat dry milk
1 tablespoon vanilla extract
2 tablespoons fructose
1 banana
1 cup ice cubes

Place all ingredients in a blender and blend until smooth. Serve immediately, preferably in a chilled glass. (90 calories per shake)

CRANBERRY COCKTAIL PUNCH

Serves 30

2 (32 ounce) bottles cranberry juice cocktail, chilled
2 cups orange juice, chilled
1 cup pineapple juice, chilled
1/2 cup sugar
1/2 cup lemon juice, chilled
1 (28 ounce) bottle ginger ale, chilled
1 tray ice cubes
Lemon slices for garnish

In large punch bowl, stir first 5 ingredients until sugar is dissolved. Add remaining ingredients, except lemon slices, which should be added just before serving.

HOT MULLED CIDER

1 quart apple juice
1 quart pineapple juice
2 cinnamon sticks
12 whole cloves

Combine all ingredients and simmer gently for about 5 minutes. Save time by mixing the day before and then heating when ready to serve on the day of the breakfast.

Pour boiling water over tea bags; cover and let stand 4 minutes. Remove tea bags. Add next 4 ingredients, stirring until honey dissolves. Stir over low heat until thoroughly heated. Serve with lemon slices.

HOT TEA PUNCH

½ cup sugar
½ cup water
1 (2-inch) stick cinnamon
1 teaspoon grated lemon rind
1½ teaspoons grated orange rind
¼ cup orange juice
2 tablespoons lemon juice
¼ cup canned pineapple juice
3 cups boiling water
3 tablespoons tea leaves *or* 9 tea bags

In saucepan combine sugar, water, cinnamon, lemon and orange rinds; boil 5 minutes. Remove cinnamon stick. Add orange, lemon and pineapple juice; keep hot. Pour boiling water over tea; steep 5 minutes; strain. Combine with juice. Serve hot, float orange slices with cloves on top.

ORANGE EGGNOG

Serves 2

1 egg
½ cup orange juice
1 tablespoon lemon juice
Crushed ice
2 tablespoons sugar
Dash nutmeg

Dissolve sugar in the fruit juices. Add egg and crushed ice. Shake until egg is thoroughly beaten and foamy. Strain and serve over crushed ice. Put a few grains of nutmeg on top.

CAFE SWISS MOCHA

1/4 cup powdered non-fat dairy creamer or non-fat dry milk
1/4 cup instant coffee
1/3 cup sugar
2 tablespoons cocoa

Shake in jar to mix. Use 1 level tablespoon, to 6 ounces boiling water. Put 1 heaping teaspoon into 1 cup cold water; heat in microwave for 1 minute, 15 seconds; let sit a moment; stir.

ICED TEA A LA MODE

Serves 3

2 cups double-strength cold tea
1 pint vanilla ice cream

Blend tea and ice cream until smooth and pour into a tall glass.

SWEET CHERRY SODA

Serves 2

1/3 cup ruby-red cherry sauce
2 scoops vanilla ice cream
Club soda
2 whole sweet cherries

In a blender container, combine cherry sauce and ice cream. Cover and process until smooth. Pour half of mixture into each of 2 tall glasses. Fill glasses with club soda. Garnish each serving with a whole cherry.

HONEY-SPICED TEA

Makes 1 quart

1 quart boiling water
2 large tea bags
½ cup honey
2 tablespoons lemon juice
¼ teaspoon ground allspice
⅛ teaspoon ground nutmeg
Lemon slices, halved

PEANUT BUTTER SHAKE

Makes 4 cups

2 cups milk
1 pint vanilla ice cream
1/4 cup creamy peanut butter

Combine all ingredients in container of electric blender; process until smooth. Serve at once.

CITRUS ICED TEA A LA MODE
Serves 5

3 cups double-strength cold tea
1/2 cup chilled orange juice
1 pint vanilla ice cream

Blend ingredients until smooth and pour into a tall glass.

PINEAPPLE-ORANGE PUNCH
Makes 5 quarts

½ gallon orange sherbet
1 (46-ounce) can pine-
   apple juice, chilled
1 (33½-ounce) bottle
   ginger ale, chilled
3 cups orange-flavored
   drink, chilled
3 cups lemon-lime
   carbonated beverage,
   chilled

Place sherbet in a large punch bowl; add remaining ingredients and stir well. Chunks of orange sherbet will remain in punch.

HOT CHOCO-MALLOW MIX
Makes 6 cups

4 cups dry non-fat dry milk
1 cup dry non-dairy
   creamer
¾ cup sugar
¾ cup cocoa
1 cup colored, miniature
   marshmallows

Stir together dry non-fat milk, non-dairy creamer, sugar and cocoa in large bowl. Stir in marshmallows.

Spoon mix into glass jar with tight-fitting lid. Use smaller containers, if desired. Attach instruction label: For each serving combine ¼ cup mix and 6 ounces boiling water in mug. Stir and serve.

PACIFIC FRUIT PUNCH

1 large can orange juice
1 large can apricot nectar
1 large can pineapple juice
1 quart ginger ale
1 cup fresh strawberries
1 quart orange sherbet, soften in refrigerator

Combine juices and ginger ale in punchbowl. Add sherbet, strawberries, and ice. Garnish individual glasses with pineapple spears and small umbrellas.

SPICED TEA MIX
Makes ¾ cup

⅔ cup Tang Orange
   Flavored Breakfast
   Beverage Crystals
3 tablespoons instant tea
1 teaspoon nutmeg
1 teaspoon allspice

Combine all ingredients and blend well. Store in tightly covered jar. For 1 serving, combine ½ cup *each*, water and apple juice in saucepan, and bring just to a boil. Pour over 1 well-rounded teaspoon Tea Mix in mug and stir until dissolved. Serve hot or over ice. For 1 quart, combine 2 cups each water and apple juice, and bring just to a boil. Add ⅓ cup mix; stir until dissolved. Serve hot or over ice.

ICED TEA SODA
Serves 8

4 cups double-strength cold tea
1/2 cup light corn syrup
1 pint vanilla ice cream
Carbonated water

Blend tea and corn syrup. Fill a tall glass half-full with mixture. Add a scoop of ice cream, then fill the glass to the top with carbonated water.

LOW-CAL SPICED TEA MIX
Makes 48 servings

1 cup lemon-flavored instant tea, sweetened with NutraSweet
1 tablespoon Tang, sweetened with NutraSweet
1 tablespoon apple pie spice
1 (1 1/2-ounce) package lemonade drink mix, sweetened with NutraSweet

Combine all ingredients in a bowl and mix well. Store mixture in air-tight container. For each serving, place 1 1/4–1 1/2 teaspoons mix in cup. Add 3/4 cup hot water. Stir well. (3 calories per serving)

HOLIDAY PUNCH
Serves 50

3 cups sugar
3 cups water
4 cups cranberry juice
   cocktail
3 cups lemon juice
2 cups orange juice
2 cups unsweetened
   pineapple juice
2 quarts ginger ale

Combine sugar and water in sauce-pan; stir over heat until sugar dissolves. Bring to boiling point; let boil, without stirring, for about 7 minutes. Cool; add fruit juices. When ready to serve pour over ice; add ginger ale. Garnish with sprigs of mint.

SPICED TEA

1 cup instant tea
2 cups Tang
1/3 cup lemonade mix (crystals)
2 tablespoons sugar
1 teaspoon cinnamon
1 teaspoon ground cloves

Mix thoroughly. Keep in airtight container. Use 1 rounded teaspoonful per cup hot water.

SPICED TEA

1-1/2 cups instant tea
1 cup Tang
1 (3-ounce) package lemonade mix
2-1/2 cups sugar
1 teaspoon cloves
2 teaspoons cinnamon

Mix all ingredients. Use 2 teaspoonfuls to one cup hot water.

NEW ENGLAND SWEET CIDER PUNCH

3 oranges
1 lemon
1/4 cup maraschino cherries
1 quart cider

Extract juices from oranges and lemon; add to cider together with cherries. Chill thoroughly before serving.

FRUIT SMASH PUNCH
Makes 1 gallon

2 cups hot water
1 package raspberry gelatin
1 package cherry gelatin
6 cups cold water
1-1/2 cups lime or lemon juice
5 cups fresh or frozen orange juice
1/2 to 1 cup sugar
5 or 6 ripe bananas
1 quart chilled ginger ale

Make gelatin in usual manner; add cold water and fruit juices; stir in sugar. Just before serving, mash or whip bananas until smooth and creamy. Beat into mixture. Add ginger ale, the last minute.

PEACH PICK ME UP
Makes 3-1/2 cups

2 containers (8-ounce each) peach yogurt
6 ounces frozen apple juice concentrate
1/2 teaspoon almond extract
3 ice cubes

Place all ingredients in blender container; cover. Blend on high speed until ice is reduced to small pieces and mixture is well combined. Serve immediately in tall chilled glasses.

CHOCOLATE TOFU NUTRITIONAL SHAKE
Serves 4

3 cups milk
1 cup Silken Tofu, drained
2 bananas, broken into chunks
4 tablespoons instant cocoa mix powder
2 tablespoon honey
1 tablespoon wheat germ

Combine ingredients in blender, 1/2 at a time; whirl until smooth and creamy. Serve cold. Wonderful as a complete protein breakfast drink or for snack any time.

Any fresh fruit in season such as berries, cantaloupe or papaya can be substituted for the chocolate flavor.

Pour into tall glasses, sprinkle with nutmeg.

COFFEE EGGNOG

2 eggs, separated
1/3 cup sugar
1/3 cup instant coffee
Dash salt
1 teaspoon vanilla extract
2 cups milk, chilled
3/4 cup water
1 cup heavy cream, whipped
Shaved unsweetened chocolate

In small bowl, beat egg whites at high speed until soft peaks form. Gradually, beat in sugar until stiff peaks form. In large bowl, beat egg yolks until lemon colored. Gradually beat in coffee, salt, vanilla, milk, and 3/4 cup water. Stir in egg-white mixture and whipped cream; mix well. Serve well chilled, with chocolate shavings sprinkled over each serving.

EGGNOG
Makes 6 large glasses

4 eggs
4 cups milk
4 tablespoons lemon juice
1/2 cup cream
1/8 teaspoon nutmeg
1/8 teaspoon salt
1/3 cup sugar

Beat eggs until thick and lemon colored. Add sugar, salt, nutmeg, and lemon juice; add ice cold milk and cream. Beat with mixer until frothy.

FRIENDSHIP TEA

1 pound 2 ounce jar Tang
3/4 to 1 cup instant tea
2 tablespoons cinnamon
1 pound package dry lemonade
2-1/2 cups sugar

Mix together; store in closed container. To use: add 2 spoonfuls of mixture to one cup of hot water.

ZESTY FRUIT REFRESHER

1 cup cranberry cocktail juice
1 cup prune juice (Welch's)
2 cups apple juice

Mix all the above juices and place in refrigerator. When ready to serve, place 1/2 cup fruit juice mixture into glass tumbler and fill rest of glass with ginger ale.

FRUIT LOW-BALL
Serves 6

1 (10-ounce) package frozen peaches
1/4 cup firmly-packed light brown sugar
1/4 teaspoon cinnamon
1 quart buttermilk
1 medium orange

Thaw peaches. Combine peaches, sugar, and cinnamon in blender. Whirl at medium speed until smooth. Add buttermilk; whirl again.

To serve, pour into six 8-ounce glasses. Slice orange very thin; garnish each glass edge with an orange wheel. Top with dash of cinnamon. Very zesty and refreshing with the buttermilk!

ORANGE-TOMATO COCKTAIL
Serves 6

1-1/2 cups chilled tomato juice
1 cup chilled orange juice
1 tablespoon lemon juice
1/2 teaspoon salt
1 slice onion

Blend all ingredients in blender about 30 seconds or until thoroughly mixed. Add 4 ice cubes, one at a time, and blend until mixed.

PINEAPPLE SLUSH
Makes 3 cups

1 (5-1/4 ounce) can pineapple tidbits, undrained
1 medium banana, chilled
1/4 cup milk
2 cups pineapple sherbet

Combine all ingredients in container of electric blender; process until smooth.

MOCHA
Serves 8-10

2/3 cup instant cocoa mix
1/2 cup instant coffee
8 cups boiling water
Sweetened whipped cream or Cool Whip

Mix cocoa and coffee in pot or pitcher. Pour in boiling water and stir. Serve hot and topped with Cool Whip or whipped cream.

CHOCOLATE-PEANUT-BUTTER MILK SHAKE
Makes 2 cups

2 tablespoons powdered chocolate drink mix
3 tablespoons crunchy peanut butter
1 cup milk, chilled
1 teaspoon honey
Dash cinnamon
Dash nutmeg
8 ice cubes

Place all ingredients in blender. Cover and process until frothy. Pour into vacuum containers.

MELON SHAKE
1 serving

1/2 cup watermelon, cantaloupe or honeydew melon balls
2 large scoops vanilla ice cream (about 1 cup)
1/4 cup milk

Place melon balls in blender. Add ice cream and milk. Cover and blend until smooth. Serve immediately.

LO-CALORIE BANANA MILK SHAKE

6 ounces skimmed milk
1/2 teaspoon vanilla
1 banana, sliced frozen
1/2 teaspoon Sprinkle Sweet or sweetener

Put milk in blender. Add vanilla and frozen banana, a little at a time. If a thicker shake is desired, add ice cubes until desired thickness.

SPICY MILK TEA
Serves 4

6 whole cloves
4 thin slices fresh ginger or 1/2 teaspoon ground ginger
2 cinnamon sticks
4 cups water
4 teaspoons jasmine tea
1 cup milk or half-and-half
Honey
Cardamom, optional
Mint sprigs for garnish

Bring water to boil. Add cinnamon, cloves, and ginger. Cover; simmer 10 minutes. Add tea and steep for a few minutes. Add milk. Bring to boil again. Remove from heat. Strain into a teapot. Serve with a sprinkle of cardamom and a bit of honey. Garnish with mint.

For 1 serving:
Boil 1 cup water. Add 1/2 cinnamon stick, 3 cloves, 2 slices fresh ginger, and 1 teaspoon tea.

EASY PARTY PUNCH

3-ounce package raspberry gelatin
3-ounce package cherry gelatin
3 cups boiling water
5 cups cold water
3 cups pineapple juice
12 ounces frozen orange juice
2 pints pineapple or lemon sherbet

Dissolve gelatins in boiling water; add next 3 ingredients. Stir in one tray ice cubes until melted. Spoon in sherbet. Serve immediately or let stand at room temperature.

GOOD LUCK PUNCH
Makes 1 gallon

1 quart fresh rhubarb
Water to cover
3 cups sugar
2 cups water
Juice of 6 lemons
1 cup pineapple juice
1 quart gingerale

Cut rhubarb into 1-inch pieces; cover with water and cook until soft, about 12-15 minutes. Drain through cheesecloth. Should be about 3 quarts of juice. Dissolve sugar in the 2 cups water and cook 10 minutes to make a syrup.

Combine all juices, except ginger ale, pouring over chunk of ice in punch bowl. Just before serving, add ginger ale.

PARTY PINK PUNCH

1 (46-ounce) can pineapple juice
1 large bottle lemon lime pop
1 small can pink lemonade, frozen
1 can water
2 large bottles strawberry pop
Sugar, if desired
Raspberry sherbet

Mix first six ingredients. Drop spoonfuls of sherbet on top before serving. Delicious!

AUTUMN PUNCH
Makes 7-1/2 quarts

1-1/2 cups honey
3/4 cup lemon juice
6 whole cardamom seeds
3 (3-inch) sticks cinnamon
1 teaspoon whole allspice
2 teaspoons whole cloves
1-1/2 quarts cranberry juice
5 cups apple juice
5 cups apricot nectar
3 quarts ginger ale
Crushed ice

Combine first 6 ingredients in a saucepan; bring to a boil; reduce heat; simmer 10 minutes. Strain and discard spices. Chill. Combine chilled mixture with remaining juices and ginger ale. Serve over ice.

HOT SPICED CIDER

1   gallon apple cider
½   cup brown sugar
2   lemons, sliced
2   oranges, sliced
8   whole cloves, studded into orange/lemon slices (1 clove to a slice)
4   cinnamon sticks

Combine all ingredients in a saucepan. Bring to a boil over medium heat; reduce and simmer for about 10 minutes.

PINK PUNCH
Makes 8 cups

2   (6-ounce) cans frozen pink lemonade
1   (46-ounce) can pineapple juice
1   (46-ounce) can Hawaiian Punch
4   cups ginger ale

Add water to lemonade to make 8 cups. Add other ingredients and mix well. Chill.

SPICY CALIFORNIA PUNCH

4 cups unsweetened grapefruit juice
4 cups orange juice
2 cups honey
1/4 cup lime juice
1 teaspoon allspice
1 teaspoon nutmeg

In a 3-quart container, combine 4 cups each of both grapefruit juice and orange juice, then add honey, lime juice, and spices. Let stand at room temperature for 1 hour to allow flavors to blend. Chill. To serve, pour over ice in a punch bowl or several pitchers.

TROPICAL FRUIT SMOOTHIE
Makes 5 cups

1 (15-ounce) can cream of coconut
1 medium banana
1 (8-ounce) can juice packed crushed pineapple
1 cup orange– juice
1 tablespoon bottled lemon juice
2 cups ice cubes

In blender, combine all ingredients, except ice; blend well. Gradually add ice; blend until smooth. Serve immediately; refrigerate leftovers.

COFFEE COOLER

4 quarts strong coffee, cold
1 cup sugar
2 quarts vanilla ice cream
1 tablespoon vanilla
1 quart whole milk

Combine coffee, milk, and vanilla. Add sugar and stir until dissolved. Chill thoroughly and pour over ice cream that has been spooned into a punch bowl. Serves about 50 small punch cups.

19

Brunch BUFFET

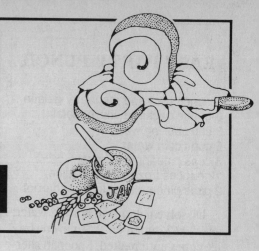

BASIC WAFFLE RECIPE

- 2 cups flour
- 2 teaspoons baking powder
- 1½ teaspoons baking soda
- ⅛ teaspoon salt
- 3 eggs, separated
- 1 tablespoon melted margarine
- 2 cups cold milk

Sift flour, baking powder, baking soda and salt together. Set aside. Separate eggs and beat yolks. Gradually add milk and melted margarine, stirring well. Stir in flour mixture. Beat egg whites until stiff and fold into mixture.

Blueberry Waffles:
- 1 cup blueberries, washed and dried
  Basic Waffle Recipe

Fold blueberries into Basic Waffle Recipe and cook in waffle iron.

Strawberry Waffles:
- 1 cup strawberries, washed and uniformly sliced
  Basic Waffle Recipe

Fold sliced strawberries into Basic Waffle Recipe. Cook.

Hint: Both of these recipes taste extra-special when served with a small amount of whipped cream topping!

Cheese Waffles:
- 1 cup grated cheddar cheese
  Basic Waffle Recipe

Fold the grated cheddar cheese into the Basic Waffle Recipe and cook.

Hint: These enticing waffles can be served with creamed tuna fish, ham, chicken or vegetables!

Corn Waffles:
- 2 cups canned corn, drained
  Basic Waffle Recipe

After preparing the Basic Waffle Recipe, mix in the corn and cook in waffle iron.

Hint: These waffles taste great at a barbecue with butter served beside fried chicken or barbecued beef.

COTTAGE CHEESE WAFFLES

- ½ cup sifted flour
- ½ teaspoon salt
- 4 eggs
- ½ cup milk
- ⅓ cup vegetable oil
- 1 teaspoon vanilla
- 1 cup cottage cheese

Sift flour and salt together. Set aside. Beat eggs, milk, vegetable oil and vanilla together. Add cottage cheese and beat until smooth. Combine with flour. Cook as usual.

GET-UP-AND-GO FRENCH TOAST
Serves 4

- ½ cup creamy peanut butter
- ¼ cup apple butter *or* favorite jelly
- 8 slices white bread
- 1 egg, beaten
- ½ cup milk
- 2 teaspoons sugar
  Dash salt
  Margarine

Make 4 peanut butter and jelly sandwiches. Mix egg, milk, sugar and salt. Melt enough margarine over medium heat to cover bottom of skillet. Dip both sides of sandwiches in egg mixture. Fry until brown on both sides.

CHEDDAR EGG BAKE

- 6 eggs, slightly beaten
- 1 cup shredded cheddar cheese (4 ounces)
- ½ cup milk
- 2 tablespoons margarine, softened
- 1 teaspoon prepared mustard
- ½ teaspoon salt
- ¼ teaspoon pepper

Heat oven to 325 degrees. Mix all ingredients. Pour into an ungreased 8 x 8 x 2-inch pan. Bake 25–30 minutes, or until eggs are set. A simple and delicious way to make eggs!

TOPPINGS

PINEAPPLE SAUCE

2 tablespoons margarine
1½ cups canned crushed pineapple
1 tablespoon brown sugar

Combine all ingredients in a saucepan and cook until heated through. This can be served hot or cold over waffles along with vanilla ice cream.

CREAM CHEESE TOPPING

1 (8-ounce) package cream cheese
¼ cup milk (or less)
1 cup chopped dates

Beat cream cheese and add milk gradually until desired consistency.

BLUEBERRY TOPPING

1½ cups blueberries, washed and drained
¼ cup sugar
1 tablespoon cornstarch
⅓ cup hot water

Combine blueberries and sugar together. Heat water and cornstarch in a saucepan. Add blueberries and heat slightly. Again, this can be served hot or cold.

HAM PANCAKE PIE
Serves 6

2 medium sweet potatoes, peeled and thinly sliced

3 cups diced, cooked ham
3 medium apples, peeled, cored and sliced
½ teaspoon salt
¼ teaspoon pepper
3 tablespoons brown sugar
¼ teaspoon curry powder
⅓ cup apple juice *or* water
1 cup pancake mix
1 cup milk
½ teaspoon dry mustard
2 tablespoons butter, melted

In a 2-quart greased casserole dish, layer half the potatoes, half the ham and half the apples. Combine salt, pepper, brown sugar and curry powder; sprinkle half the mixture over layers in dish. Repeat this process with remaining potatoes, ham, apples and brown sugar mixture. Pour apple juice or water over all. Cover dish and bake at 375 degrees until potatoes are tender, about 40 minutes. Beat together pancake mix, milk, mustard and butter. Remove casserole from oven when potatoes are done; pour pancake batter over top. Bake 20 minutes more, uncovered, or until pancake is puffed and golden.

NIGHT-BEFORE FRENCH TOAST
Serves 4–6

1 loaf French bread, cut into ¾-inch slices
4 tablespoons butter
⅔ cup brown sugar
4 eggs, beaten
2 cups milk
½ teaspoon cinnamon

The night before serving, melt butter and brown sugar in a small pan, stirring. Pour into a 9 x 13-inch baking dish. Lay bread slices on top of brown sugar mix. Combine eggs with milk and cinnamon. Pour over the bread. Cover with plastic wrap and refrigerate overnight. In the morning preheat oven to 350 degrees and uncover baking dish. Bake for 30 minutes. Serve with syrup, honey or chopped blueberries mixed with 2 tablespoons orange juice.

PIMIENTO-CHEESE SOUFFLE

6 tablespoons butter
6 tablespoons flour
⅛ teaspoon dry mustard
Dash cayenne pepper
1½ cups milk
6 large eggs, separated
1½ cups shredded Swiss cheese
1 (4-ounce) jar pimientos, drained and chopped

Heat oven to 350 degrees. Lightly grease a quart soufflé dish. Melt butter in a medium saucepan. Stir in flour, mustard and cayenne. Gradually stir in milk over medium heat until mixture thickens and begins to boil, about 5 minutes. Stir in cheese and pimientos. When cheese is melted, set aside. Beat yolks in a large bowl until light and lemon colored. Stir cheese mixture into beaten yolks. Beat egg whites in a large bowl until soft peaks form.
Gently fold beaten whites into cheese-yolk mixture. Pour mixture into soufflé dish. Bake until golden, puffy and a knife inserted comes out clean, approximately 45 minutes.

PEACH AND COTTAGE CHEESE SALAD
Single serving

2/3 cup cottage cheese
1/8 teaspoon cinnamon
Artificial sweetener to equal 2 teaspoons sugar
1/2 cup cooked, enriched rice
1 medium peach, sliced
1/4 cup skim milk

Combine cottage cheese, cinnamon, and sweetener; mix well. Add rice and peach. Toss lightly until well-mixed. Chill. Just before serving, pour skim milk over mixture.

BREAKFAST BAKED FRENCH TOAST
Serves 4

- 3 eggs
- 1 tablespoon all-purpose flour
- ¼ cup sugar
- ½ teaspoon cinnamon
- ¼ teaspoon allspice
- ¼ teaspoon salt
- ½ teaspoon baking powder
- ½ teaspoon vanilla extract
- 1 cup milk
- 8 (1-inch) slices French bread
- 2 tablespoons butter *or* margarine, melted

Beat eggs; add flour, sugar, cinnamon, allspice, salt, baking powder and vanilla; mix until smooth. Beat in milk; pour into baking dish. Dip bread into mixture; turn over; cover; refrigerate overnight. Before baking turn slices over; melt butter; drizzle over top. Bake at 400 degrees for 10 minutes; turn bread; bake an additional 5 minutes until golden brown. To serve, sprinkle with confectioners' sugar, maple syrup, honey, sour cream, jelly or preserves of your choice. Can be sprinkled with cinnamon-sugar or topped with fruit.

BAKED DOUGHNUTS

- ⅓ cup sugar
- 2 teaspoons nutmeg
- 2 teaspoons salt
- ⅓ cup shortening
- 2 eggs
- 2 cakes yeast
- ¼ cup lukewarm water
- 3¾ cups flour

In saucepan add sugar, nutmeg salt and shortening to milk. Stir until shortening is melted over low heat. Cool to lukewarm; add well-beaten eggs and yeast dissolved in ¼ cup lukewarm water. Add flour and beat briskly. Let rise until double in bulk, or about an hour. Roll to ½-inch thickness and cut with floured cutter.

place on greased pan and brush with melted butter. A cookie sheet is good for this. Let rise about ½ hour, or until about double. Bake at 450 degrees for about 10 minutes. Brush with butter when done, then dust with confectioners' sugar. These are also great with a brown-sugar frosting.

QUICK & EASY PUFFY OMELET

- 2 tablespoons bread crumbs
- 3 eggs
- ⅛ teaspoon pepper
- 4 tablespoons milk
- ½ teaspoon salt
- 3 tablespoons butter

Soak bread crumbs in milk. Separate eggs. Beat yolks until thick and lemon colored. Add crumbs and milk, salt and pepper. Beat egg whites until stiff. Gradually, fold the egg yolk mixture into the whites. Melt butter in the omelet pan or frying pan and allow it to run around the sides of the pan. Pour mixture into the pan and cook slowly for 10 minutes, or until lightly brown underneath. Put pan in a moderate 350-degree oven for 5–10 minutes until it is dry on top. Fold and turn onto a hot platter. Serve at once.

CINNAMON RAISIN BATTER BREAD

- 1 package active dry yeast
- 1-1/2 cups warm water (105-115 degrees)
- 2 tablespoons honey
- 2 tablespoons butter
- 1 teaspoon salt
- 3 cups flour, divided
- 1 tablespoon cinnamon
- 1 cup raisins

In a large bowl, dissolve yeast in warm water. Stir in honey. Add butter, salt, and 2 cups of the flour. Beat with electric mixer on low speed until blended. Beat 1 minute on high speed.

Stir in remaining flour with a wooden spoon. Cover and let rise in a warm place until doubled in size. Punch down by stirring with a heavy spoon. Add cinnamon and raisins. Spoon batter into a loaf pan. Let rise again until batter reaches the top of the pan (not over!). Bake in preheated 350-degree oven for about 40 minutes or until loaf sounds hollow when lightly tapped. Cool on wire rack.

This batter bread is a wonderful treat for breakfast or in the "munchkin's" lunch sack as a peanut-butter-and-jelly sandwich.

THANKSGIVING MORN PUMPKIN COFFEE CAKE
Serves 12

- ½ cup butter
- ¾ cup sugar
- 1¼ teaspoons vanilla extract
- 3 eggs
- 2 cups all-purpose flour
- 1 teaspoon baking powder
- 1 teaspoon baking soda
- ½ cup sour cream
- 1¾ cups solid-pack pumpkin
- 1 egg, lightly beaten
- ⅓ cup sugar
- 1½ teaspoons pumpkin pie spice
- Streusel (recipe follows)

Cream butter, ¾ cup sugar and vanilla; add eggs; beat well. Combine dry ingredients; add to butter mixture alternatly with sour cream. Combine pumpkin, beaten egg, ⅓ cup sugar and pie spice. Spoon half of batter into 13 x 9 x 2-inch baking pan; sprinkle half of streusel mixture over batter; spread remaining pumpkin mixture over streusel; sprinkle remaining streusel over top. Bake at 325 degrees for 50–60 minutes, or until tested done in middle.

Streusel:

- 1 cup brown sugar
- ⅓ cup butter
- 2 teaspoons cinnamon
- 1 cup chopped nuts

SAUSAGE WEDGES

½ pound bulk pork sausage
1 cup (4 ounces) shredded cheddar cheese *or* American
2 tablespoons diced onion
¾ cup milk
4 eggs, beaten
1 teaspoon dried parsley
2 tablespoons butter

Crumble sausage in a 9-inch pie plate. Cover with paper towel and microwave for 3–4 minutes on HIGH. Drain off fat; sprinkle cheese over sausage; stir in onion. In a medium bowl combine milk and eggs; add parsley and butter. Pour over sausage; cover with plastic wrap and microwave 4 minutes on HIGH. Stir; cover and microwave for 6–8 minutes on MEDIUM (50 percent). Let stand, covered, 5 minutes.

BAKED WESTERN OMELET
Serves 4

4 large eggs
1/4 cup water
4 ounces cooked ham, cut into thin strips
1 cup sliced mushrooms
1/2 cup chopped tomato
1/4 cup sliced scallions
1/4 cup chopped green bell pepper
1/8 teaspoon freshly ground pepper

Preheat oven to 375 degrees. Lightly spray a 10-inch glass pie pan with non-stick cooking spray. In medium bowl, with wire whisk, beat eggs with 1/4 cup water until well-blended. Stir in remaining ingredients. With rubber spatula, scrape into prepared pie pan. Bake 20-30 minutes until omelet is set, slightly puffed, and browned. Cut into four servings and serve at once. (141 calories per serving)

BREAKFAST HONEY MUFFINS
Makes 9

1 cup sifted all-purpose flour
2 teaspoons baking powder
½ teaspoon salt
½ cup unsifted whole-wheat flour
½ cup milk
1 egg, well-beaten
½ cup honey
½ cup coarsely chopped, cooked prunes
1 teaspoon grated orange peel
¼ cup salad oil *or* melted shortening

Preheat oven to 400 degrees, and lightly grease 9 (2½-inch) muffin pan cups. In large bowl, sift the all-purpose flour with the baking powder and salt. Stir in whole-wheat flour. Combine milk and rest of ingredients in medium bowl. Add, all at once, to flour mixture, stirring only until mixture is moistened. Spoon into cups; bake 20–25 minutes, or until nicely browned. Serve warm.

FRUIT DELIGHT

Prepare this ahead of time to allow flavors to develop.

1 (20-ounce) can pineapple chunks, juice pack
2 (11-ounce) cans mandarin orange sections, drained
½ to 1 cup seedless grapes, halved
2 kiwis, halved lengthwise and sliced
½ cup orange juice
¼ cup honey
1 tablespoon lemon juice

Drain pineapple; reserve juice. In a large bowl combine pineapple, mandarin oranges, grapes and kiwi. Combine pineapple liquid, orange juice, honey and lemon juice. Pour over fruit. Cover and chill until ready to serve.

HAM GRIDDLE CAKES
Makes 11

1 cup milk
1 cup quick-cooking oats, uncooked
2 tablespoons vegetable oil
2 eggs, beaten
½ cup all-purpose flour
2 tablespoons sugar
2 teaspoons baking powder
1 cup diced, cooked ham
   Maple syrup

Combine milk and oats in a large bowl; let stand 5 minutes. Add oil and eggs, stirring well. Combine flour, sugar and baking powder; add to oat mixture, stirring just until moistened. Stir in ham.

For each pancake, pour about ¼ cup batter onto a hot, lightly greased griddle. Turn pancakes when tops are covered with bubbles and edges look cooked. Serve with maple syrup.

SCRAMBLED EGGS AND SAUSAGE

¼ pound bulk sausage
6 eggs
3 tablespoons milk
½ cup herb-seasoned croutons

Put sausage in a 9-inch pie plate and microwave on HIGH for 2–3 minutes; drain and crumble meat. Beat eggs and milk together. Stir in sausage and microwave on HIGH for 3 minutes; stir twice. Fold croutons into eggs and microwave on HIGH for 1–2 minutes, or until eggs are soft and moist. Do not overcook.

OMELET SUPREME
Serves 3

3 slices bacon, cut into small pieces
2 small potatoes, peeled and sliced
8 fresh spinach leaves, stems removed, sliced into 1/4 inch slices
6 eggs, lightly beaten with fork
1/2 cup yogurt
Salt and pepper to taste

In skillet, heat bacon; add potatoes; fry until bacon is crisp, and potatoes lightly browned. Add spinach; remove mixture to bowl. In shallow bowl, mix eggs, yogurt, salt, and pepper; pour into skillet. Distribute potato mixture evenly over eggs; cook over low heat without stirring. As eggs set on bottom, lift edges; let uncooked mixture run underneath. When omelet is set, fold with fork. Serve immediately.

BROCCOLI OVEN OMELET
Serves 6

9 eggs
1 (10 ounce) package frozen chopped broccoli, thawed and drained
1/3 cup finely chopped onion
1/4 cup grated Parmesan cheese
2 tablespoons milk
1/2 teaspoon salt
1/2 teaspoon dried basil
1/4 teaspoon garlic powder
1 medium tomato, cut into 6 slices
1/4 cup grated Parmesan cheese

Beat eggs with whisk in bowl until light and fluffy. Stir in broccoli, onion, 1/4 cup Parmesan cheese, milk, salt, basil, and garlic powder. Pour into ungreased 11x7x2 inch baking dish. Arrange tomato slices on top. Sprinkle with 1/4 cup Parmesan cheese. Bake uncovered in 325 degree oven until set, 25-30 minutes.

Great for holiday brunch, also as vegetable side dish.

GARDEN MEDLEY
Serves 6

1/4 cup butter or margarine
2 cups cauliflower
1/4 cup chopped onion
2 cups sliced zucchini
1/2 cup halved cherry tomatoes
1/4 teaspoon salt
1/4 teaspoon thyme leaves, crushed
2 tablespoons grated Parmesan cheese, if desired

In large skillet, melt butter. Add cauliflower and onion; sauté 2-3 minutes. Add zucchini; cover and cook over medium heat, stirring occasionally, 3-5 minutes, or until vegetables are crisp-tender. Stir in tomatoes, salt, and thyme; cook 1-2 minutes until thoroughly heated. Spoon into serving dish; sprinkle with Parmesan cheese. (100 calories per serving)

OLD FASHIONED BREAD OMELET

Combine and soak for 10 minutes:
2 cups bread cubes
1 cup milk

Preheat oven to 325 degrees.
Combine in bowl:

5 eggs, beaten
1/2 cup grated cheese
1 cup alfalfa sprouts, chopped
1 small onion, finely chopped
1 tablespoon parsley flakes
1 teaspoon garlic powder
Salt and pepper to taste
Bread and milk mixture

Heat in skillet:
1/4-1/2 cup bacon pieces until done

Pour in egg mixture and cook over medium heat without stirring, about 5 minutes. When browned underneath, place pan in oven for 10 minutes to finish cooking the top. Turn out onto hot platter. Omelet can be folded in half.

QUICHE LORRAINE

1 (9-inch) pie crust
1 tablespoon soft butter
12 bacon slices
4 eggs
2 cups whipping cream
3/4 teaspoon salt
1/8 teaspoon nutmeg
1/4 pound natural Swiss cheese, shredded (1 cup)

Spread crust with soft butter; beat eggs, cream, salt, and nutmeg with wire whisk; stir in cheese and pour egg mixture into crust. Fry bacon until crisp and brown. Drain on paper towels and crumble; sprinkle in pie crust. Bake 15 minutes at 400 degrees; turn oven to 325 degrees and bake 35 minutes. Quiche is done when knife inserted in center comes out clean. Let stand 10 minutes before serving.

QUICK AND EASY BUCKWHEAT PANCAKES

1/2 cup bread crumbs
2-1/2 cups scalded milk
2 cups buckwheat flour
1/2 teaspoon salt
1/2 yeast cake
2 tablespoons molasses
1/4 teaspoon baking soda

Add bread crumbs and salt to scalded milk. Cool. When lukewarm add yeast and stir until yeast is dissolved. Add buckwheat flour and stir until smooth. Put in warm place overnight. In the morning add molasses and soda mixed with a little lukewarm water. Beat smooth. Bake on hot griddle.

These pancakes are delicious and more healthful than the regular kind. Your family will love them!

LUNCHEON TUNA IN TOAST CUPS

2 ribs celery, thinly sliced
1 medium onion, chopped
1 small green pepper, chopped
1 tablespoon vegetable oil
1 package white sauce mix
1 cup American cheese, cut into small cubes
1 (7-ounce) can tuna, drained and flaked
3 tablespoons pimiento, chopped
Toast cups (recipe follows)

In a skillet, cook celery, onion, and green pepper, in vegetable oil until tender. Prepare white sauce as instructed on package. Into the white sauce, stir the celery, onion, green pepper, cheese, tuna, and pimiento; heat until cheese melts and is hot and bubbly. Serve in warm toast cups.

Toast Cups:
Trim crusts from fresh wheat or white bread; spread lightly with soft butter. Press buttered side down into muffin cups. Bake 10-12 minutes in a 350 degree oven or until lightly toasted.

ELEGANT QUICHE LORRAINE

3 eggs, slightly beaten
1 cup light cream
5 slices bacon, crisply cooked and crumbled
3 tablespoons Dijon type mustard
1/4 cup finely minced onion
1 cup grated Swiss cheese
1/4 teaspoon salt
1/8 teaspoon pepper
1 unbaked 9-inch pie shell

Combine all ingredients, except pie shell. Pour into pie shell and bake in a pre-heated 375 degree oven for 35-40 minutes, or until knife inserted in filling comes out clean.

BACON ROLL-UPS
Makes 6 dozen

1/2 cup margarine
3 cups herb-seasoned stuffing mix
2 eggs, beaten
1/4 pound ground beef
1/4 pound hot sausage, crumbled
1 pound sliced bacon, cut slice into thirds

Melt margarine in 1 cup water in saucepan. Remove from heat. Combine with stuffing. Mix in large bowl, mixing well; chill. Add remaining ingredients except bacon, mixing well.

Shape into pecan-shaped balls. Wrap with bacon; secure with toothpicks. In baking dish, bake at 375 degrees for 35 minutes or until bacon is crisp.

CHEESE, HAM 'N OLIVE SWIRLS
Makes 45

1-one pound loaf frozen ready-dough
6 thin slices cooked ham (4 x 7 inches)
4 ounces softened cream cheese
6 tablespoons chopped olives (black or green)

Let frozen dough thaw until pliable. (To thaw dough in the microwave, wrap in plastic wrap and cook on lowest setting for six minutes, rotating occasionally.) On a lightly floured board, roll thawed dough out to a 14-inch square. Cut in half. Cover each half with three slices of meat. Spread each half with two ounces softened cream cheese and sprinkle with 3 tablespoons chopped olives.

Beginning with 14-inch sides, roll each half in jelly-roll fashion. Pinch long edge to seal. Cut rolls into 1/2 inch slices. Place slices on greased baking sheets. Let rise for 30 minutes. Bake in 350 degree oven for 15 minutes or until golden brown. Remove from pan immediately.

ZUCCHINI QUICHE
Serves 8

2 cups zucchini, sliced thin
1 cup onion, sliced
3 tablespoons oil
1 clove garlic, minced
1-1/2 teaspoons salt
4 eggs, beaten
1 cup milk
1 cup heavy cream
1/2 cup mozzarella cheese, grated
10-inch pie crust

Saute zucchini, onion, and garlic in oil. Season with salt. Cover pie crust with this mixture. Combine remaining ingredients and pour into pie shell. Bake in preheated 375 degree oven 30-35 minutes until custard is set. Serve hot.

COCONUT CRUNCH CEREAL
Yields 8 cups

3 cups rolled oats
1-1/2 cups shredded coconut
1/3 cup wheat germ
1 cup toasted, unsalted sunflower kernels
1/3 cup sesame seeds
1/4 cup soy flour
2 teaspoons cinnamon
1/4 cup honey
1/4 cup vegetable oil
1/2 cup water
1 cup almonds, chopped

Mix first seven ingredients. Heat honey and water; pour slowly over cereal. Pour oil over cereal and mix until crumbly. Pour mixture into a heavy, shallow baking pan that has been oiled. Bake in a 325 degree oven for 1-1/2 hours; stirring every 15 minutes. Add chopped almonds and bake for 30 additional minutes. Cereal should be crisp. Turn off the oven; cool. Store cereal mixture in a tightly covered container. Serve plain with fresh fruit or milk.

BACON PUFFED PANCAKES

Makes about 15

2 eggs
3/4 cup sweet milk
2-1/3 cups baking mix (I use Bisquick)
2 tablespoons sugar
1/4 cup oil
8 slices bacon, fried and crumbled

Beat eggs with mixer on high speed for about 5 minutes or until thick and lemon colored. Add remaining ingredients. Pour about 1/4 cup batter onto hot, ungreased griddle or use skillet. Cook as usual, turning once.

Kids love these because they are so light and have the bacon right inside. Awfully good on a cold day or any day!

OATMEAL PANCAKES

2 cups milk
1-1/2 cups quick rolled oats (uncooked)
1 cup sifted flour
2-1/2 teaspoons baking powder
1 teaspoon salt
2 tablespoons sugar
2 eggs, beaten
1/3 cup melted butter or margarine

Pour milk over oats and let stand 5 minutes. Sift together flour, baking powder, salt, and sugar. Add beaten eggs to rolled oats mixture. Add butter. Add sifted dry ingredients; mix quickly and lightly. If not used right away, store in refrigerator and mix again just before using. Keeps for several days in refrigerator.

POTATO PANCAKES

Serves 6

4 large potatoes
1 small onion
1/2 cup milk
1 teaspoon salt

1 egg, beaten
2 tablespoons flour
Fat for frying

Peel and grate potatoes; mix with onion and milk. Mix with salt, egg, and flour. Drop by tablespoonsful into hot fat in skillet. Brown on both sides and serve immediately.

POTATO PANCAKES WITH CHEDDAR

Serves 4

1 egg
1/3 cup milk
1/2 teaspoon salt
3 tablespoons flour
1 small onion, grated or chopped fine
1/2 cup grated Cheddar cheese
4 medium potatoes
Shortening or salad oil for frying
Applesauce

In bowl, beat egg; beat in milk, salt and flour. Add grated or chopped onion and grated cheese. Wash and peel potatoes. Grate directly into egg mixture, working rapidly as grated potatoes tend to darken.

In heavy skillet, heat shortening or salad oil, using enough to coat surface generously. Add potato mixture by tablespoons; cook until brown and crisp on both sides. Serve hot with applesauce.

SOUFFLE PANCAKES

Serves 6

6 egg yolks
1/3 cup pancake mix
1/3 cup sour cream
1/2 teaspoon salt
6 egg whites

Beat egg yolks until thick and lemon colored; fold in pancake mix, sour cream and salt, until well blended. Beat egg whites until stiff but not dry. Carefully fold into yolk mixture. Drop by tablespoonsful onto hot, well greased griddle. Cook until golden brown on both sides.

Serve hot with butter, maple syrup, honey or favorite fruit sauce.

MAPLE PANCAKE SYRUP

Makes 2-1/2 cups

2 cups sugar
2 cups water
1 teaspoon maple flavoring

Combine sugar, water, and maple flavoring in small saucepan. Bring to boil; cook for 5 minutes. Bottle and refrigerate.

CORN FRITTERS

1 to 2 cups corn
1 egg, well beaten
1 teaspoon sugar
1/2 teaspoon salt
1 tablespoon butter, melted
2 teaspoons baking powder
1 cup flour
2/3 cup milk

Mix thoroughly. Drop spoonfuls of batter into fat in hot frying pan. Brown both sides.

BUFFET RYE SLICES

1 cup Swiss cheese, grated
1/4 cup bacon, cooked and crumbled
1/4 cup mayonnaise
1 teaspoon Worcestershire sauce
1/4 cup green onions, chopped
1/2 cup chopped ripe olives

Mix all ingredients and spread on party rye slices. Bake in 375 degree oven for 8-10 minutes; serve warm.

BREAKFAST EGG DISH

Serves 6

8 slices bread
1/2 cup melted butter
1 cup grated Cheddar cheese
Bacon or ham bits
Chopped green pepper
Sliced mushrooms, optional
2 cups milk
1/4 teaspoon salt
1/8 teaspoon pepper

Cut crust off the slices of bread and cube bread. Put in a 9x13 inch buttered pan. Pour the melted butter over the bread cubes; sprinkle on bacon bits, green pepper, and mushrooms.

Separate the eggs. Beat the yolks with the milk, salt, and pepper; pour over ingredients in the pan. Beat egg whites until stiff. Seal above mixture with egg whites. Cover and keep in the refrigerator overnight.

Bake at 325 degrees for 40-45 minutes.

EGG 'N' CHIPS

Serves 6

6 hard-boiled eggs, chopped
2 tablespoons chopped green pepper
1/2 teaspoon salt
2/3 cup mayonnaise or salad dressing
1-1/2 cups diced celery
3/4 cup coarsely chopped walnuts
1 teaspoon minced onion
1/4 teaspoon pepper
1 cup grated Cheddar cheese
1 cup crushed potato chips

Combine eggs, celery, walnuts, green pepper, onion, salt, pepper and salad dressing or mayonnaise. Toss lightly, but thoroughly, so ingredients are evenly moistened. Use additional salad dressing if needed. Place in a greased 1-1/2 - quart baking dish. Sprinkle with cheese and top with crushed chips. Bake at 375 degrees for about 25 minutes or until thoroughly heated and cheese has melted.

FOOLPROOF SCRAMBLED EGGS

Serves 3-4

6 eggs
1/3 cup light cream
3/4 teaspoon salt
1/8 teaspoon pepper
1/2 teaspoon Worcestershire sauce

Beat eggs; beat in cream and seasonings. Cook in upper part of double boiler, over hot water, until just set, stirring often. Serve at once with toast.

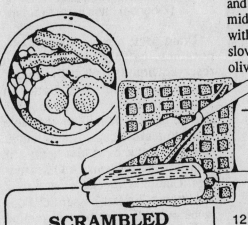

SCRAMBLED BAGEL ROYALE

Serves 2

2 bagels
1-1/2 tablespoons butter
  or margarine
4 eggs
2 tablespoons milk
3 tablespoons chopped onion
1/4 cup lox pieces or smoked salmon
2 ounces cream cheese
2 slices tomato garnish

Slice bagels in half horizontally. Lightly spread with one tablespoon of butter or margarine; toast lightly. Over medium high heat, saute chopped onion in remaining half tablespoon of butter or margarine until translucent. Beat eggs with milk; add to onions. Stir eggs. When eggs are almost set, add lox pieces and cream cheese that has been cut into small chunks; scramble in pan until cheese begins to melt.

Spoon mixture over bagels. Garnish with tomato slices.

TOLEDO HAM AND EGGS

Serves 6

1 cup chopped, cooked ham
1 tablespoon olive oil
2 cups cooked peas
2 canned pimentos, chopped
1/4 cup chopped green olives
Salt and pepper, if desired
6 eggs
2 tablespoons olive oil

Saute ham in olive oil for 2-3 minutes. Combine with peas, pimento, and olives. Heat well; add salt and pepper if desired. Put in the middle of a hot platter and surround with the eggs, which have been slowly cooked in the 2 tablespoons of olive oil.

TUNA STUFFED EGGS

Makes 24 halves

12 eggs
6 slices bacon
1 - 3-1/4 to 3-1/2 - ounce can tuna, drained and finely flaked
3/4 cup mayonnaise
1 tablespoon lemon juice
1/2 teaspoon hot pepper sauce
1/2 teaspoon salt

In 4-quart saucepan, place eggs and enough water to come one inch above tops of eggs over high heat; heat to boiling. Remove saucepan from heat; cover tightly and let eggs stand in hot water 15 minutes; drain.

Meanwhile, in 10-inch skillet, cook bacon until browned, remove to paper towel to drain. Crumble bacon, set aside.

Peel and slice eggs lengthwise in half. Remove yolks and place in medium bowl. With fork, finely mash yolks. Stir in tuna, mayonnaise, lemon juice, hot pepper sauce and salt until smooth. Pile egg yolk mixture into egg whites center. Sprinkle with bacon. Cover and refrigerate.

Casseroles
CREATIVE

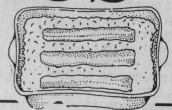

AMISH-STYLE YUM-A-SETTA
Serves 6–8

2 pounds hamburger
Salt and pepper to taste
2 tablespoons brown sugar
¼ cup chopped onion
1 (10¾-ounce) can tomato soup, undiluted
1 (10¾-ounce) can chicken soup, undiluted
1 (16-ounce) package egg noodles
1 (8-ounce) package processed cheese, such as Kraft or Velveeta

Brown hamburger with salt, pepper, brown sugar and onion. Add tomato soup. Cook egg noodles according to package; drain. Add cream of chicken soup. Layer hamburger mixture and noodle mixture in 9 x 12-inch casserole with processed cheese between layers. Bake at 350 degrees for 30 minutes.

TUNA BAKE
Serves 6–8

1 (1-pound, 1-ounce) can green peas
1½ cups diced potatoes
1 cup diced carrots
½ cup chopped onion
4 tablespoons butter
4 tablespoons flour
Milk
1 teaspoon salt
⅛ teaspoon pepper
2 teaspoons soy sauce
2 (7-ounce) cans tuna, drained

Drain peas; reserve liquid. Cook potatoes, carrots and onions in reserved liquid for 8–10 minutes. Drain; save liquid. Melt butter in saucepan; stir in flour to make a smooth paste. Add milk to vegetable liquid to make 2 cups. Add to butter mixture. Cook over low heat; stir until mixture thickens. Add seasonings. Combine vegetables and tuna in buttered 2-quart casserole. Pour sauce over all (may be refrigerated overnight). To serve, bake covered in 325-degree oven for 1 hour.

HAM & RICE CASSEROLE
Serves 6

2 cups Spam, cut up in small squares
3 cups cooked rice *or* 2 cups uncooked rice
1 cup peas, drained
1 teaspoon salt
1 teaspoon prepared mustard
¼ teaspoon pepper
1 cup grated cheddar cheese
1 (10-ounce) can cheddar cheese soup, undiluted
¼ cup milk

Preheat oven to 350 degrees. Grease a 3-quart casserole. Combine ham, rice, peas, salt, mustard, pepper, ½ cup cheddar cheese, cheddar cheese soup and milk. Turn into casserole. Top with remaining ½ cup cheese. Bake 30 minutes, until bubbly. If chilled before baking, bake 1 hour.

ROMAN RICE

1 (2¼-ounce) can sliced black olives, drained
1 (11-ounce) can Green Giant Delicorn, drained
1 (15-ounce) can red kidney beans, drained
6 slices bacon strips
1 cup uncooked regular rice
1 small onion, chopped
1 teaspoon salt
⅛ teaspoon pepper
1½ cups water
½ cup chicken broth
¼ cup ketchup
Dash minced garlic
1 (16-ounce) can tomatoes, undrained and cut up
½ cup mozzarella cheese, shredded
½ cup Monterey Jack cheese, shredded
¼ cup mixture Parmesan and Romano cheese, grated
1 tablespoon sugar

Fry bacon, saving 2 tablespoons of drippings. Cook rice and onion in it until onion is tender. Add drained Delicorn, beans, olives, seasonings and tomatoes. Stir well. Add grated cheese mixture, ketchup, water and broth. Cover and simmer for 30–45 minutes. Sprinkle shredded cheeses on top.

RANCHO SAUSAGE SUPPER
Serves 6

1 pound pork sausage
1 cup chopped onions
1 green pepper, chopped
2 cups stewed tomatoes
2 cups dairy sour cream
1 cup uncooked elbow
  macaroni
1 teaspoon chili powder
1 teaspoon salt
1 tablespoon sugar

In a large skillet fry sausage until pink color disappears. Drain. Add onions and green pepper; cook slowly for 5 minutes. Stir in tomatoes, sour cream, macaroni, chili powder, salt and sugar. Cover. Simmer 30 minutes, stirring frequently, until macaroni is done. Serve hot.

Serve with a green salad and hard rolls.

FAMILY GOULASH
Serves 4

4 ounces noodles
1 pound ground beef
1 medium onion, chopped
2 cups sliced celery
½ cup ketchup
1 (2½-ounce) jar sliced
  mushrooms
1 (14½-ounce) can tomatoes
1 teaspoon salt

Cook noodles as directed on package. While noodles cook, cook and stir ground beef and onion in large skillet until meat is brown and onion tender. Drain off fat. Stir in drained noodles, celery, ketchup, mushrooms (with liquid), tomatoes and salt. Cover; simmer 30–45 minutes.

MARDI GRAS MAGIC
Serves 6

1 pound red beans
1 pound smoked sausage, cut into
  bite-size pieces (kielbasa is fine)
1-2 stalks celery, chopped
1 onion, chopped
1 garlic clove, crushed
1 teaspoon sugar
1 teaspoon salt
1 bay leaf
8-10 cups water
1-1/2 cups uncooked rice (white,
  wild,or brown rice)

Rinse beans. In a large pot combine beans, sausage, celery, onion, garlic, sugar, salt, bay leaf, and 8-10 cups water. Bring to boil and stir frequently so mixture does not stick.

Reduce heat to low and cook, covered, until beans are tender, 1-1/2-2 hours. Add uncooked rice and cook until tender, about 15-20 minutes.

HEARTY CASSEROLE
Serves 6–8

1 (11-ounce) can cheddar cheese
  soup
1 (1-pound) can julienne carrots,
  drained (reserve 1/3 cup liquid)
3/4 teaspoon crushed rosemary
1/4 teaspoon pepper
1 (9-1/4-ounce) can tuna, drained
  and flaked
1 (15-ounce) can macaroni and
  cheese
1/4 cup minced parsley
1 (3-1/2-ounce) can french-fried
  onion rings

Heat oven to 375 degrees. Mix soup with reserved liquid from carrots. Stir in rosemary and pepper. Spread tuna in oblong baking dish, 11-1/2 x 7-1/2 x 1-1/2-inch. Layer with macaroni and cheese, carrots and parsley. Pour cheese soup mixture over layers. Bake, uncovered, for 30–35 minutes, or until bubbly. Top with onion rings and bake 5 minutes longer.

DRIED BEEF CASSEROLE
Serves 4–6

1 cup uncooked elbow
  macaroni
1 (10½-ounce) can condensed
  cream of mushroom soup
½ cup milk
1 cup shredded cheddar
  cheese
3 tablespoons finely chopped
  onion
¼ pound dried beef, cut into
  bite-size pieces
2 hard-cooked eggs, sliced

Heat oven to 350 degrees. Cook macaroni according to package directions. Blend soup and milk. Stir in cheese, onion, drained macaroni and dried beef; fold in eggs. Pour into an ungreased 1½-quart casserole. Cover; bake 30 minutes, or until heated through.

MEXICAN DINNER PRONTO
Serves 4

2 tablespoons vegetable oil
1 onion, chopped
1 (15-ounce) can tamales in
  chili gravy
1 (15-ounce) can chili without
  beans
1 (15-ounce) can chili with
  beans
¼ teaspoon oregano
½ cup Monterey Jack cheese,
  shredded

In a skillet heat oil; sauté onion until tender; transfer to ovenproof baking dish. Unwrap tamales; arrange ½ over onions. Add the 2 cans of chili; sprinkle with oregano; top with remaining tamales. Bake at 350 degrees for 30 minutes, or until bubbling hot. Remove from oven; sprinkle with cheese; bake 15 minutes longer, or until cheese has melted.

PORK CHOW MEIN
Serves 6

1 pound pork steak
3 tablespoons cooking oil
1 cup sliced onion
1 cup sliced celery
1 (8-ounce) can mushrooms
1 (8-ounce) can water
  chestnuts, drained and sliced
1 (13¾-ounce) can
  chicken broth
¼ cup soy sauce
1 (16-ounce) can chop suey
  vegetables, undrained
5–6 tablespoons cornstarch
1 chicken bouillon cube
  Hot cooked rice

Boil celery and onion in ½ cup water. Add 1 chicken bouillon cube. Cook until tender. Set aside. Slice partially frozen pork in thin, bite-size slices, across the grain. Preheat a large skillet or wok. Add cooking oil. Stir-fry pork for 2–3 minutes. Add bouillon mixture, mushrooms, water chestnuts, chicken broth, soy sauce and chop suey vegetables. Cook to a boil. Add cornstarch. Stir after each tablespoon of cornstarch. Serve over rice. Enjoy!! It is my favorite!.

ONION LOVERS' CASSEROLE
Serves 4–6

1 pound ground beef
3 large onions, sliced
1 large green pepper, chopped
1 (1-pound) can tomatoes
½ cup uncooked regular rice
1 teaspoon chili powder
1 teaspoon salt

Heat oven to 350 degrees. In large skillet, cook and stir ground beef until light brown; drain off fat. Add onions and green pepper; cook and stir until onion is tender. Stir in tomatoes, rice, chili powder and salt. Pour into an ungreased 2-quart casserole. Cover; bake 1 hour.

MACARONI HOT DISH
Serves 6

2 cups warm, cooked macaroni
1-1/2 cups grated cheese
1-1/2 cups bread crumbs
1 green pepper, diced
3 eggs, beaten
1 onion, diced
2 tablespoons margarine, melted
Pepper and salt to taste
1-1/2 cups milk
1 can mushroom soup

Mix all ingredients, except mushroom soup, and place in pan set in hot water. Bake at 350 degrees for 45 minutes. Cut in squares and then pour over undiluted mushroom soup which has been heated.

NO-FUSS SHORTCUT PAELLA
Serves 6

2 cups cooked chicken, cut into 1-inch pieces
1-1/2 cups chicken broth
10 ounces shrimp, shelled
1 (8-1/2-ounce) can peas, drained
2 cups rice
1 (3-ounce) can mushrooms, sliced and drained
1 envelope onion soup mix
1 teaspoon paprika

Combine chicken, chicken broth, shrimp, peas, rice, mushrooms, onion soup mix and paprika. Pour into 3-quart casserole; bake at 350 degrees, covered, for 1-1/4 hours until rice is tender.

CHICKEN-IN-A-SHELL
Serves 6

6 baking potatoes
2 tablespoons butter or margarine
1 (10-3/4 ounce) can cream of chicken soup
1 cup Parmesan cheese, grated
3 tablespoons fresh parsley, chopped
1-1/2 cups cooked chicken, cubed

Bake potatoes until done; cut potatoes in half lengthwise; scoop out insides and reserve, leaving a thin shell. Mash potatoes with butter; add 1/2 cup cheese and remaining ingredients. Spoon into potato shells; sprinkle with remaining cheese. Arrange potatoes in shallow 3-quart baking dish. Bake 375 degrees for 15 minutes.

CHEESEBURGER PIE

1 package crescent rolls
1 pound hamburger
1/2 small onion, chopped
1/2 teaspoon oregano
1/4 teaspoon basil
Salt and pepper to taste
1 (6-ounce) can tomato paste
1 (8-ounce) package Mozzarella cheese

Press crescent rolls into pie crust for 9-inch pan. Brown hamburger, onion, oregano, basil, salt, and pepper to taste. Drain. Add tomato paste; pour into pie shell. Top with cheese. Bake at 425 degrees for 15-20 minutes.

BAKED CHICKEN WITH ORANGE SOY SAUCE
Serves 4

1 (2-1/2 pound) chicken, cut up (skin removed)
2 tablespoons soy sauce
1/4 teaspoon salt
1/2 teaspoon celery seed
1/2 teaspoon garlic powder
1/4 teaspoon ground ginger
2/3 cup orange juice

Preheat oven to 400 degrees. Place chicken in 13x9-inch baking pan in a single layer. Top with soy sauce, salt, celery seed, garlic powder, and ginger. Pour orange juice over chicken. Bake 40-45 minutes, until juices run clear when chicken is pierced with a fork. (220 calories per serving)

GRITS CASSEROLE
Serves 10-12

1 pound sausage
1/2 cup chopped green peppers
1 cup chopped onion
1 cup chopped celery
1 cup grits, uncooked
4 cups water
1 teaspoon salt
1 can cream of chicken soup
1 cup grated cheese

Preheat oven to 375 degrees. Brown sausage. Add peppers, onion, celery, and sauté. Cook grits in 4 cups water with 1 teaspoon salt. Combine cooked grits with sausage, peppers, onion, and celery. Pour mixture into 2-quart buttered casserole. Spread soup on top and sprinkle with cheese. Bake 30 minutes.

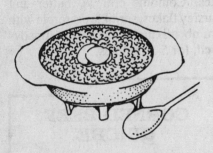

BEEF-ONION RING CASSEROLE
Serves 4–6

1-1/2–2 pounds ground chuck
Salt and pepper
1 can condensed cheddar cheese
    soup
1 can condensed cream of mush-
    room soup
1 package frozen Tater Tots
1 package frozen onion rings

Press raw meat into bottom of casserole; season with salt and pep-per. Combine the 2 soups and spread half over meat. Add Tater Tots. Pour rest of soup over Tater Tots. Top with onion rings. If canned onion rings are used, stir them into last half of soup mixture. Bake at 350 degrees for 1–1-1/2 hours.

JIFFY MINESTRONE
Serves 8

4   cups coarsely chopped
    cabbage (½ medium-
    size head)
1   medium onion, coarsely
    chopped
¼   cup parsley, chopped
1   clove garlic, chopped
1   teaspoon salt
1   teaspoon oregano
¼   teaspoon pepper
3   tablespoons oil
5   cups beef broth
1   (16-ounce) can toma-
    toes *or* 2 cups chopped
    fresh
¼   pound spaghetti, broken
    up
1   medium zucchini, sliced
1   (16-ounce) can red
    kidney beans

In Dutch oven, over medium heat, sauté cabbage, onion, parsley, garlic ,salt, oregano and pepper in oil, stir-ring often, 5 minutes, or until cabbage is crisp-tender. Add broth and toma-toes; bring to boil. Stir in spaghetti, zucchini and beans. Cook, stirring oc-casionally, for 10 minutes, or until spaghetti is of desired doneness. (200 calories per serving)

ZUCCHINI AND CHICKEN SKILLET

2   medium zucchini, sliced
2   tablespoons shortening
½   cup tomatoes, drained
2   pounds chicken
1   can cream of celery
    soup
1   teaspoon paprika
1   teaspoon basil
    Salt and pepper to taste

In skillet brown chicken in shorten-ing. Pour off excess fat. Add soup, tomatoes and seasonings. Cover. Cook on low heat for 30 minutes. Add zuc-chini. Cook about 15 minutes longer.

SMOKED SAUSAGE AND SAUERKRAUT
Serves 4

1 pound smoked sausage
1 can sauerkraut
1 tablespoon cooking oil
1/2 pint water
1 potato, grated
1 carrot, grated
Pinch salt
1/3 cup sugar
2 onions, chopped

Heat oil in skillet and fry chopped onions; add sauerkraut and simmer for 2 minutes. Add water and sau-sage; cook until done. Add grated potato, salt, sugar, and grated carrot. Cook 4-5 additional minutes.

PIZZA RICE PIE
Serves 4-5

2-2/3 cups cooked rice
1/3 cup minced onion
2 eggs, beaten
2 tablespoons melted butter or
   margarine
1 (8-ounce) can tomato sauce with
   cheese
1/4 teaspoon oregano
1/4 teaspoon basil
1 cup shredded mozzarella cheese
1 (4-1/2-ounce) package sliced
   pepperoni or salami
1/2 cup sliced stuffed olives

Mix together rice, onion, eggs, and melted butter. Line a 12-inch pizza pan with rice mixture and bake 12 minutes at 350 degrees, or until set. Spread tomato sauce with cheese over rice crust. Sprinkle with spices and cheese. Top with pepperoni and olives. Bake at 350 degrees for 20-25 minutes. After removing from oven, allow to stand a few minutes before serving.

SAUCY PIZZA SURPRISE
Serves 6

3 cups cooked rice
2 cups (8 ounces)
   cheese, shredded
½ teaspoon basil
2 eggs, beaten
2 (8-ounce) cans tomato
   sauce
½ teaspoon oregano
½ teaspoon garlic powder

Combine rice, eggs and 1 cup cheese. Press firmly into 2 (9-inch) pans. Spread evenly. Bake at 450 degrees for 20 minutes. Combine tomato sauce and seasonings. Spread evenly over rice crust. Top with remaining cheese. Bake 10 minutes longer. *Note:* Other ingredients, such as cooked sausage, green pepper, mushrooms, etc., may be added before baking.

This pizza is great. A good way to use leftover rice, which makes a crust like deep-dish.

CHICKEN-BROCCOLI BAKE
Serves 4-5

1 (10-ounce) package broccoli cuts
2 cups chopped, cooked chicken
4 ounces medium noodles
1 cup sour cream
1 (10 3/4-ounce) can cream of
   chicken soup
2 tablespoons chopped pimiento
1 tablespoon minced onion
1 teaspoon salt
1/2 teaspoon Worcestershire sauce
1 tablespoon melted butter
1/2 cup soft bread crumbs
1 cup grated Swiss cheese

Prepare broccoli as directed on package; drain. Cook noodles and drain. Combine chicken, sour cream, soup, pimiento, onion, salt and Worcestershire sauce. Add butter to bread crumbs and mix well. Place noodles in greased, shallow 2-quart baking dish. Sprinkle with 1/3 of the cheese. Add broccoli. Sprinkle with 1/2 of the remaining cheese. Pour on the chicken mixture. Sprinkle with rest of cheese, and then with bread crumbs. Bake at 350 degrees for 1 hour.

BEEFY CASSEROLE
Serves 4

1 large eggplant
1 medium onion, chopped
2 tablespoons butter
1 pound ground beef
Salt and pepper to taste
1 bay leaf

Peel eggplant and cut into slices 1 or 1 1/2 inches thick. Cook in boiling, salted water for 10-15 minutes, or just until tender. Drain. Sauté onion in butter until soft; add beef and seasonings. Cook until meat is nicely browned. Place slices of eggplant in a greased baking dish. Remove bay leaf and add meat/onion mixture to eggplant. Cover with thin slices of cheese. Bake at 400 degrees for 20 minutes, or until cheese is melted.

TOWN AND COUNTRY CASSEROLE

1 package French's Real Cheese
   Scalloped Potatoes
1 pound smoked kielbasa or Polish
   sausage, cut in 1/4-inch slices
1 cup thinly sliced carrots
1 tablespoon freeze-dried chives
1 cup soft bread crumbs
1 tablespoon butter or margarine
1 tablespoon parsley flakes

Follow microwave method on package, except *increase* water to 3 cups and add carrots; microwave, covered, for 15 minutes. Add seasoning mix, milk, sausage, and chives. Microwave, covered, for 3-5 minutes. Combine crumbs, butter and parsley flakes; sprinkle casserole with crumb mixture; microwave, uncovered, for 5-7 minutes.

CORNED BEEF QUICHE

1 (9-inch) pie shell, unbaked
1 (15-ounce) can corned beef hash
1 small onion, finely shredded
1 cup Swiss cheese, shredded
2 teaspoons flour
1/4 teaspoon salt
Dash allspice
2 eggs, slightly beaten
1-1/4 cups milk

Pre-bake pie shell at 375 degrees for 7 minutes; remove from oven; set aside. Reduce oven temperature to 325 degrees. Crumble corned beef hash into pie shell; sprinkle onion over meat; top with Swiss cheese. Combine remaining ingredients; pour over hash and cheese. Bake 35-40 minutes, or until set. Cool 20 minutes before serving.

VEGETABLE CASSEROLE

1 can French-style green beans, drained
1/2 cup chopped celery
1/2 cup chopped green pepper
1/2 cup sour cream
1 can white shoepeg corn, drained
1/2 cup chopped onion
1/4 cup grated sharp cheese
1-1/2 cups crushed cheese crackers
1 can cream of mushroom soup
1/4 cup margarine
1/2 cup sliced almonds

Mix drained beans, corn, celery, green pepper, and onion. Alternate one layer vegetables with a layer of soup, grated cheese, then sour cream. Bake 25 minutes at 350 degrees.

Melt margarine and stir in crackers and almonds. Spread this on top of casserole and cook for 10 more minutes.

CORN AND SAUSAGE CASSEROLE

1 pound sausage
1/4 cup bell pepper, chopped
1 can whole kernel corn, drained
1 large can evaporated milk
2 tablespoons flour
1/4 teaspoons salt
1-1/2 cups grated cheese

Brown sausage and pepper until sausage is cooked. Drain and save 2 tablespoons sausage drippings. Add sausage to casserole dish with corn. Blend sausage drippings with flour in skillet over medium heat. Add milk and salt; simmer 2-3 minutes until thickened, stirring constantly. Pour over sausage and corn mixture; stir together. Top with grated cheese. Bake in a 350 degree oven for 25-30 minutes until bubbly.

SPAGHETTI RING

1/2 pound spaghetti
2 cups hot milk
1/4 cup butter
2 cups shredded Cheddar cheese
2 cups soft bread crumbs
2 eggs, well beaten
2 tablespoons minced onions
2 tablespoons minced parsley
2 tablespoons minced pimento
1 teaspoon salt
1/4 teaspoon pepper

Cook and drain spaghetti. Combine remaining ingredients. Mix thoroughly. Pour into well-greased 10-inch ring mold. Set in pan of hot water 1-inch deep. Bake at 350 degrees until set, about 30 minutes. Unmold on hot platter. Fill center with choice of creamed chicken, creamed seafood or any combination of creamed vegetables.

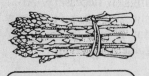

HASH BROWN POTATO CASSEROLE

1 (32-ounce) package frozen hash brown potatoes
1/2 cup melted margarine
8 ounces shredded Cheddar cheese
1 cup onions, chopped
1 pint sour cream
1 can cream of chicken soup
1 teaspoon salt
1/2 teaspoon garlic salt
1 cup corn flakes
1/4 cup melted margarine

Partially defrost hash browns. Mix potatoes, 1/2 cup margarine, cheese, onions, sour cream, soup, and spices. Put into greased 9 x 13-inch dish. Sprinkle corn flakes on top of potatoes; pour the 1/4 cup margarine over corn flakes. Bake uncovered in 350 degree oven for 1 hour and 15 minutes.

LAZY DAY LIMA BEAN CASSEROLE

2 cups grated American cheese
2/3 cup undiluted evaporated milk
1/2 teaspoon prepared mustard
2 cups cooked, large lima beans
2 medium tomatoes
Salt and pepper to taste

Combine cheese, milk and mustard. Cook and stir over hot water until cheese melts and sauce is smooth. Put lima beans into ovenproof casserole. Cover with 3/4 of sauce. Top casserole with tomato slices, salt and pepper and the remaining sauce. Bake in a 375 degree oven for 25 minutes or until lightly browned and bubbly on top.

SKILLET MACARONI AND CHEESE

Serves 6 to 8

1/4 cup butter or margarine
1 cup chopped onion
1 tablespoon all-purpose flour
1-1/2 teaspoons salt
1/4 teaspoon oregano
7 or 8 ounce package elbow macaroni
3-1/2 cups milk
2 cups shredded Cheddar cheese

Melt butter in skillet; add onion and saute until tender. Stir in flour, salt and oregano; add macaroni and milk. Cover and bring to boil; reduce heat and simmer 15 minutes or until macaroni is tender, stirring occasionally. Add cheese and stir until cheese is melted (do not boil).

CREAMY CHIPPED BEEF CASSEROLE

2 packages chipped beef
1/2 package (16-ounce) frozen hash brown's (thawed)
1 can cream of mushroom soup
1 cup evaporated milk
2 tablespoon Crisco
1 can Durkee French fried onion rings

Snip beef in bite size pieces. Brown in Crisco until edges curl; drain. Mix milk and soup. Add beef, hash brown's and 1/2 can onion rings. Place in 2-quart casserole dish; bake covered for 30 minutes in 350 degree oven. Remove lid; crumble remainder of onion rings over top. return to oven for 5 to 10 minutes. NOTE: Also good with hamburger or leftover ham.

REUBEN CASSEROLE

5 cups herb seasoned croutons
1 cup hot water
1 (8-ounce) package Swiss cheese (sliced), set aside 2 slices
6-9 slices of canned corn beef
1/2 cup melted margarine
2 cups sauerkraut (drained)
1 teaspoon caraway seeds (if desired)

In a large bowl, put in croutons and margarine; toss gently. Add hot water, sauerkraut, and caraway seeds. Set aside 1 cup of mixture. Grease casserole dish. Layer crouton mixture, corn beef, and cheese slices. End up with the 1 cup of crouton mixture. Cover and bake in a 350 degree oven for 20 minutes. Top with the 2 cheese slices and bake uncovered 10 minutes until cheese melts.

DRESSING CASSEROLE

Serves 12

2 cups diced celery
1 clove garlic
12 cups toasted bread cubes
4 cups cubed corn bread
1/2 teaspoon pepper
4 cups turkey or chicken broth
1-1/2 cups chopped onion
1/2 cup butter
1 tablespoon sage
2 tablespoons salt
1 (13 ounce) can evaporated milk
2 eggs, slightly beaten

Cook celery, onion, and garlic in butter until light brown. Crumble bread cubes and corn bread in large bowl. Add sage, salt, and pepper. Stir celery mixture into bread cubes. Add evaporated milk, broth, and eggs. Mix well. Pour into greased 9 x 13" pan. Bake at 325 degrees for 35 to 40 minutes.

This is a good way to use up leftover corn bread. Recipe can easily be cut in half and baked in an 8 x 8" pan for smaller families. Bouillon may be substituted for the broth.

NIGHT BEFORE CASSEROLE

Serves 10

2 cups macaroni, cooked
2 cups chicken, turkey, *or* tuna (if using chicken or turkey, it should be cooked)
2 cans mushroom soup
1/2 pound American cheese, cut into fine pieces
3 eggs, hard-cooked, cut into small pieces
2 cups milk
Chopped pimiento and green pepper to taste

Mix all ingredients together and refrigerate overnight or for at least 6-12 hours. Remove from refrigerator and bake for 1 hour in 350 degree oven.

PENNYWISE CASSEROLE

1 pound lean stewing beef, cut into 1" cubes
(Lamb or pork can also be used for this recipe)
Salt and pepper
1/3 cup vegetable oil
2 medium onions, sliced
2 teaspoons honey
1/2 teaspoon ground cinnamon
1/2 teaspoon ground nutmeg
1/2 teaspoon parsley
1/2 teaspoon basil
8 ounce can tomatoes
4 slices wheat (or white) bread, buttered and quartered

Lightly salt and pepper beef. In skillet over moderate heat, fry beef cubes until browned. Transfer meat to ovenproof dish. In the same skillet, fry onions for 5 minutes until soft, but not browned. Stir in remaining ingredients (except bread); bring to a boil. Pour over meat; cover. Bake in a 350 degree oven for 1 hour. Taste and adjust seasonings, if necessary. Arrange bread slices neatly on top; return to oven for 30 minutes (or until the bread is golden and crisp).

MEXICAN COMBO

1 pound ground beef
1 medium onion, diced
1 medium green pepper, diced
2 tablespoons chili powder
1-1/2 cups hot water
1/2 pound sharp cheese, diced
1 can red kidney beans
Salt & pepper to taste

Brown ground beef, onion, and pepper in a large skillet, using fork to break up meat. Mix chili powder and hot water; pour over meat mixture. Simmer 5 to 10 minutes. Add cheese, beans with juice, salt, and pepper. Simmer until cheese melts. Be careful not to let it burn.

PORK CHOP CASSEROLE
Serves 4

6 pork chops
1 teaspoon salt
1/8 teaspoon pepper
4 medium apples, peeled and sliced
1 cup water
4 medium sweet potatoes, peeled and sliced
1 teaspoon Worcestershire sauce
1 medium onion, chopped

Wipe chops; brown them in a little fat in frying pan. Place chops in a large casserole; sprinkle with half the salt and pepper. Place apples and sweet potatoes in layers on chops and sprinkle with remaining salt and pepper. Sauté onion in the same frying pan where chops were browned. Add water and Worcestershire sauce. Mix and pour over chops, apples and potatoes. Cover and bake 1-1/2 hours in a moderate 375-degree oven.

LEMON DILLED BEEF

2 1/2 pounds stewing beef
1/2 cup butter
2 1/2 cups chopped celery
1 1/2 cups chopped onion
1 cup chopped green pepper
1/3 cup lemon juice
2 cups beef stock
3 cloves garlic, finely chopped
1 1/2 teaspoons dill weed
Salt to taste
1 1/2 cups sour cream
3 tablespoons butter, softened
3 tablespoons flour
1 medium package noodles

Lightly brown beef in butter. Add vegetables, liquid and seasoning. Cover and simmer on low for 2 hours. Add sour cream and simmer, uncovered, for 30 minutes. Combine flour and butter; add by spoonfuls to bubbling mixture. Simmer 10 minutes and serve on prepared noodles.

DELI REUBEN CASSEROLE
Serves 6.

3 cups sauerkraut, drained
1-1/2 cups tomatoes, drained
2 tablespoons Thousand Island dressing
2 tablespoons butter or margarine
3 packages corned beef, shredded
1 (10-ounce) can refrigerated flaky biscuits
3 rye crackers, crushed
1/4 teaspoon caraway seeds

Spread sauerkraut in a 13x9x2-inch baking dish; arrange tomatoes on top; spread with dressing; dot with butter. Place shredded corned beef and cheese over all. Separate each biscuit into halves; arrange over casserole. Sprinkle with the rye crackers and caraway seeds. Bake at 350 degrees, 12 minutes, or until biscuits are flaky and golden.

HAM & NOODLE BAKE

2 cups cooked ham, cubed
1/4 cup onion, chopped
1/8 teaspoon thyme leaves, crushed
2 tablespoons margarine
1 (10-3/4-ounce) can cream of chicken soup
3/4 cup water
2 cups cooked noodles (5 ounces)
1 cup canned, cut green beans, drained
1/2 cup shredded cheddar cheese

In saucepan, brown ham, cook onion with thyme in margarine until tender. Stir in remaining ingredients, except cheese. Pour into 2-quart casserole. Bake at 350 degrees for 30 minutes. Top with cheese; bake until cheese melts, 8 minutes longer. If refrigerated before cooking, bake 45 minutes longer.

This is made quickly and is nice for a company dinner.

CHICKEN AND BROCCOLI RICE CASSEROLE
Serves 6

1/2 cup chopped onions
1/2 cup sliced mushrooms
1 tablespoon butter
2 cups hot, cooked rice
2 cups cubed chicken breast
2 cups chopped, fresh broccoli (steamed) *or*
1 (10-ounce) package frozen broccoli, thawed
1 (10-3/4-ounce) can cream of mushroom soup, condensed
1/2 cup (2 ounces) shredded cheddar cheese

Simmer onions and mushrooms in large skillet with butter until tender. Stir in rice, chicken, broccoli, and soup. Pour into buttered 1-1/2-quart baking dish. Top with cheese. Bake at 350 degrees for 20-25 minutes.

My husband is fussy about casseroles, but he *loves* this one.

CHICKEN CASSEROLE SUPREME

3   cups cooked chicken, deboned
1   (6-ounce) package Uncle Ben's rice, cooked
1   can cream of celery soup, undiluted
1   can cream of chicken soup, undiluted
1   can French-style green beans, drained
1   medium jar pimientos, sliced
1   cup mayonnaise
1   small can water chestnuts, sliced
    Salt and pepper to taste

Mix all ingredients together and pour into 3-quart casserole. Bake 25–30 minutes at 350 degrees.

MOCK OYSTER CASSEROLE
Serves 6

1 large eggplant
1 cup cracker crumbs (approx. 25 soda crackers, crushed)
2 eggs
1/2 cup milk
3 tablespoons butter
1/4 cup chopped celery
1/4 cup chopped green pepper
1/4 cup chopped onion
1 (11 ounce) can mushroom soup
Tabasco sauce to taste

Peel eggplant and cut into cubes. Boil eggplant for 3 minutes in salt water; set aside. Place 1/3 of the crushed crumbs in a buttered 2 quart casserole dish; add 1/2 the eggplant. Repeat layering the cracker crumbs and eggplant. Beat eggs slightly, add 1/2 cup milk, mushroom soup, peppers, onions, celery and Tabasco sauce, mixing well. Pour slowly over eggplant mixture. Dot with butter. Cover and bake at 375 degrees for 30 minutes. Uncover and add more milk if needed. Bake 15 minutes more uncovered, until golden brown.

RICE OLE
Serves 3-4

2 slices bacon
1/3 cup chopped onion
1/4 cup finely chopped green pepper
1-1/2 cups water
2 envelopes Lipton Tomato Cup-a-Soup
1 cup uncooked instant rice
1/2 teaspoon garlic salt

In skillet cook bacon until crisp; drain, reserving 2 tablespoons drippings. Crumble bacon; set aside. Add onion and green pepper to skillet; cook until tender. Add water and bring to boil. Stir in Cup-a-Soup, uncooked rice, garlic salt, and crumbled bacon; cover and remove from heat. Let stand for 5 minutes.

LAZY BEEF CASSEROLE
Serves 4

1 pound lean beef chuck, cut into 1-1/2-inch cubes
1/2 cup red wine
1 (10-1/2-ounce) can consomme, undiluted
1/4 cup all-purpose flour
Freshly ground black pepper, to taste
1 medium onion, chopped
1/4 cup fine dry bread crumbs
1/4 teaspoon rosemary

Put meat in a casserole with the wine, consomme, pepper, rosemary, and onion. Mix flour and bread crumbs and stir into the liquid. Cover and bake at 300 degrees, about 3 hours. Serve with rice or noodles. (206 calories per serving)

EASY BEEF GOULASH
Serves 4

1 to 2 tablespoons vegetable oil
1 pound ground beef (chuck)
3 cups uncooked medium egg noodles
2 cups water
1 (8-ounce) can tomato sauce
1 envelope dry onion soup mix

Heat oil in a medium-size skillet over medium heat. Add ground beef and cook until lightly browned, stirring occasionally with a fork to break up meat. Drain off any excess fat. Sprinkle uncooked noodles over meat. Combine water, tomato sauce, and onion soup mix. Pour over noodles in skillet. Do not stir. Cover and bring to a boil. Reduce heat to moderately low and simmer about 30 minutes, or until noodles are tender. Stir and serve.
Note: You may have to add a small amount of water if the noodles seem to be sticking. This is very easy and quick for those hectic days.

GERMAN POTATO CASSEROLE

6 medium-size potatoes, peeled and sliced
1 pound hot pork sausage, cooked and drained
8 ounces sour cream
2 teaspoons dry onion soup mix
2 teaspoons lemon juice
1 can cream of mushroom soup
2 teaspoons Dijon mustard
1 can sauerkraut, washed and drained
1 cup buttered bread crumbs
Salt and pepper to taste

Peel, wash, and slice potatoes. Boil in salted water until tender. Mix sour cream, dry onion soup mix, mushroom soup, lemon juice, and mustard. Heat sauerkraut in 2 tablespoons sausage drippings. Alternate layers of potatoes, cream mixture, and sauerkraut. Put bread crumbs on top and bake in 350-degree oven until hot and bubbly, about 20-25 minutes.

INDIAN CASSEROLE

1 can hominy, drained
1 pound ground beef
1/2 cup chopped onion
1/2 cup chopped green pepper
1-3/4 cups canned tomatoes
1/2 teaspoon salt
1/4 teaspoon pepper
1 cup grated cheese

Brown beef, salt, onions, and green pepper. Add tomatoes and hominy. Pour into buttered casserole and bake at 350 degrees for 40 minutes. Remove from oven and sprinkle cheese on top. Return to oven and bake 15 minutes.

Note: I tried this recipe and cooked it in an electric skillet. I cooked it on low until thick, then placed slices of cheese over the top and put lid of skillet on until cheese melted. I served it with French bread and a cottage cheese and peach salad.

YELLOW SQUASH CASSEROLE
6-8 Servings

2 pounds yellow squash, sliced
  (6 cups)
1/4 cup chopped onion
1 can cream of chicken soup
1 cup sour cream
1 cup shredded carrots
1 (8-ounce) package herb-seasoned
  stuffing mix
1/2 cup melted margarine

Cook squash and onion in boiling, salted water for 5 minutes; drain. Mix soup and sour cream. Stir in the carrots; fold in squash and onion. Combine stuffing mix and margarine. Spread half stuffing mixture in lightly buttered 12 x 7-1/2-inch baking dish; spoon vegetable mixture over stuffing. Sprinkle remaining stuffing mixture over vegetables. Bake in preheated 350 degree oven for 25-30 minutes, until heated thoroughly.

PINTO BEAN CASSEROLE
Serves 4-6

1 to 1-1/2 pounds ground beef
1/2 cup chopped onion
1/2 cup chopped green pepper
1 clove garlic, minced
1 (15-ounce) can tomato sauce
2 teaspoons chili powder
1 teaspoon salt
1 cup cooked rice
1 (15-ounce) can pinto beans
1-1/2 cups grated Cheddar cheese

Brown beef, onion, green pepper, and garlic. Blend in tomato sauce, chili powder, and salt. In greased 2-quart casserole, layer part of meat sauce, beans, half of cheese, and remainder of meat sauce. Top with other half cheese. Bake 350 degrees for 15-20 minutes. Let stand a few minutes before serving.

Rolls or garlic toast and salad with this casserole make a complete meal.

YAM AND CRANBERRY CASSEROLE
Serves 8

1 (40 ounce) can yams, drained
3 cups fresh, whole cranberries
1-1/2 cups sugar
1 small orange, sliced
1/2 cup pecan halves
1/4 cup orange juice or brandy
3/4 teaspoon cinnamon
1/4 teaspoon nutmeg
1/4 teaspoon mace

Combine cranberries, sugar, orange slices, pecans, orange juice, and spices in 2-quart casserole. Bake uncovered at 375 degrees for 30 minutes. Stir yams into cranberry mixture. Bake until heated through—about 15 minutes.

Nice to serve with your holiday turkey.

CABBAGE CASSEROLE

1 medium onion, chopped
3 tablespoons butter
1/2 pound ground beef
1 teaspoon salt
1/8 teaspoon pepper
6 cups chopped cabbage
1 can tomato soup

Sauté meat and onion. Place 3 cups cabbage in 2 quart casserole; cover with meat mixture; top with remaining cabbage. Pour soup over top. Bake 350 degrees for 1 hour.

GREEN TOMATO CASSEROLE

4 large green tomatoes, sliced
Salt and pepper to taste
3/4 cup Cheddar cheese, grated
1 tablespoon butter

Preheat oven to 400 degrees. Butter casserole dish. Lay 1/3 of tomato slices on bottom. Sprinkle with salt and pepper and 1/4 cup of cheese. Repeat with remaining slices. Top with 1/2 cup of cheese and dot with butter. Bake covered 40 to 60 minutes. Brown under broiler if desired.

This is a simple way to use green tomatoes and it tastes great.

ROUND-UP BEAN CASSEROLE

1 pound ground beef
1 can red (kidney) beans
1 can butter beans
1 can pork and beans
1/2 cup catsup
3/4 cup brown sugar
1 teaspoon mustard
2 tablespoons vinegar
Chopped onion and bell pepper (optional)

Brown beef; season with salt and pepper. (Add onion and bell pepper at this time.) Combine with remaining ingredients. Put into casserole dish. Bake about 1 hour at 350 degrees.

This is also good cooked in a slow pot. It is simple to prepare, and with a salad makes a quick meal.

SPINACH CASSEROLE

1 package frozen spinach
1 (8 ounce) package cream cheese
1 can cream of mushroom soup
1 can French onion rings
6 tablespoons butter or margarine
Cracker crumbs

Cook spinach according to package directions. Heat soup and cream cheese to soften. Mix with spinach; add onion rings. Pour into casserole. Melt butter; add enough cracker crumbs to absorb butter. Spread buttered crumbs on top and bake at 350 degrees for 20 minutes.

DYNASTY CASSEROLE

Serves 4-6

1 (8-ounce) can water chestnuts sliced
1 (3-ounce) can chow mein noodles
1 carrot sliced
1 can bean sprouts, drained
1 can cream of mushroom soup
1 cup half-and-half cream
1 cup chopped celery (cut on the diagonal)
Dash of hot–pepper sauce and black pepper
2 tablespoons soy sauce
1-1/2 cups cooked chicken chunks or strips
1/4 cup minced green onion
3/4 cup chopped cashew nuts
Hot cooked rice

Preheat oven to 350 degrees and set aside 1/2 cup of crisp chow mein noodles. Mix all other ingredients (except rice) in a large buttered 2-quart casserole or long baking dish. Bake, uncovered, for about 30 minutes. Sprinkle remaining chow mein noodles on top of casserole and bake 10 minutes longer. Serve casserole over hot cooked rice. Pass the soy sauce at the table.

BAKED BEANS WITH SAUSAGE

Serves 6

1/4 cup molasses
2 tablespoons prepared mustard
2 tablespoons vinegar
2 teaspoons Worcestershire sauce
1/4 teaspoon Tabasco sauce
2 (1-pound) cans baked beans
1 (20-ounce) can apple slices
1 pound pork sausage links, cooked

Mix all ingredients, except sausages, and place in a bean pot. Bake at 350 degrees for 40 minutes. Top with hot sausages and serve.

This is a complete meal with French or garlic bread and a crisp salad.

CHILI RELLENOS CASSEROLE

16 ounces Ortega whole green chilies
12 ounces Cheddar cheese, grated
12 ounces Monterey Jack cheese, grated
2 eggs, separated
2 egg whites
3 tablespoons flour
12 ounces evaporated milk
14 ounces Ortega green chili salsa

Remove seeds from chilies; flatten and drain. In a greased 9x9-inch pan, layer half the chilies and top with Cheddar cheese. Cover with rest of chilies and top with Monterey Jack cheese. Mix egg yolks, flour, and milk. Whip the 4 egg whites until stiff, then fold into yolk mixture. Pour the whole mixture over chilies and cheese. Bake in a 325 degree oven for 45 minutes. Pour green chili salsa over the top and return to oven for 30 minutes. After baking, allow to sit for 10 minutes. Cut into squares.

SHRIMP CASSEROLE

Serves 4-5

1 can condensed mushroom soup
1/2 cup milk
2 tablespoons minced parsley
1 tablespoon instant minced onion
1/2 teaspoon salt
2-3 dashes Tabasco sauce
2-1/2 cups cooked rice
2 cups cooked shrimp
1 cup corn flakes
2 tablespoons melted butter
2 tablespoons toasted slivered almonds (optional)

Combine soup, milk, parsley, onions and seasonings. Add rice and shrimp; mix thoroughly. Pour into greased 10x6x2-inch baking dish. Slightly crush corn flakes; combine with melted butter and almonds; sprinkle over top of casserole. Bake at 375 degrees for about 20 minutes or until bubbly.

BACON MACARONI 'N CHEESE

Serves 4-6

3/4 pound bacon, diced
1 cup onions, chopped
1 quart milk
2 teaspoons celery salt
1/2 teaspoon pepper
1/4 teaspoon Tabasco sauce
2 cups elbow macaroni
1 cup cheese, grated
1/2 cup pimiento, chopped

In large skillet, cook bacon and onion over low heat for 15 minutes. Drain drippings. Add milk, celery salt, pepper, and Tabasco. Heat to boiling; gradually add macaroni, so that milk continues to boil. Simmer, uncovered, for 20 minutes, stirring often. Add cheese and pimiento; stir until cheese melts. Serve hot.

QUICK CHILI-RICE DINNER

Serves 4

3/4 pound ground beef
1/3 cup chopped onion
1 tablespoon chili powder
1/2 teaspoon dry mustard
1 (10-ounce) package whole-kernel corn
1 cup diced green pepper
1 (15-ounce) can tomato sauce
1/2 cup water
1 cup Minute Rice
1/2 cup shredded cheddar cheese

Brown beef and onion in skillet. Add spices, corn, green pepper, tomato sauce, and water. Cover and bring to a full boil, stirring occasionally. Stir in rice; reduce heat; cover and simmer for 5 minutes. Sprinkle with cheese.

Good for when time is limited; takes only 20 minutes to prepare.

MACARONI LOAF

2 cups cooked macaroni
1/2 cup bread crumbs
1/2 cup grated cheese
3 tablespoons butter
1/2 tablespoon chopped parsley
1/2 tablespoon chopped onion
1/2 teaspoon salt
1/2 cup milk
1 egg, beaten

Place a layer of cooked macaroni into a greased baking dish. Sprinkle bread crumbs, grated cheese, parsley, onions, salt, and butter between each layer. Repeat until all ingredients are used. Pour egg and milk over mixture. Bake in 350 degree oven for 30 minutes or until it is set.

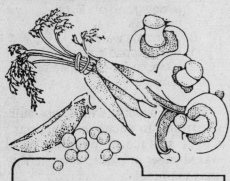

ORIENTAL RICE CASSEROLE

6-8 servings

1 pound ground beef
1 cup chopped celery
1 cup chopped onions
4 ounce can mushrooms
8 ounce can water chestnuts, sliced
.8 ounce can bamboo shoots, drained
1/3 cup soy sauce
1 can cream of mushroom soup
2 beef bouillon cubes
2 cups hot water
3/4 cup rice

Brown beef, celery and onions. Drain off excess fat. Mix in mushrooms, water chestnuts, bamboo shoots and soy sauce. Dissolve bouillon cubes in hot water, stir in mushroom soup. Add to beef mixture. Stir in rice, place in 13 x 9 inch baking pan. Bake uncovered for 1 hour in a 350 degree oven. Delicious!

TOSTADO CASSEROLE
Serves 6

1 pound ground beef
15-ounce can (2 cups) tomato sauce
1 envelope taco seasoning mix
2-1/2 cups corn chips
15-1/2 - ounce can refried beans
2 ounces (1/2 cup) shredded Cheddar cheese

In skillet, brown ground beef. Add 1-1/2 cups of tomato sauce and seasoning mix, stirring to mix well. Line bottom of 11 x 8 x 2-inch baking dish with 2 cups corn chips. Crush remaining corn chips; set aside. Spoon meat mixture over corn chips in baking dish. Combine remaining tomato sauce and refried beans; spread over ground beef mixture. Bake at 375 degrees for 25 minutes. Sprinkle with shredded cheese and crushed corn chips. Bake 5 minutes more.

POT LUCK CASSEROLE

8 ounces noodles
1-1/2 pounds hamburger
1 onion, chopped
1 teaspoon salt
Pepper
2 (8 ounce) packages cream cheese
1 cup cottage cheese
1/ 4 cup sour cream
1/3 cup chopped green pepper
1/3 cup chopped green onion

Cook noodles. Simmer hamburger, onion, salt, pepper and tomato sauce. Cream in blender the cottage cheese, cream cheese and sour cream. Add chopped peppers and green onions. Layer noodles, meat and cheese sauce. Top with grated cheese and bake at 350 degrees for 30-40 minutes.

HAMBURGER CASSEROLE
Serves 4

1 pound lean ground beef
1 (26 1/4 ounce) can of Franco-American Spaghetti
1 medium onion, chopped
1 medium green pepper, chopped

Saute onions and green pepper in 2 tablespoons margarine until nearly done, remove from pan and drain. Saute ground beef until brown; drain grease. Add spaghetti from can. Slightly chop while mixing. Add peppers and onions. Mix well. Pour into 1-1/2 quart casserole. Bake 375 degrees for 30-45 minutes.

Optional additions:
Mushrooms, sliced
Black and or green olives, sliced
1 small can green beans

Serve with Parmesan cheese, garlic bread and tossed salad.

HAMBURGER MACARONI CASSEROLE

2 cups macaroni
1 pound ground beef
1 can condensed tomato soup
1 can condensed mushroom soup
1 medium green pepper
1/4 cup colby cheese, cubed
1/4 cup chopped pimiento, optional
1 (3-ounce) can French fried (Durkee) onions

Cook macaroni; drain. Brown the ground beef; drain. Add soups, green pepper, pimiento, macaroni, and the ground beef. Place half the mixture in a greased 2-quart casserole. Sprinkle with half the cheese and onions. Top with remaining macaroni mixture and cheese. Bake at 350 degrees for 25 minutes. Sprinkle with remaining onions, bake 5 additional minutes.

Desserts
DELICIOUS

ICE CREAM GELATIN DESSERT
Serves 5

1 (3-ounce) package gelatin, any flavor
1 cup boiling water
½ cup cold water
1 cup vanilla ice cream (or your favorite flavor)
1 cup canned fruit, drained (fruit cocktail, sliced peaches or mandarin oranges)

Dissolve gelatin with boiling water in an 8-inch or 9-inch metal pan. (The pan helps the gelatin cool faster.) Then remove ½ cup and pour into a bowl. Add ½ cup cold water to the gelatin in the pan and place in the freezer until it thickens (10–15 minutes).

Meanwhile, add 1 cup ice cream to the gelatin in the bowl; stir until smooth. Remove thickened gelatin from the freezer and, if desired, stir in fruit, reserving a few pieces for garnish.

Spoon thickened gelatin and fruit into individual dessert glasses.

Top with ice cream/gelatin mixture. Chill 30 minutes. Garnish and serve.

CHERRY WHIP

1 stick margarine
2 cups graham cracker crumbs

1 cup cold milk
2 envelopes whipped topping mix
1 teaspoon vanilla
1 cup sugar
1 (8-ounce) package cream cheese
1 large can cherry pie filling

Melt margarine over low heat. Mix with 2 cups graham cracker crumbs. Put into 9 x 13 x 2-inch pan. In a large bowl, whip until stiff, 1 cup cold milk with 2 envelopes whipped topping mix. Add 1 teaspoon vanilla, cup sugar and cream cheese (softened). Spread over crumb mixture. Spoon 1 large can cherry pie filling over whipped mixture. Set in refrigerator overnight. Slice and serve.

CANDY CANE DESSERT
Serves 9

1 graham cracker crust (your favorite recipe)
1 (8-ounce) container frozen whipped topping, thawed
1 small package miniature marshmallows
4 large candy canes, crushed (about ½ cup)

Place graham cracker crust in bottom of 11 x 7-inch pan. Combine whipped topping, marshmallows and ¾ of the candy. Spoon on crust. Spread remaining crushed candy cane over mixture. Chill thoroughly.

CHOCOLATE WAFER PUDDING
Serves 6–8

1 (3¼-ounce) package vanilla pudding and pie filling
2 cups milk
8 chocolate waters
1 cup whipped cream
2 tablespoons chocolate syrup (optional)

Prepare pudding with 2 cups milk according to package directions. Cover surface of pudding with waxed paper or plastic wrap; refrigerate until cool.

Alternate layers of chocolate wafers and pudding in a 1-quart casserole, ending with vanilla pudding. Garnish with whipped cream and drizzle with chocolate syrup, if desired.

PEANUT BUTTER INSTANT PUDDING
Serves 4

⅓ cup creamy peanut butter
2 cups cold milk
1 (3¾-ounce) package vanilla, 1 (4-ounce) package butterscotch or 1 (4½-ounce) package chocolate *instant* pudding

Stir peanut butter and milk together. Add pudding mix and beat slowly with rotary beater for 1–2 minutes, or until well-blended. Pudding will be soft. Let stand for 5 minutes and serve.

PISTACHIO TORTE

Crust:
- 1 cup flour
- ½ cup butter *or* margarine
- ½ cup chopped nuts
- ¼ cup confectioners' sugar

Filling:
- 1 (8-ounce) package cream cheese, softened
- 1 cup confectioners' sugar
- 1 cup whipped topping

Topping:
- 2 packages instant pistachio pudding
- 2½ cups milk

Garnishes:
- Crushed nuts
- Whipped topping

Combine ingredients for crust and press onto bottom of 9 x 13-inch pan. Bake at 350 degrees for about 15 minutes, or until golden brown. Cool.

Combine ingredients for filling and spread over cooled crust. For topping, combine pudding and milk. Spread over cream cheese mixture. Top with nuts and frost with whipped topping.
Variation:

Add 1 small can of crushed pineapple (drained) to filling ingredients.

HEAVENLY HASH CAKE
Serves 12–16

- 1 (12-ounce) package semisweet chocolate chips
- 4 eggs, separated
- 2 tablespoons sugar
- 1 teaspoon vanilla extract
- ½ teaspoon salt
- 1 pint whipping cream
- 1 cup pecans, broken
- 1 large angel food cake

Melt chocolate chips over low heat.

Beat egg yolks and add to chocolate. Beat egg whites and add 2 tablespoons sugar. Add egg whites to chocolate mixture. Stir and add pecans, vanilla and salt. Whip cream and fold in last.

Break angel food cake into chunks and cover bottom of tube pan or deep bowl. Cover with layer of chocolate mixture; add another layer of cake pieces and cover with chocolate mixture. Then add another layer of cake pieces and cover with remaining chocolate mixture.

Chill in refrigerator overnight. Turn onto cake plate and slice to serve.

CREAMY CHOCOMINT TORTE
Serves 12

- 2 envelopes unflavored gelatin
- ½ cup sugar
- 4 eggs, separated
- 1½ cups milk
- ½ cup creme de menthe
- 2½ cups chocolate sandwich cookie crumbs
- ¼ cup butter *or* margarine, melted
- 2 cups (1 pint) whipping *or* heavy cream, whipped

In medium saucepan, mix unflavored gelatin with ¼ cup sugar; blend in egg yolks beaten with milk. Let stand 1 minute. Stir over low heat until gelatin is completely dissolved, about 5 minutes; add liqueur. Pour into large bowl and chill, stirring occasionally, until mixture mounds slightly when dropped from spoon. Meanwhile, in small bowl, combine cookie crumbs and butter. Reserve 1½ cups mixture. Press remaining onto bottom of 9-inch springform pan; chill.

In medium bowl, beat egg whites until soft peaks form; gradually add remaining sugar and beat until stiff. Fold egg whites, then whipped cream into gelatin mixture. Turn ⅓ mixture into prepared pan and top with ¾ cup reserved cookie crumbs; repeat, ending with gelatin mixture. Chill until set. Garnish, if desired,

with additional whipped cream and miniature chocolate-mint candy bars.

FESTIVE RASPBERRY FRAPPÉ
Serves 8

- 4 packages frozen whole red raspberries, plus syrup
- ¼ cup lemon juice
- ¼ cup sugar
- 1½ cups heavy cream, whipped
- 1 pint vanilla ice cream, softened

Purée thawed raspberries and syrup in blender or food processor; strain to remove seeds. Combine purée with lemon juice and sugar. Stir in whipped cream and ice cream; chill. Fill individual serving dessert bowls; serve ice-cold.

BRANDIED MINCEMEAT MOUSSE
Makes 1½ quarts

- 2 egg whites
- 2 cups whipping cream
- 1 cup sugar
- ⅛ teaspoon salt
- 1 teaspoon brandy *or* rum extract
- 1½ cups mincemeat

Place egg whites and cream in mixing bowl; beat until stiff. Add sugar gradually and continue beating until blended. Fold in salt, brandy (or rum) and mincemeat. Spoon into freezing tray or small paper cups. Place in freezing compartment of refrigerator and set control for coldest temperature. Freeze until firm; about 2–3 hours.

LINCOLN LOG
Serves 5

Cake:
- 5 eggs, separated
- 6 tablespoons sugar
- ½ cup all-purpose flour
- ½ teaspoon vanilla extract

Mocha Cream Filling and Frosting:
- 1 cup butter *or* margarine, softened
- 4½ tablespoons confectioners' sugar
- 2 tablespoons unsweetened cocoa
- 2 tablespoons strong, cooled coffee
- 2 cups whipping cream, whipped

Beat egg yolks with sugar; mix in flour and vanilla. Fold in stiffly beaten egg whites; spread mixture on a buttered waxed-paper–lined jelly roll pan. Bake at 350 degrees for 15 minutes; transfer to a dampened cloth dusted with confectioners' sugar. Roll cake in cloth; cool. Beat butter and confectioners' sugar; stir in cocoa and coffee. Unroll pastry; cover with a thin layer of mocha cream and whipped cream. Reroll cake (without cloth); cut off 2 ends diagonally; reserve. Cover cake and 2 slices with remaining mocha cream; place 1 slice on top of cake, the other slice on the side of cake (to resemble branches). With a fork, trace lines into the cream to simulate the bark.

PEACH BLUEBERRY COBBLER
Serves 8

- ½ cup sugar
- 1 tablespoon cornstarch
- ¾ cup orange juice
- 1½ cups fresh *or* frozen peach slices
- 1½ cups blueberries
- ½ cup all-purpose flour
- ½ cup whole-wheat flour
- 1½ teaspoon baking powder
- ⅓ cup milk
- 1 tablespoon vegetable oil
- 1 teaspoon sugar

In small saucepan, stir together ½ cup sugar, cornstarch and orange juice. Cook until bubbly; add peaches and blueberries; cook until hot. Keep warm. Stir together flours and baking powder; add milk and oil and stir until mixture forms a ball. On floured surface, pat into an 8-inch circle. Cut into wedges. Spoon hot berry mixture into 9-inch pie plate and top immediately with pastry wedges. Sprinkle with sugar. Bake in 425-degree oven for 20–30 minutes, or until pastry is browned. This cobbler has a grandmother flair!

CREAM CHEESE AND CHERRY DESSERT
Serves 18–20

Crust:
- 2 cups crushed pretzels
- 1 cup melted butter *or* margarine
- ¾ cup sugar

Filling:
- 1 (8-ounce) package cream cheese, softened
- 1 cup confectioners' sugar
- 1 (8-ounce) container whipped topping

Topping:
- 1 (30-ounce) can cherry pie filling

For crust: Combine ingredients and press into a 9 x 13-inch pan, reserving some for garnish.

For filling: Combine and beat cream cheese with confectioners' sugar. Add whipped topping to the cheese mixture, ½ cup at a time, mixing gently. Spread over crust.

Spread pie filling over top and sprinkle with reserved pretzel mixture. Refrigerate 2–3 hours.

PEACHES AND CREAM DESSERT

- 3/4 cup all-purpose flour
- 4 serving size package regular vanilla pudding mix
- 1 teaspoon baking powder
- 1 beaten egg
- 1/2 cup milk
- 3 tablespoons margarine, melted
- 16-ounce can peach slices
- 8-ounce package cream cheese, softened
- 1/2 cup sugar
- 1 teaspoon sugar
- 1/2 teaspoon ground cinnamon

Stir together flour, pudding mix and baking powder. Combine egg, milk and melted margarine; add to dry ingredients. Mix well; spread in greased 8-inch square baking pan. Drain peaches, reserving 1/3 cup liquid. Chop peaches; sprinkle on top of batter. Beat together cream cheese 1/2 cup sugar and reserved peach liquid; pour on top of peaches in pan. Combine 1 tablespoon sugar and cinnamon; sprinkle over all. Bake at 350 degrees for 45 minutes. Cool in refrigerator.

FLUFFY PUMPKIN CHEESECAKE

- ¾ cup pumpkin
- 1 (8-ounce) package cream cheese, softened
- ¾ cup confectioners' sugar
- 2 tablespoons milk
- 1 teaspoon ground cinnamon
- ¼ teaspoon ground cloves
- ½ teaspoon ground ginger
- ½ teaspoon nutmeg
- 1 (8-ounce) container frozen whipped topping, thawed
- 1 graham cracker pie crust

In small bowl beat cream cheese and sugar together until fluffy. Add pumpkin, milk and spices, beating until creamy. Fold whipped topping into pumpkin mixture. Turn into graham cracker pie crust. Chill 5 hours. (May be frozen for later use.)

FUDGE RICE

2 cups milk
1 cup cooked rice
1/4 cup sugar
2 tablespoons flour
1/4 teaspoon salt
2 eggs, beaten
1/2 teaspoon vanilla
1/4 cup chopped walnuts

Scald milk in heavy saucepan. Stir in rice. Mix sugar, flour and salt. Whisk into scalded milk. Cook, stirring over medium heat, for 5 minutes. Stir small amount of hot mixture into eggs. Then stir back into saucepan. Cook stirring for 1 minute. Add vanilla. Pour into shallow, 1-1/2 - quart buttered baking dish. Bake at 300 degrees for 30 minutes until knife inserted comes out clean. Cool slightly. Spread with fudge topping. Sprinkle with nuts. Let stand until firm.

Fudge Topping:
1 cup powdered sugar
Dash of salt
1-1/2 tablespoons milk
1 tablespoon softened butter
1-1/2 squares unsweetened chocolate, melted
1/4 teaspoon vanilla

Beat powdered sugar, salt and milk together; stir in butter, chocolate and vanilla. Beat until blended and of spreading consistency.

IRISH COFFEE PUDDING

Use this for your centerpiece.

6 eggs
1/3 cup Irish whiskey
3/4 cup sugar
1 1/4 cups heavy cream
1 cup strong, black espresso
2 tablespoons finely crushed walnuts
3 tablespoons gelatin
1 cup whipped cream
2 tablespoons chopped walnuts

Separate eggs and beat yolks with sugar. Heat coffee and dissolve gelatin in it. Add to egg-sugar mixture. Heat over double boiler until thickened; add whiskey or extract; beat until creamy. Place bowl over cracked ice and stir until it begins to set. Whip cream and fold in; then whip egg whites and fold in.

Pour into mold or waxed-paper–lined bowl; press an oiled jar into center to form a well. Chill to set. Fold nuts into whipped cream; fill center.

BAKED BLUEBERRY PUDDING

½ cup plus 1 tablespoon margarine
½ cup brown sugar
2 cups blueberries
½ cup sugar
1 egg, lightly beaten
½ cup milk
1 cup flour
1 teaspoon baking powder
Whipped cream

Preheat oven to 350 degrees. In saucepan, combine 1 tablespoon margarine and brown sugar. Cook over medium heat until sugar melts. Stir in blueberries and pour into greased baking dish. Beat together the remaining margarine and ½ cup white sugar; beat in egg and milk. Sift together flour and baking powder. Combine with mixture and cover blueberry mixture with the batter and bake for 30 minutes. Serve with whipped cream.

LIME CHEESECAKE
Serves 10–12

1 cup shredded coconut
2 tablespoons flour
2 tablespoons margarine, melted
1 envelope unflavored gelatin
2 (8-ounce) packages cream cheese
3 eggs, separated
3/4 cup sugar
1/4 cup lime juice
Grated lime rind
Green food coloring (optional)
1 cup whipping cream, whipped

Combine coconut, flour and margarine; press into a 9-inch springform pan. Bake at 350 degrees for 12–15 minutes. Soften gelatin in 1/4 cup cold water. Soften cream cheese. Combine egg yolks, 3/4 cup water and sugar in saucepan; cook, stirring constantly, over medium heat for 5 minutes. Stir in gelatin until dissolved. Add gelatin mixture gradually to cream cheese; mix until blended. Stir in lime juice, 1 teaspoon lime rind and several drops of green food coloring, if desired. Fold in whipped cream and stiffly beaten egg whites; pour over crust. Chill until firm. Garnish with lime rind. A dreamy, delightful dessert!

CRESCENT APPLE PASTRIES
Makes 16

2 cups (2 large) apples, peeled and finely chopped
1/3 cup sugar
2 tablespoons flour
1/4 teaspoon cinnamon
2 (8 ounce) cans Pillsbury Quick Crescent Dinner Rolls

Glaze:
1/2 cup powdered sugar
2-3 teaspoons water

Heat oven to 350 degrees. Combine first 4 ingredients. Stir until apples are well coated. Separate crescent dough into 16 triangles. Spoon about 1 rounded tablespoon apple mixture onto center of each triangle. Fold 3 points of dough over filling, overlapping like an envelope. Place 1 inch apart on ungreased cookie sheet. Bake at 350 degrees for 20-25 minutes until golden brown. Remove and cool on rack. Blend glaze; drizzle over warm rolls.

EASY CHERRY COBBLER

2 cans tart cherries, undrained
1 package white cake mix
1 stick margarine, melted
1 cup nuts

Pour cherries in bottom of 9 x 13-inch pan, then sprinkle dry cake mix over cherries and *do not stir*. Pour melted margarine over cake mix; sprinkle nuts on top. *Do not mix.* Bake at 400 degrees for 30 minutes, or until set. Delicious topped with ice cream.

HAPPY DAY CAKE
Serves 8–10

1 (3¾-ounce) package chocolate fudge pudding and pie filling
2 cups milk
1 (11¼-ounce) frozen pound cake
⅓ cup coconut
½ gallon vanilla ice cream (optional)

Prepare pudding with 2 cups milk according to package directions. Cover surface of pudding with waxed paper or plastic wrap; refrigerate until cool.

Slice pound cake lengthwise into 3 layers. Spread pudding between each layer and frost top with pudding. Sprinkle with coconut. Serve with a scoop of vanilla ice cream, if desired.

PEANUT BUTTER PARFAIT
Serves 4

1 cup brown sugar
⅓ cup milk
¼ cup white corn syrup
1 tablespoon butter
¼ cup peanut butter
Vanilla ice cream
Peanuts

Combine first 4 ingredients in medium saucepan. Cook over medium heat until sugar dissolves and butter melts, stirring constantly. Remove from heat; add peanut butter. Beat with rotary beater or mixer until smooth; cool. Alternate layers of peanut sauce and ice cream in parfait glasses, beginning and ending with ice cream. Top with peanuts.

MILK DUD DESSERT

6 egg yolks
1 cup sugar
1 cup rusk crumbs
½ cup chopped walnuts
1 teaspoon vanilla
1 teaspoon baking powder
6 egg whites
4 small packages Milk Duds
¹/₂ cup milk
1 cup confectioners' sugar
2 tablespoons butter
½ pint whipping cream

Beat egg yolks; add sugar and beat again.

Mix together rusk crumbs, nuts, vanilla and baking powder. Add to egg mixture. Fold in stiffly beaten egg whites. Bake in 9 x 13-inch greased pan at 350 degrees for 30 minutes. Cool. Melt Milk Duds, milk, confectioners' sugar and butter until smooth, stirring constantly. Let stand until cool and creamy. Whip the cream; spread over baked portion. Pour sauce on top and refrigerate overnight.

FRUIT COCKTAIL DESSERT

The topping melts as it cooks and makes a tasty dessert.

1 (16-ounce) can fruit cocktail, drained
1 egg, beaten
1 cup sugar
1 teaspoon soda
1 cup flour
⅛ teaspoon salt
½ cup chopped nuts
½ cup brown sugar

Add egg to fruit and then fold in dry ingredients. Pour the batter into a 9-inch round or square microwave-safe baking dish.

Combine nuts and brown sugar and pour over batter.

Place small glass or custard cup, open end up, in center of baking dish before placing batter in dish. Microwave, uncovered, 7–8 minutes. For varying power, use 5 minutes on 50 percent power and 4–5 minutes on HIGH.

CARAMEL CHRISTMAS CUSTARD
Serves 5

¾ cup sugar
3 eggs
⅛ teaspoon salt
2 cups milk, scalded
1 teaspoon vanilla extract

Heat ½ cup sugar slowly in a small heavy skillet, stirring constantly, until sugar melts and turns a light caramel color. Pour into 5 (6-ounce) custard cups. Let stand until slightly cooled. Lightly beat eggs with remaining ¼ cup sugar, salt, milk and vanilla. Pour mixture into the cups, being careful not to disturb the caramel. Place cups in pan of hot water (water should be almost level with top of cups) and bake at 350 degrees for 40 minutes, or until a knife inserted in center comes out clean. Remove immediately from water. Chill if desired. To serve, loosen edges with knife and turn out onto serving dishes.

PRETTY PUMPKIN CUSTARD

- 2 cups canned pumpkin
- 1 cup soft bread crumbs
- 2 eggs, separated
- 1½ cups sweet milk
- 1 cup sugar
- 3 tablespoons butter, melted
- ¼ teaspoon salt
- 1¼ teaspoons orange extract

Combine all ingredients 1 at a time, except egg whites; mix well after each addition. Pour into ovenproof dish or individual custard cups. Bake at 325 degrees until mixture thickens and browns. Beat egg whites until stiff; add 2 tablespoons sugar. Spread on top of custard; place under broiler until golden brown.

CRANBERRY PUDDING

- 1 cup flour
- ½ cup sugar
- 1½ teaspoons baking powder
  Salt
- 1 cup halved cranberries
- 1½ tablespoons melted butter
- ½ cup milk

Mix the dry ingredients. Blend in butter and milk. Add cranberries. Bake in greased 9 x 9-inch pan at 375 degrees for 30 minutes.

Sauce:
- ½ cup butter
- 1 cup brown sugar
- ¾ cup cream (evaporated milk is fine)

Place ingredients in saucepan on medium heat until well-blended. Serve pudding in squares with warm sauce.

HOLIDAY MINCEMEAT-STUFFED APPLES
Serves 8

- 8 medium-size Granny Smith apples
- 4 tablespoons butter *or* margarine
- 1 tablespoon rum extract
- 8 tablespoons mincemeat

Wash and core apples; do not peel. Place apples in an ovenproof dish. Fill cavities with butter, rum extract and mincemeat. Bake at 350 degrees for 25 minutes, or until apples are tender. Serve with baked pork loin, lamb or baked ham.

BLUEBERRY SALAD
Serves 12

- 1 (3-ounce) package blackberry gelatin
- 2 cups boiling water
- 1 (15-ounce) can blueberries with juice (*or* 1 pound of your own, frozen)
- 1 (8-ounce) can crushed pineapple, drained

Topping:
- 1 (8-ounce) package cream cheese, softened
- ¼ cup sugar
- ¼ pint sour cream
- ½ teaspoon vanilla
- ½ cup nuts

Dissolve gelatin in boiling water. Add blueberries and pineapple; pour into 9 x 12-inch glass baking dish. Refrigerate until set.

Blend cream cheese and sugar. Add sour cream slowly and then vanilla. Spread over gelatin salad and sprinkle with nuts. Refrigerate until serving time.

This salad may be varied with the use of black raspberry gelatin.

BAKED BANANAS

- 2 bananas
  Lemon juice
  Brown sugar *or* granulated sugar with cinnamon
  Butter

Peel bananas and slice in half lengthwise. Place in a buttered pie plate or casserole. Sprinkle with lemon juice and sugar. Dot with butter. Bake at 350 degrees for 15 minutes. This is also a delicious way to make a dessert using pears or apples.

FRUIT PARFAITS

- 2 tablespoons frozen orange juice concentrate
- 1 tablespoon sugar
- ½ cup whipped topping
- 1 orange, peeled, sectioned and cut up
- 1 banana, sliced
- ½ cup pineapple chunks
- ⅓ cup marshmallows

Combine orange juice and sugar; mix well. Fold in whipped topping. In another bowl, combine fruit pieces. In 2 parfait glasses, alternately layer fruit, marshmallows and then whipped topping; repeat. Chill. May be topped with a maraschino cherry.

QUICK BAKED ALASKA
Serves 4

- 4 packaged dessert shells
  Jam *or* jelly
- 4 scoops of favorite ice cream
  Whipped cream

Turn oven temperature to 475 degrees. Spread dessert shells with jam or jelly. Place on baking sheet. Bake dessert shells with jam or jelly for 5 minutes. Place a scoop of ice cream in center; top with whipped cream; serve.

MOCHA FLUFF
Serves 4

1 envelope gelatin
¼ cup water
¼ cup sugar
¼ teaspoon salt
1½ cups hot, strong coffee
2 tablespoons lemon juice
2 egg whites, stiffly beaten

Soften gelatin in cold water. Add sugar, salt and hot coffee, stirring thoroughly to dissolve. Add lemon juice and cool. When nearly set, beat until stiff. Add egg whites and continue beating until mixture holds its shape. Turn into molds and chill.

GINGER PEACH CAKE
Serves 6–8

2 tablespoons margarine
1 package ginger bread mix
½ cup water
2 cups sliced peaches
Whipped cream for topping

Preheat oven to 375 degrees. Grease bottom and sides of baking pan. In bowl, combine gingerbread mix and water. Blend at low speed; then beat 2 minutes at medium speed. Stir in peaches. Pour into baking pan. Bake in oven for 35 minutes. Serve warm topped with whipped cream.

BANANA SPLIT
Serves 4

1 (3⅝-ounce) package chocolate pudding and pie filling
2 cups milk
4 bananas, sliced lengthwise
½ gallon vanilla ice cream

1 (8½-ounce) can pineapple tidbits, drained
½ cup chopped pecans
1 cup whipped cream
4 maraschino cherries, drained

Prepare pudding with 2 cups milk according to package directions. Cover surface of pudding with waxed paper or plastic wrap; refrigerate until cool.

Put 1 sliced banana in each of 4 serving dishes. Top with 3 scoops of ice cream; cover with ¼ of pudding; sprinkle with pineapple tidbits and pecans. Garnish with whipped cream and a cherry.

CREAMY RICE PUDDING AND MERINGUE
Serves 6

⅓ cup rice
1 quart milk
4 eggs, separated
½ teaspoon salt
1 teaspoon vanilla
½ cup, plus 3 tablespoons sugar, divided

Wash rice and cook slowly in milk until tender. Beat yolks slightly; add to rice-milk mixture with vanilla, salt and ½ cup sugar. Cook for 5 minutes, or until slightly thickened. Pour into a buttered casserole. Beat egg whites until stiff; add 3 tablespoons sugar. Place meringue over pudding; bake in a 350-degree oven for 15 minutes, or until meringue is golden brown.

AMBROSIA PARFAITS

1 (8-ounce) can mandarin orange segments, drained
¼ cup chopped, toasted blanched almonds

2 cups prepared whipped topping
1 package *instant* toasted coconut pudding
2 cups cold milk
Mint sprigs

Reserve 5 orange segments for garnish. Fold oranges and almonds into topping. Combine pudding with milk; beating slowly for 2 minutes. Alternate topping and pudding in parfait glasses. Garnish with oranges and mint.

MAGIC MALTED PARFAIT
Serves 2

4 scoops vanilla ice cream
1 cup caramel topping
½ cup crushed malted milk balls
2 whole malted milk balls
Whipped cream

Put a scoop of ice cream into each parfait glass. Pour a tablespoon of caramel topping over ice cream, followed with a layer of crushed malted milk balls.

Repeat these steps by adding another scoop of ice cream, a layer of caramel topping and a sprinkling of milk balls. Top off with whipped cream, and garnish with a malted milk ball.

CRANBERRY FLUFF
Serves 6

1 pound cranberries, chopped
1 cup sugar
½ cup seeded grapes, halved
½ cup small marshmallows
½ cup chopped pecans
½ cup maraschino cherries, halved
½ pint whipping cream, whipped

Combine fruits, marshmallows and nuts; fold in whipping cream. Transfer mixture to a serving bowl. Chill in refrigerator 1–2 hours.

APPLE ROLY POLY
Serves 6-8

2 cups prepared baking mix
1/2 cup honey
3/4 teaspoon cinnamon
1/4 teaspoon nutmeg
1/4 teaspoon cloves
3 tablespoons sugar
5 large tart apples, peeled, cored, finely chopped
2 tablespoons butter or margarine

Prepare biscuit mix as directed on package. On lightly floured board, roll dough into 1/4 inch oblong (about 10x12 inches). Spread with honey to within 1 inch of the edges of dough. Combine spices and sugar. Toss with apples. Spread apples evenly over the honey, and dot apples with butter. Roll up like a jelly roll and seal well. Bake in greased pan with sides at 350 degrees for 40 minutes. Slice and serve hot with whipped cream, hot lemon, or vanilla sauce.

COLONIAL BAKED APPLES
Serves 8

3 medium sweet potatoes
1/2 teaspoon finely shredded orange peel
2 tablespoons orange juice
1 tablespoon brown sugar
1 tablespoon butter or margarine
1/4 teaspoon nutmeg, ground
1/4 teaspoon salt
1 beaten egg
2 tablespoons milk
8 large cooking apples, peeled and cored
1/2 cup corn syrup
2 tablespoons lemon juice

Cook sweet potatoes, covered in enough boiling salted water to cover, for 25 to 35 minutes or until tender. Drain, peel, dice and mash with electric mixer on low speed until smooth. Should have about 1-3/4 cups mashed potatoes. Add orange peel, orange juice, sugar butter, nutmeg and salt. Add egg and milk; set aside. Remove a slice from top of each apple. Score apple by going around the outside surface with tines of a fork in circular pattern. Using pastry bag fitted with star tip, fill apples with sweet potato mixture. Place apples in 12 x 7-1/2 x 2-inch baking dish. Stir corn syrup and lemon juice together and pour over apples. Bake uncovered in 325 degree oven for 45 minutes or until tender, basting several times with the corn syrup mixture. Serve hot.

BOILED APPLE DUMPLINGS

3 cups flour
4 teaspoons baking powder
1/2 teaspoon salt
2 tablespoons sugar
2 tablespoons vegetable shortening
1/4 cup milk
3 large tart apples
6 teaspoons sugar
Milk
Sugar

Sift baking powder, salt, and sugar with flour into bowl. Cut in shortening until mixture is in crumbs the size of peas. Stir in 1/4 cup milk. On floured board, roll dough to 1-1/2 inch thickness. Cut into six squares. Pare and core apples and cut in half. Place a half on each square of dough and sprinkle with 1 teaspoon sugar.

Pull the four corners of the dough together, dampen slightly, and press edges to seal. Tie each dumpling in a clean piece of white muslin. Drop dumplings into a large kettle of boiling water. Cook 20-25 minutes depending on size of apple. Serve with milk, cinnamon, and sugar, if desired.

MAPLE APPLE BROWN BETTY
Serves 4

1-1/2 cups fine bread crumbs, toasted lightly
3/4 stick (6 tablespoons) unsalted butter
4 apples, peeled and diced
1/2 cup maple syrup
3/4 teaspoon cinnamon
Vanilla ice cream, as an accompaniment

Sprinkle bottom of well-buttered baking dish with one fourth of the crumbs; dot the crumbs with one fourth of the butter. Spread one third of apples over the crumbs. In a small bowl combine the syrup and cinnamon; drizzle one third of mixture over apples. Layer the remaining crumbs, butter, apples and syrup mixture, ending with a layer of crumbs and butter. Bake in a preheated 375 degree oven for 40 minutes or until apples are tender. Serve the dessert with ice cream, if desired.

MARSHMALLOW APPLE CRISP
Serves 6

4 cups peeled, sliced apples
1/4 cup water
3/4 cup flour
1/2 cup sugar
1 teaspoon cinnamon
1/4 teaspoon salt
1/2 cup margarine
1/2 cup miniature marshmallows

Place apples and water in 8-inch square baking dish. Combine flour, sugar, cinnamon, and salt; cut in margarine until mixture is like coarse crumbs. Sprinkle over apples. Bake at 350 degrees for 35 to 40 minutes or until apples are tender. Sprinkle with marshmallows. Broil until lightly browned.

CARAMEL CORN

Serves 6-8

6 toffee bars, (1-1/8 ounce each)
1/4 cup light corn syrup
8 cups popped popcorn
1 cup unsalted roasted peanuts

In heavy saucepan, heat toffee bars and corn syrup over low heat until melted, stirring often. Pour popcorn into large, deep pan. Add warm toffee mixture and peanuts. Toss well until popcorn is coated. Cool; break into chunks.

Children and adults all enjoy caramel corn.

CARAMEL CRUNCH

1 cup light brown sugar, firmly
   packed
1/2 cup butter or margarine
1 (6 ounce) package chocolate
   chips
1 cup coarsely chopped nuts

Combine sugar and butter in saucepan; boil 7 minutes. Melt chocolate chips in saucepan over low heat. Spread nuts over bottom of buttered 8x8 inch pan. Pour butter and sugar mixture slowly over nuts. Pour melted chocolate over top. Cool. Cut into pieces.

DATE NUT BALLS

Cook together for 5 minutes:
1 stick margarine
1 cup sugar
1 egg, beaten
1 (8 ounce) package dates, cut up
Pinch of salt

Remove from heat and cool.
Add:

1 cup chopped nuts
2 cups Rice Krispies
1 teaspoon vanilla
   Stir well and shape in small balls.
Roll in flaked coconut.

EASTER EGG CANDY

1 cup hot mashed potatoes
2 tablespoons butter
1 cup shredded coconut
1 teaspoon vanilla
3 - 1 pound boxes confectioners'
   sugar
1 - 8 ounce package of chocolate
   chips
1/8 cake paraffin

Combine potatoes and butter; stir in coconut and vanilla. Add sugar gradually, mixing well after each addition. Form into egg shapes, using 1 tablespoon mixture for each egg; place on waxed paper. Let harden for 1-3 days. Melt chocolate over hot water; dip eggs into chocolate, using 2 spoons. Place on waxed paper to harden. Chopped nuts, candied fruits, or peanut butter may be used instead of coconut.

EASTER PEANUT BUTTER EGGS

2 eggs, well beaten
1/8 teaspoon salt
1-1/2 to 2 cups peanut butter
4-5 cups powdered sugar
1 teaspoon vanilla
1 Hershey chocolate bar
1 - 6 ounce package chocolate chips

Mix the eggs, salt, peanut butter, sugar, and vanilla in order listed. Form dough into egg shapes. Melt the chocolate bar and the chocolate chips in a double boiler. Dip egg shapes into chocolate mixture. Arrange on waxed paper until set.

ICE CREAM SANDWICHES

Makes 15

32 graham cracker squares
2 tablespoons milk
1 tablespoon cornstarch
1 tub Creamy Deluxe ready to spread
   frosting (any flavor)
1-1/2 cups chilled whipping cream.

Line 13x9x2 inch pan with aluminum foil. Arrange 16 graham crackers on foil, cutting about 6 of the squares to completely cover foil. Mix milk and cornstarch in large bowl; stir in frosting and whipping cream. Beat on medium speed, scraping bowl constantly, 2 minutes. Beat on high speed until thick and creamy; scrape bowl occasionally. Beat about 3 minutes. Spread over graham crackers in pan. Arrange remaining graham crackers over frosting mixture, cutting about 6 of the squares to completely cover mixture. Cover and freeze until firm, about 8 hours. Cut into 2-1/2 inch squares.

HOMEMADE MARSHMALLOWS

2 cups granulated sugar
3/4 cup water
2 tablespoons gelatin
1/2 cup cold water
1 teaspoon vanilla
1/2 teaspoon salt
Cornstarch
Confectioners' sugar

Mix granulated sugar with 3/4 cup water. Simmer to soft ball stage. Remove from fire. Soften gelatin in cold water. Place on large platter. Pour hot syrup over softened gelatin. Stir until dissolved. Let stand until partially cooled; whip until thick and white, and mixture will nearly hold its shape. Add vanilla and salt. Pour into straight sided pans lined with equal parts of cornstarch and confectioners' sugar, mixed together. Let stand in cool place until firm (not in ice box). Cut into squares with scissors and dust with confectioners' sugar.

CHOCOLATE DELIGHT

Crust:
1/2 cup chopped pecans
1-1/2 cups flour
1-1/4 sticks margarine

Melt margarine; add flour, nuts, and mix well. Pat into 9x13-inch pan. Bake 20-25 minutes at 350 degrees until slightly brown.

First layer:
1 cup powdered sugar
1 medium size Cool Whip
1 (8 ounce) cream cheese

Mix powdered sugar and cream cheese; blend well. Add 1 cup of Cool Whip; spread over crust.

Second layer:
2 (6 ounce) boxes instant chocolate pudding mix
3 cups milk

Combine pudding mix and milk. Pour mixture over first layer.

Third layer:
Spread remaining Cool Whip over top. Make dessert 24 hours before serving and refrigerate, but do not freeze.

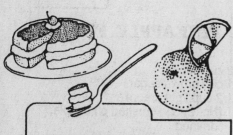

LEMON DELIGHT

Serves 12-15

1-1/2 cups flour, sifted
1-1/2 sticks margarine
1/2 cup chopped pecans
1 - 8 ounce package cream cheese
1 cup sifted powdered sugar
1 - 9 ounce container frozen whipped topping
2 - 6 ounce packages instant lemon pudding mix
2 tablespoons lemon juice
3 cups milk
1/2 cup chopped pecans

Blend together flour, margarine and 1/2 cup pecans. Press into a 13 x 9 inch pan. Bake 20 minutes at 350 degrees. Cool.

Blend together cream cheese, powdered sugar, and 1/2 of 9 ounce carton of whipped topping. Spread over crust. Combine 2 packages instant lemon pudding mix with 2 tablespoons lemon juice and 3 cups milk. Pour over previous layer. When firm, top with remainder of whipped topping. Sprinkle with 1/2 cup pecans. Chill overnight and keep in refrigerator. A delightful tasting dessert.

APPLE DUMPLING DESSERT

1 can (10) country-style refrigerator biscuits
2 cups thinly sliced peeled apples
1/2 cup packed brown sugar
1/2 cup evaporated milk
1/2 cup dark corn syrup
1/4 cup margarine

Preheat oven to 375 degrees.

Grease an 8-inch square baking dish. Separate biscuits into 10 individual ones. Place on bottom of buttered baking dish. Arrange apple slices over top.

In small saucepan combine all remaining ingredients and bring to a boil, stirring constantly. Pour hot syrup mixture over apples and biscuits. Bake at 375 degrees for 25-35 minutes or until golden brown and biscuits are done in the center. Serve warm.

For extra goodness, top with whipped cream.

APPLE DESSERT

1 box yellow cake mix
1/2 cup margarine
1/2 cup coconut
2-1/2 cups sliced apples
1/2 cup sugar
1 teaspoon cinnamon
1 cup sour cream
1 egg

Put yellow cake mix, margarine and coconut in bowl and mix like you would for pie crust. Pat into ungreased 13 x 9 inch pan. Bake 10 minutes at 350 degrees. Mix sugar, cinnamon, and apples and put over baked crust. Blend the sour cream and egg; drizzle over top. Bake at 350 degrees for 25 minutes. You can use any flavor cake mix or any kind of fruit. This is a really delicious dessert you will enjoy.

BANANA SPLIT DESSERT

First layer:
2 cups graham cracker crumbs
1/2 cup sugar
1 stick melted margarine
Mix and spread in bottom of 11 x 14-inch casserole.

Second layer:
2 egg whites, stiffly beaten
1 stick softened margarine
1 (1-pound) box powdered sugar

Beat with mixer for 10 minutes, spread over crumbs.

Third layer:
Slice 2-3 bananas over sugar mixture.

Fourth layer:
Spread 1 large can crushed pineapple, drained, over banana layer.

Fifth layer:
Spread 1 large or 2 small cartons Cool Whip over pineapple.

Sixth layer:
Sprinkle chopped pecans and maraschino cherries over all.

BUTTERSCOTCH-PEANUT FUDGE

Makes 4 dozen squares

1 (12 ounce) package butterscotch pieces
1 (14 ounce) can condensed sweetened milk
1-1/2 cups miniature marshmallows
2/3 cup chunk-style peanut butter
1 teaspoon vanilla
1 cup chopped peanuts
Dash of salt

In saucepan combine butterscotch pieces, milk, and marshmallows. Stir over medium heat until marshmallows melt. Remove from heat; beat in peanut butter, vanilla, and dash salt. Stir in nuts. Pour into buttered 9x9x2 inch pan. Chill. Cut in squares. Store in refrigerator.

CHUNKY MACADAMIA ORANGE FUDGE

3 cups sugar
3/4 butter
2/3 cup evaporated milk
12 ounce package semi-sweet chocolate morsels
7 ounce jar marshmallow cream
1 cup macadamia nuts
2 tablespoons orange flavored liquer

In heavy saucepan, combine sugar, butter and milk. Bring to full rolling boil over moderate heat, stirring constantly; boil 5 minutes, stirring constantly. Remove from heat. Add morsels; stir until morsels melt and mixture is smooth. Add marshmallow cream, nuts and liquer; beat until well blended. Pour into foil-lined 9" x 13" pan. Chill until firm.

HONEYPOT FUDGE

1/2 cup butter or margarine
2 tablespoons honey
1 pound confectioners' sugar
1/8 teaspoon cream of tartar

Mix all ingredients in 3-quart saucepan. Bring slowly to boil, stirring constantly. Bring to full rolling boil for about 8 minutes, stirring occasionally (a small amount dropped into cold water should form a soft ball at 235 degrees.) Remove pan from heat; cool slightly; beat mixture until thick. Pour into greased shallow pan. When nearly set, mark into squares. Separate pieces, when set, and leave to harden on plate.

MAPLE SYRUP FUDGE

Makes about 25 - 1-1/2" pieces

2 cups maple syrup
1 tablespoon light corn syrup
3/4 cup half and half
1 teaspoon vanilla
3/4 cup coarsely chopped walnuts

Combine maple syrup, corn syrup and half and half in 1-1/2 - quart saucepan. Place pan over moderate heat; stir constantly until mixture starts to boil. Continue cooking mixture without stirring until it reaches 234 degrees on candy thermometer or until a small amount of syrup forms a soft ball in cold water. Remove pan from heat; do not stir. Let mixture stand until it cools to lukewarm, about 110 to 120 degrees. Beat mixture until it thickens and begins to lose its gloss. Add vanilla and walnuts; pour immediately into a buttered 8 x 8 x 2-inch pan. When cool, cut into squares.

NOEL FUDGE

2 cups sugar
3/4 cup milk
1 teaspoon Karo syrup
1 teaspoon vanilla
2 tablespoons butter
1 cup diced red or green candied cherries
1/2 cup chopped nuts

Mix together sugar, milk, and Karo in saucepan. Bring to boil; lower heat and simmer for 8 to 10 minutes, stirring occasionally. When a drop forms a firm ball in cold water, remove from heat; stir in butter and vanilla. Let cool. Beat well with large spoon until mixture loses gloss. Quickly stir in candied fruit and nuts; pour into buttered 8 or 9 inch square pan. When set, cut in squares.

Variations: For chocolate fudge, stir 4 tablespoons cocoa into sugar before adding milk. For peanut butter flavor, substitute 3 tablespoons peanut butter for the butter. Use chopped or diced dates, if desired, or coconut, instead of fruits and nuts. Wrap in foil to store.

This is an excellent fudge which keeps well.

PINEAPPLE FUDGE

2 cups sugar
1 cup brown sugar
1/2 cup light cream
1 (No. 2) can crushed pineapple, drained
2 tablespoons butter
1/2 teaspoon ginger
2 teaspoons vanilla
1 cup walnuts, broken

Combine sugars, cream, and pineapple; cook, stirring occasionally, to soft ball stage, 236 degrees. Remove from heat. Add butter, ginger, and vanilla. Cool to room temperature, stirring, until lukewarm. Beat until mixture loses its gloss. Add nuts. Pour into buttered 8x8x2 inch pan. Score candy in squares. Press walnut half on each. Finish cutting when firm.

Meat
DISHES

BREADED PORK CHOPS
Serves 6

- 6 pork chops
- ¾ cup fine bread crumbs
- 1 teaspoon salt
- ⅛ teaspoon pepper
- 1 egg, beaten
- ¼ cup milk
- ¼ cup boiling water

Add salt and pepper to bread crumbs. Beat egg and add milk. Dip chops in liquid and roll in crumbs. Put 3 tablespoons fat into skillet; brown chops. Place chops in a baking pan or dish and add boiling water. Cover and bake at 400 degrees for about 50 minutes. (I take the cover off for about the last 10 minutes.) These are delicious and so easy to prepare, too. The chops turn out very tender. This is one of my favorite pork chop recipes.

HERB-STUFFED HAM SLICES
Serves 6

- 4 tablespoons butter *or* margarine
- 1 onion, finely chopped
- 10 mushrooms, finely chopped
- 1¼ teaspoons prepared mustard
- 2 tablespoons parsley, finely chopped
- 2 tablespoons chives, finely chopped
- ¼ teaspoon ground sage
- ¾ cup herb bread crumbs
- ½ to 1 cup chicken stock
  Salt and pepper to taste
- 6 large slices cold boiled *or* baked ham, ¼–½ inch thick

Heat half the butter in a skillet; add onion and mushrooms; sauté 5 minutes; remove to bowl.

Add rest of ingredients with enough chicken stock to moisten the mixture and hold it together. Spread the prepared mixture on ham slices; fold slices in half; arrange on shallow, buttered baking dish. Melt remaining butter; pour over ham slices. Cover; bake at 375 degrees for 20 minutes.

SASSY SAUSAGES
Serves 5–6

- 1 cup water
- ⅓ cup red cinnamon candies
  Red food coloring
- 3 red tart apples, cored and cut into ½-inch rings
- 1 pound pork sausage links
- 3 tablespoons water

In skillet, heat 1 cup water, the cinnamon candies and a few drops red food coloring until candies are melted. Place apple rings in syrup; cook slowly, turning occasionally, about 20 minutes, or until tender. Place links in another skillet; add 3 tablespoons water. Cover tightly; cook slowly for 8 minutes. Uncover; cook, turning sausages until well-browned. To serve, insert hot sausage link in center of each apple slice.

SOUPY PORK CHOPS

- 6 pork chops, ½ inch thick, fat removed
- 1 can tomato soup
- 1 package dry onion soup mix
- 1 medium onion, sliced
- 1 green pepper, sliced
- 1 cup mushrooms, sliced

Arrange chops in an oblong casserole. Mix remaining ingredients and pour over chops. Cover with waxed paper. Microwave at 70 percent for 30 minutes.

SPARERIBS "ALOHA"

- 3 pounds spareribs
- ½ cup finely chopped onion
- ¼ cup green pepper, chopped
- 1 (16-ounce) can tomato sauce
- ½ teaspoon dry mustard
- 1 tablespoon Worcestershire sauce
- 1 (2½-cup) can crushed pineapple
- ¼ cup brown sugar

Cut every third rib about halfway through the strip. Sprinkle with salt and pepper. Place in shallow pan. Bake 1¼ hours at 350 degrees. Pour off fat. Mix remaining ingredients and let stand to blend flavor. Pour over ribs. Bake 45–50 minutes, basting frequently to glaze ribs.

ROAST GOOSE
Serves 6

1 (6–8 pound) goose

Preheat oven to 400 degrees. Place goose, breast side up, on rack about 1 inch from bottom of roaster. After 30 minutes, turn down to 375 degrees and prick goose with fork around breast, back and drumsticks, letting excess fat escape. Let cook about 20 minutes per pound.

Apple Stuffing:
- 3 cups stale bread
- 1 egg
- ¼ cup chopped onion
- ½ cup melted butter
- ½ teaspoon salt
- ½ teaspoon poultry seasoning
- ¼ teaspoon sage
- ¼ teaspoon white pepper
- 1 cup chopped apples
  Chicken stock, enough to moisten

Sauté onions in butter until transparent. Cool. Add egg, bread, seasoning and apples; mix thoroughly, moistening with the stock until wet, but not soupy. Place in heavily buttered small baking dish and bake at 300 degrees for 1 hour 15 minutes.

Tangerine Sauce:
- 2 tablespoons sugar
- 1 lemon
- 1 orange
- ¾ cup red current jelly
- ¼ cup wine vinegar
- ½ cup orange juice concentrate
- 1 pint brown gravy
- 2 tangerines

Grate peel from orange and lemon; save. Place sugar in heavy-bottomed saucepan and caramelize with lemon and orange split in two. Add jelly, orange juice and vinegar. Bring to a boil; remove lemon and orange. Add brown gravy and simmer for 15 minutes. Strain. Add tangerine segments and peel as garnish.

CHICKEN-VEGETABLE-FRENCH-FRY CASSEROLE
Serves 8

This provides meat, potatoes and vegetables in 1 dish. Put together ahead of time, and it is ready to eat 35 minutes after popping in the oven.

- 2 fryer chickens, cut up
- ¼ cup (½ stick) butter
- ¼ cup flour
- 1 teaspoon salt
- 2 cups reserved chicken broth
- 1 (10½-ounce) can cream of celery soup
- 1 (10-ounce) package frozen peas and carrots
- ½ cup (1 stick) butter
- 1 (1-pound) box frozen french fries
  Parmesan cheese

Cook, cool and bone chicken. Save 2 cups of broth. In a buttered 9 x 13-inch pan, put good-sized pieces of chicken. Melt butter; add flour, salt, broth and soup. Cook until thick and smooth. Cook peas and carrots for 3 minutes. Drain. Mix with sauce and pour over chicken.

Melt stick of butter; stir frozen french fries in butter until coated. Place on top of other ingredients. Sprinkle generously with Parmesan cheese. Bake, uncovered, at 450 degrees for 20–25 minutes. If it has been put together earlier and refrigerated, bake for 35 minutes.

CHICKEN NOODLE MEDLEY
Serves 6

- 10 ounces green noodles
- 1 medium-size onion
- 1 bay leaf
- 2 tablespoons butter
- 1 teaspoon onion salt
- ⅛ teaspoon pepper

- 3 pounds broiler-fryer chicken, cut up
- 1 (10¾-ounce) can cream of mushroom soup
- ¾ cup milk
- ⅔ cup grated Parmesan cheese
- 2 tablespoons chopped chives
- ½ teaspoon sage
  Paprika
- 1 (1-pound) package frozen baby carrots, drained and cooked

Preheat oven to 350 degrees. Cook noodles according to package directions, adding onion and bay leaf to cooking water. Drain noodles; discard onion and bay leaf. Toss together noodles, butter, onion salt and pepper. Spoon into buttered 13 x 9-inch baking dish. Sprinkle chicken pieces with salt and pepper; place on noodles. Combine soup, milk, ⅓ cup cheese, chives and sage; pour over chicken. Sprinkle with remaining cheese and paprika. Bake 45 minutes; add carrots. Bake additional 20 minutes, or until chicken is tender.

CRUSTY BAKED CHICKEN
Serves 4

- 2 cups potato chips, finely crushed
- ¼ teaspoon salt
- ¼ teaspoon pepper
- ¼ teaspoon curry powder
- ⅛ teaspoon ginger
- 1 (3-pound) frying chicken, cut up
- 2 eggs, beaten
- ¼ cup milk
- ½ cup butter *or* margarine, melted

Mix potato chips, salt, pepper, curry powder and ginger. Combine eggs and milk; pour butter into shallow baking dish. Dip chicken in chips, then in egg mixture, then in chips again. Put pieces side by side in dish; bake at 375 degrees for 45 minutes.

BAKED CHICKEN

2 chicken breasts
1 tablespoon butter *or* margarine, melted
½ cup Parmesan cheese
2 tablespoons butter *or* margarine

Preheat oven to 400 degrees. Dip chicken in melted butter and coat with cheese. Melt remaining butter in a pie plate and place chicken in pie plate, skin-side up. Bake at 400 degrees for 50 minutes. Baste with juice during baking. Cover with foil if chicken browns too quickly.

CHICKEN AND BISCUITS
Serves 4

Filling:
2 tablespoons vegetable oil
1 small onion, peeled and chopped
½ green pepper, finely chopped
⅔ cup sliced mushrooms
2 tablespoons cornstarch
1½ cups milk
2 cups cooked chicken, cubed
Salt and pepper

Biscuits:
2 cups flour
2½ teaspoons baking powder
⅓ cup margarine
⅔ cup milk

Heat oil in skillet. Add onion, green pepper and mushrooms. Sauté for a few minutes. Add cornstarch; cook 1 minute, stirring constantly. Add milk gradually; stir until boiling. Add chicken and seasoning. Turn into deep 9-inch pie plate. In bowl, sift flour and baking powder. Cut in margarine with pastry blender. Stir in milk with fork to make soft dough. Knead lightly on floured board; roll to about ½-inch thickness. With cookie, cut into 1½-inch rounds. Place rounds on top of chicken; brush with milk. Bake at 425 degrees for 10–15 minutes, or until biscuits are done.

PATRICIA NIXON'S HOT CHICKEN SALAD
Serves 8

4 cups cold chicken, cut up into chunks (cooked)
2 tablespoons lemon juice
⅔ cup finely chopped toasted almonds
¾ cup mayonnaise
1 teaspoon salt
½ teaspoon monosodium glutamate
1 cup grated cheese
2 cups chopped celery
4 hard-cooked eggs, sliced
¾ cup cream of chicken soup
1 teaspoon onion, finely minced
2 pimientos, finely cut
1½ cups crushed potato chips

Combine all ingredients, except cheese, potato chips and almonds. Place in a large rectangular dish. Top with cheese, potato chips and almonds. Let stand overnight in refrigerator. Bake in a 400-degree oven for 20–25 minutes.

GINGER AND RUM ROASTED CORNISH GAME HENS

4 Cornish game hens
Salt and freshly ground pepper
1 large garlic clove, crushed
¼ cup honey
¼ cup chicken stock
¼ cup soy sauce
¼ cup rum
1 tablespoon peanut *or* vegetable oil
1 teaspoon ground ginger

Preheat oven to 375 degrees. Season Cornish hens well with salt and pepper, inside and out. Combine remaining ingredients in bowl. Spoon 2 tablespoons of the mixture into each hen cavity. Tie the legs together and fold the wings back. Place the hens in a roasting pan.

Brush each hen with the sauce. Roast for 55 minutes, or until tender. Baste the hens twice during the cooking time with the sauce.

CHICKEN CHOLUPAS

4 chicken breasts, cooked, deboned and diced
3 cans cream of chicken soup
1 large can green chilies, diced
1 onion, finely diced
16 ounces sour cream
¾ pound Monterey Jack cheese, grated
¾ pound mild cheddar cheese, grated
12 small flour tortillas

Mix all ingredients together, except tortillas and only half the cheeses. Put 3 tablespoons mixture in each tortilla. Roll up and place in a greased baking dish. Pour rest of mixture over tortillas. Sprinkle remaining cheeses over all. Bake at 350 degrees for 45 minutes.

FAVORITE CHICKEN LOAF
Serves 6

1 cup soft bread crumbs
2 cups milk
2 eggs, lightly beaten
½ teaspoon salt
¼ teaspoon paprika
3 cups cooked chicken, diced ¼ inch thick
½ cup cooked peas
¼ cup chopped pimiento
1 (10½-ounce) can condensed cream of mushroom soup for sauce

In a bowl blend bread crumbs, milk, eggs, salt and paprika. Stir in chicken, peas and pimiento. Turn into a well-greased loaf pan (9 x 5 x 3-inch). Bake in a moderate 325-degree oven until firm, about 40 minutes. Serve with mushroom sauce made from soup.

QUICK CHICKEN BAKE
Serves 6

2 cups cooked chicken, cubed
1 can cream of chicken soup
1 cup sour cream
½ cup celery, diced
½ cup onion, chopped
½ cup water chestnuts, thinly sliced
1 cup cooked rice
Bread crumbs

Mix together and place in a buttered 2-quart casserole. Sprinkle bread crumbs on top. Microwave on HIGH for 6–8 minutes.

If you prefer cream of mushroom soup or cheddar cheese soup—go for it. Do not be afraid to experiment.

CRISPY SESAME CHICKEN
Serves 6–8

10 pieces chicken
½ cup butter
½ cup bread crumbs
1 cup grated Parmesan cheese
6 tablespoons sesame seeds

Preheat oven to 350 degrees. Rinse chicken and pat dry with paper towels. Combine bread crumbs, cheese and sesame seeds. Melt butter. Dip chicken into the butter and then the seasoned crumbs. Place chicken in a shallow pan (lining with foil helps with cleanup). Bake at 350 degrees for 1 hour.

TUNA AND CHEESE CASSEROLE

⅓ cup chopped onion
1 teaspoon butter or margarine
7 tablespoons (⅓ of a 10¾-ounce can) condensed cream of celery soup

2 teaspoons lemon juice
⅔ cup tuna, drained and flaked
1 cup cooked rice
Salt to taste
Black pepper to taste
¼ cup grated cheddar cheese

Preheat oven to 350 degrees. Cook onion in butter until tender, but not brown. Stir in remaining ingredients, except cheese. Turn into a buttered, shallow 6-inch casserole for 20 minutes, or until heated through. Top with cheese and bake 5 minutes longer.

PATIO LICKIN' CHICKEN
Serves 4 to 6

1 frying chicken, cut up
1 envelope dry onion soup mix
3/4 cup uncooked rice
1 can cream of mushroom soup or cream of chicken soup
1 soup can water
1 small can mushrooms, drained
1/2 teaspoon salt
1/4 teaspoon pepper

Season chicken; brown slightly in frying pan. Mix remaining ingredients together; place in 9 x 13-inch baking dish. Arrange chicken on top. Cover with foil; bake one hour at 350 degrees. Remove foil and bake 20 minutes longer.

BARBECUED LEMON CHICKEN

3 roasting or broiling chickens
1 cup salad oil
¾ cup fresh lemon juice
1 tablespoon salt
2 teaspoons paprika
2 teaspoons onion powder
1 teaspoon garlic powder
2 teaspoons crushed sweet basil
2 teaspoons crushed thyme

Have butcher split chickens and remove wings, backbone and tail. Clean well; place in shallow pan. Combine remaining ingredients; pour into jar. Cover; shake well to blend. Pour over chicken; cover tightly. Marinate overnight in refrigerator, turning chicken occasionally. Remove to room temperature 1 hour before grilling. Barbecue chicken over hot coals for 15–20 minutes on each side, basting often with marinade.

PEPPER STEAK
Serves 6

1½ pounds round steak, ½ inch thick
1 cup sliced onion
1 cup beef broth
2 stalks celery, chopped
1 tablespoon salt
½ teaspoon garlic powder or 1 garlic clove, minced
½ teaspoon ginger
2 green peppers, cut in strips
1 cup sliced mushrooms
1 (1-pound) can tomatoes, chopped
3 tablespoons soy sauce
2 tablespoons cornstarch
1 cup water

Cut round steak into thin strips and brown in Dutch oven in small amount of oil and margarine. Add beef broth, onion, celery, salt, garlic and ginger; simmer, covered, for 35–40 minutes, or until tender. Add green peppers, mushrooms and tomatoes; cook an additional 10 minutes. Mix soy sauce and cornstarch in 1 cup water until smooth. Slowly stir into sauce and cook, stirring constantly, until thickened. Serve over rice. This can be made the day before serving and reheated in the microwave.

GREEN VEGETABLE MEAT LOAF
Serves 8

- 2 pounds lean ground meat
- 2 (10-ounce) boxes frozen chopped broccoli, thawed and drained
- 1 cup chopped onion
- ⅔ cup uncooked quick cooking oatmeal
- 2 large eggs
- ½ cup milk *or* water
- 1 (1.5-ounce) package meat loaf seasoning mix

Heat oven to 375 degrees. Lightly grease a 9 x 5 x 3-inch loaf pan. Put all ingredients into a large bowl. Mix with hands 3–4 minutes until well-blended. Press mixture into prepared pan. Bake 1 hour in the middle of oven. Remove from oven; cover loosely with foil and let stand 10–15 minutes. Drain off juice. This vegetable-laced meat loaf is delicious fresh from the oven, and even better the next day cold.

MEAT LOAF CHOW MEIN

- 1 pound ground beef
- 1 package Chow Mein Oriental Seasoning Mix
- ¾ teaspoon garlic powder
- ½ teaspoon salt
- ½ teaspoon pepper
- 2 eggs
- 1 can crispy Chinese noodles (optional)

Mix all ingredients together, except crispy Chinese noodles. Mold into 2 loaves. Bake at 350 degrees for 1 hour. Arrange Chinese noodles around loaves for garnish before serving.

MEXICAN MEAT LOAF

- 1½ pounds ground beef
- 1 medium onion, chopped
- ½ cup chopped mushrooms
- ¼ cup chopped green pepper
- ½ cup taco sauce
- 2 tablespoons barbecue sauce
- 1 egg, beaten
- ½ cup tortilla chips, finely crushed
- ½ teaspoon salt
- Dash black pepper

Combine all ingredients; mix well. Pack into an oiled 8-inch loaf pan. Bake at 400 degrees for 1¼ hours, or until done.

LAYERED MEAT LOAF WITH MUSHROOM SAUCE

- 6 ounces herb-seasoned stuffing mix
- 1½ pounds lean ground beef
- ½ pound bulk pork sausage, with sage
- 1 egg, beaten
- 2 slices bread, crumbled
- ¼ cup milk
- 1 teaspoon garlic salt
- 2 teaspoons minced onion
- 1 teaspoon Worcestershire sauce
- ½ teaspoon pepper (No salt is needed as it is seasoned enough with other ingredients)
- 1 can mushroom soup
- ¼ cup water

Prepare the stuffing mix, using 1½ cups water and 3 tablespoons melted butter. Mix well and fluff lightly. Set aside.
Combine remaining ingredients, except soup and water, in a bowl; mix well. Spread half the meat mixture in bottom of a loaf pan. Spread stuffing over, patting it down evenly. Pat remaining meat mixture over stuffing. Preheat oven to 350 degrees. Bake loaf for 45 minutes, or until top is lightly browned. Combine mushroom soup with water and pour over meat loaf. Continue baking for 30 minutes longer.

TENDER MEATBALLS IN MUSHROOM GRAVY
Serves 4-6

- 1 pound hamburger
- 4 slices soft white bread
- 1 teaspoon salt
- 1/4 teaspoon pepper
- 1 tablespoon minced onion
- 1 can mushroom soup
- 1/3 cup water

Pull apart bread into small, dime-size pieces. Combine hamburger, bread, salt, pepper, and minced onion in large mixing bowl. Using a spoon, scoop out rounds of meat, or shape into several round, 2-inch balls by hand.
Brown meatballs in a hot skillet using a small amount of butter or oil. Turn them occasionally so all sides are browned. Place meat in cooker. Add soup and water. Cook on *low* for 6 to 12 hours, *high* for up to 6 hours.

SOUPER MEAT LOAF

- 2 pounds ground chuck
- 1 package dry onion soup mix
- 1 egg
- ½ cup ketchup
- ½ cup baked crumbs
- 4 slices American cheese

Mix all ingredients, except cheese; blend well. Divide mixture in half. Place half of meat in a ring mold. Place cheese strips over meat. Add remaining meat and seal well. Cover with waxed paper. Microwave on HIGH for 15 minutes. Rest 5 minutes or microwave at 50 percent for 25–30 minutes.

HAM LOAF

- 2 pounds ground beef
- 2 pounds ground ham
- 4 slices bread, cut up
- ¼ pound soda crackers, crushed
- 1 small onion
- 2 cans tomato soup
- 4 eggs
- 1 teaspoon salt
- ½ teaspoon pepper
- 4 tablespoons mustard
- 2 tablespoons Worcestershire sauce

Mix well and add just enough milk to give a soft consistency. Bake in preheated oven at 350 degrees for 2 hours.

MUSTARD-GLAZED HAM LOAF
Serves 8–10

- 1½ pounds ground ham
- 1 pound boneless pork shoulder, trimmed and ground
- 3 eggs, slightly beaten
- ½ cup finely crushed saltine crackers (14 crackers) **or**
- ½ cup finely crushed bread crumbs (3 or 4 slices)
- ½ cup tomato juice
- 2 tablespoons chopped onion
- 1 tablespoon prepared horseradish
- ½ teaspoon salt
- ⅛ teaspoon pepper
- 1–2 recipes Mustard Sauce (recipe follows)

Mix ingredients. Shape into a 9 x 5-inch loaf in shallow baking dish. Bake in a 350-degree oven for 1¼ hours.

Meanwhile prepare Ham Loaf Mustard Sauce. Drain fat from pan.

Pour Mustard Sauce over loaf. Bake 30 minutes more, basting with sauce occasionally.

Mustard Sauce:
- ½ cup brown sugar, firmly packed
- 2 tablespoons vinegar
- ½ teaspoon dry mustard

REAL BAKED HAM

- 5 pounds ham
  Cider to cover
- ½ cup brown sugar
- 1 teaspoon mustard
- 20 whole cloves

Cover the ham with cold water and bring slowly to the boil. Throw out the water and replace with the cider to cover ham. Bring this to a boil; lower heat, keeping the liquid barely simmering for 20 minutes to the pound of ham; remove from heat and allow to stand in the liquid for 30 minutes. Take out ham; skin it and score fat with a sharp knife in a diamond pattern. Stud with whole cloves. Mix the sugar and mustard; rub well into ham. Bake in a preheated oven for an additional 10 minutes to the pound in a 400-degree oven. Carve; serve with sweet potatoes or a salad.

HAM CASSEROLE

- ½ pound egg noodles, cooked
- 2 cups ham, cubed
- 1 to 1½ cups cheddar cheese, shredded
- 1 can cream of mushroom soup
- ¾ cup milk
- 1 teaspoon dry mustard
- 1 box frozen peas

Pierce box of peas in several places. Microwave for 5 minutes; set aside. Combine ham, cheese, soup, milk and mustard in a 3-quart glass casserole. Add noodles and peas; stir to blend. Microwave on HIGH for 6–8 minutes, stirring one time.

HAM STEAK WITH PINEAPPLE GLAZE

- 1 ham steak (2 pounds)

Glaze:
- 1 (8-ounce) can crushed pineapple, drained, reserving juice
- ¾ cup brown sugar
- 3 teaspoons prepared mustard
- 1½ teaspoons dry mustard
- 1½ to 2 tablespoons reserved juice

Combine the ingredients to make a smooth paste. Place ham steak on a slotted bacon rack or oblong casse-

SWISS STEAK
Serves 6

- 2 pounds round steak
- 6 tablespoons flour
- 1 teaspoon salt
- ½ teaspoon pepper
- 4 onions
- 6 tablespoons shortening
- ½ cup chopped celery
- ¾ cup chili sauce
- ¾ cup water
- 1 green pepper

Combine flour, salt and pepper; rub into both sides of steak; cut into 6 portions. Peel and slice onions. Preheat skillet; add half of shortening, then onions; brown lightly; remove from skillet. Add remaining shortening; brown steak on both sides. Reduce heat. Add celery, chili sauce and water. Cover; simmer 1 hour. Cut green pepper into slices. Add pepper and onions to meat. Continue cooking for 30 minutes.

BURGUNDY STEAK
Serves 2

- 1 cup burgundy wine
- 1 tablespoon Worcestershire sauce
- ½ teaspoon dried leaf basil
- ½ teaspoon dried leaf thyme
- ¼ teaspoon dry mustard
  Dash garlic powder
- 2 (8-ounce) beef rib-eye steaks
- ¼ cup butter *or* margarine
- 4 frozen french-fried onion rings
- ½ cup fresh mushroom slices

In a small bowl, mix burgundy, Worcestershire sauce, basil, thyme, mustard and garlic powder. Place meat in a plastic bag; put in a shallow baking pan. Pour marinade into bag; seal bag. Marinate in refrigerator 8 hours or overnight, turning bag over occasionally. Melt butter or margarine in a large skillet. Add onion rings. Cook over medium-high heat until golden brown. Remove onion rings and keep warm; reserve butter or margarine in skillet; Drain steak; reserve ½ cup marinade. Cook steaks in butter or margarine in skillet until done as desired, turning several times. Place steaks on a platter; reserve drippings in skillet. Cook and stir mushrooms in drippings until barely tender. Stir in reserved marinade. Cook and stir until heated through. Pour over steaks. Top with cooked onion rings.

SOUR CREAM SWISS STEAK
Serves 4

- 2 pounds round steak, 1 inch thick
- ¼ cup flour
- 1 teaspoon salt
- ¼ teaspoon pepper
- 2 tablespoons vegetable oil
- 2 onions, sliced
- ½ cup water
- ¼ tablespoon steak sauce
- ½ cup sour cream
- 2 tablespoons Swiss cheese, grated
- ⅛ teaspoon paprika

Dredge steak on both sides with flour seasoned with salt and pepper. Heat oil in skillet; brown steak on both sides. Add remaining ingredients, except cheese; cover skillet. Simmer 1 hour, or until meat is fork-tender; sprinkle Swiss cheese on steak while still hot.

BARBECUED FLANK STEAK

- ¼ cup soy sauce
- 3 tablespoons honey
- 2 tablespoons vinegar
- 1 green onion, chopped, *or* 2 teaspoons onion powder
- ½ to 1½ teaspoons garlic powder
- 1½ teaspoons powdered ginger
- ¾ cup salad oil
  Flank steaks

Mix first 7 ingredients in large bowl; add steaks. Marinate at room temperature for 3–6 hours. Broil over hot coals until medium-rare or rare; slice diagonally, cutting in ½–¾-inch strips. Marinade will keep indefinitely in refrigerator if green onion is removed.

ROLLED STEAK SKILLET SUPPER
Serves 4

- 1 onion, finely cut
- 1 green pepper, finely cut
- 1 clove garlic, minced
- 3 tablespoons butter *or* margarine
- 1 (7-ounce) can tomato paste
- 30 saltine crackers, crumbled
- ¼ teaspoon salt
- ¼ teaspoon pepper
- 4 cubed steaks
- ¾ cup beef bouillon

Sauté onion, green pepper and garlic in butter. Combine half tomato paste with cracker crumbs, salt and pepper; add to onion mixture. Spoon mixture onto steaks; roll each, fasten with toothpicks; brown in butter. Blend remaining tomato paste with beef bouillon. Pour over steaks; cover skillet. Simmer gently 40–50 minutes; remove toothpicks before serving.

SWISS STEAK
Serves 4

- ¼ cup flour
- ¾ teaspoon salt
- ¼ teaspoon black pepper
- 1½ pounds round steak
- 3 tablespoons fat
- 1 medium onion, chopped
- 1½ cups stewed tomatoes
- ½ cup sliced carrots
- ½ cup sliced celery

Mix flour, salt and pepper. Dredge steak with flour; pound the flour into both sides of steak. In a Dutch oven, heat the fat; brown the steak well on both sides. Add vegetables; cover and simmer gently for 1½ hours.

SALISBURY STEAK

- 2 pounds hamburger
- 1 can onion soup
- 1 cup bread crumbs
- 2 eggs, beaten
- 1 can tomato soup
- 1 can celery soup

Mix the hamburger, bread crumbs, onion soup and eggs as for meat loaf. Add salt to taste. Add more bread crumbs, if needed. Make into patties; dip in flour and brown on each side.

Arrange in a greased baking dish. Make a gravy of 1 can celery soup, 1 can tomato soup and 1 can water.

Pour over the patties and bake in a 350-degree oven for 1 hour.

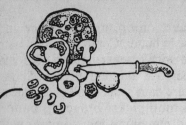

COLA ROAST
Serves 8–10

- 1 teaspoon salt
- ½ teaspoon pepper
- ½ teaspoon garlic powder
- 1 (4–5-pound) bottom-round roast
- 3 tablespoons vegetable oil
- 1½ cups cola-flavored soda
- 12 ounces chili sauce
- 2 tablespoons Worcestershire sauce
- 2 tablespoons hot sauce

Combine salt, pepper and garlic powder; rub over surface of roast. Brown roast on all sides in vegetable oil in Dutch oven. Drain off drippings. Combine remaining ingredients; pour over roast. Cover and bake at 325 degrees for 3 hours, or until tender.

BAKED PORK CHOPS & APPLES
Serves 4

- 4 pork chops
- ¼ teaspoon nutmeg
- 1 tablespoon shortening
- 1¼ cups apple juice
- 2 cups sliced raw potato
- 1 tablespoon cornstarch
- 1 cup sliced onion
- 1 teaspoon salt
- 2 apples, cored and cut into wedges

In skillet, brown chops on both sides in shortening. Remove chops from skillet; arrange in 2-quart casserole. Add potato and onion to pan drippings; heat thoroughly, stirring carefully. Sprinkle with salt and nutmeg; stir in apple wedges. Spoon mixture over chops. Add 1 cup apple juice to skillet; heat until simmering; pour over apple-potato mixture.

Cover casserole; bake at 350 degrees for 45 minutes, or until chops and vegetables are tender. Using slotted spoon, place apple-potato mixture on serving platter; arrange chops on top. Combine remaining apple juice and cornstarch, stirring until free of lumps; pour into pan juices; cook until thickened, stirring constantly. Serve sauce over chops, or separately, if desired.

PORK CHOP 'N' POTATO BAKE

- 1 can cream of celery soup
- ½ cup milk
- ½ cup sour cream
- 1 package hash brown potatoes
- 1 cup shredded cheddar cheese
- 1 can French onion rings
- 6 medium pork chops
  Seasoned salt
- ¼ teaspoon salt
- ¼ teaspoon pepper

Brown chops and sprinkle with seasoned salt. Mix soup, milk, sour cream, potatoes, salt, pepper, ½ cup of the cheese and ½ can of the onion rings. Spoon into a greased casserole or 9 x 13-inch pan, and arrange chops over top. Cover and bake at 350 degrees for 40 minutes. Top with remaining cheese and onion rings. Bake, uncovered, 5 minutes more.

OVEN FRIED PORK CHOPS
Serves 4

- 3 tablespoons margarine *or* butter
- 1 egg, beaten
- 2 tablespoons milk
- 1 cup corn bread stuffing mix

- 4 pork loin chops (about 1½ pounds), cut ½ inch thick

Set oven to 425 degrees. Place margarine or butter in a 13 x 9 x 2-inch baking pan. Place pan in the oven about 3 minutes, or until margarine melts. Stir together egg and milk. Dip pork chops in egg mixture. Coat with stuffing mix. Place chops on top of melted margarine in pan. Bake 20 minutes. Turn. Bake 10–15 minutes more, or until pork is no longer pink.

These are delicious and so tender!

CHERRY PORK CHOPS
Serves 6

- 6 pork chops, cut 3/4-inch thick
- 1/4 teaspoon salt
- 1/4 teaspoon pepper
- 1/2 can cherry pie filling (1 cup)
- 2 teaspoons lemon juice
- 1/2 teaspoon instant chicken bouillon granules
- 1/8 teaspoon ground mace

Trim excess fat from pork chops. Brown pork chops in hot skillet with butter or oil. Sprinkle each chop with salt and pepper. Combine cherry pie filling, lemon juice, chicken bouillon granules, and ground mace in cooker. Stir well. Place pork chops in Crock-pot. Cover. Cook on *low* for 4-5 hours. Place chops on platter. Pour cherry sauce over meat.

TROPICAL PORK CHOPS
Serves 4

- 4 thin pork chops
- 1 small can crushed pineapple
- 1 cup orange juice

Preheat oven to 325 degrees. Place chops in shallow baking dish. Top with pineapple and orange juice. Bake for 1 hour, uncovered.

SWEET SOUR PORK STEAKS
Serves 4

- 1 tablespoon cooking oil
- 2 pork steaks
- ¾ cup chicken broth
- ¼ cup finely chopped celery
- 1 tablespoon brown sugar
- 1 tablespoon vinegar
- 1 teaspoon prepared mustard
- ¼ teaspoon salt
  Dash of pepper
- 2 tablespoons crushed gingersnaps (2 cookies)
  Hot cooked noodles

Heat skillet over high heat. Add oil to skillet. Cook steaks in oil about 8 minutes, or until meat is no longer pink, turning once. Remove steaks and keep warm. Drain fat from skillet. In same skillet, stir together chicken broth, celery, brown sugar, vinegar, mustard, salt and pepper. Stir in gingersnaps. Cook and stir until mixture is thick and bubbly. Serve meat and sauce over hot cooked noodles.

SAUSAGE 'N' CHEESE TURNOVERS
Makes 10 sandwiches

- 1 (10-ounce) can refrigerated big flaky biscuits
- ½ pound Italian bulk sausage *or* ground beef, browned and drained
- ¼ teaspoon Italian seasoning
- 1 (4-ounce) can mushroom pieces and stems, drained
- 4 ounces (1 cup) shredded mozzarella or provolone cheese
- 1 egg, slightly beaten
- 1–2 tablespoons grated Parmesan cheese

Heat oven to 350 degrees. Grease a cookie sheet. Separate dough into 10 biscuits; press or roll each to a 5-inch circle. In a medium bowl, combine browned sausage, seasoning, mushrooms and mozzarella cheese. Spoon about 3 tablespoons meat mixture onto center of each flattened biscuit. Fold dough in half over filling; press edges with fork to seal. Brush tops with beaten egg; sprinkle with Parmesan cheese. Place on prepared cookie sheet. Bake for 10–15 minutes, or until deep golden brown.

Tip: To reheat, wrap loosely in foil. Heat at 375 degrees for 10–15 minutes.

SMOKED SAUSAGE CASSEROLE

- 2 pounds smoked sausage, cut into 4-inch lengths
- 1 teaspoon butter *or* margarine
- 1 medium onion, cut into wedges
- 2 (16-ounce) cans sauerkraut
- 1 cup apple juice
- 2 medium apples, cut into wedges
- 4 medium potatoes, cut in half
  Salt and pepper

Brown sausage in butter in a 1½-quart Dutch oven or large casserole. Arrange onion, sauerkraut, apples and potatoes around sausage. Top with apple juice; salt and pepper to taste. Cover tightly and simmer over low heat for 30–40 minutes, or until potatoes test done with a fork. Stir once during cooking time.

SUKIYAKI
Serves 8

- 2 pounds lean ground beef
- 2 tablespoons sugar
- ⅓ cup soy sauce
- ¼ cup A-1 steak sauce
- 1 teaspoon salt
- 1 (6-ounce) can sliced mushrooms
- 2 medium onions, thinly sliced
- 1 green pepper, sliced in thin strips
- 6 scallions, cut in 1-inch pieces
- 1 cup thinly sliced celery
- 1 (8-ounce) can water chestnuts, thinly sliced
- 1 (8-ounce) can bamboo shoots
- 1 tablespoon cornstarch
  Cooked rice

In large skillet, brown beef until crumbly. In small bowl, mix sugar, soy sauce, A-1 steak sauce and salt. Set aside. Drain mushrooms, reserving liquid. When meat is cooked, mix in vegetables. Add sauce. Simmer for 3 minutes, or until vegetables are just crisp-tender. Combine cornstarch and reserved mushroom liquid. Stir into sukiyaki. Cook just until thickened. Serve over rice.

BAKED BEEF CUBES CACCIATORE
Serves 4

- 3½ pounds lean beef, cut into 1-inch cubes
  Flour for dredging
  Vegetable oil
- 1 large onion, chopped
- 1 clove garlic, minced
- ¼ teaspoon salt
- ½ teaspoon oregano
- ½ teaspoon red pepper, crushed
- 1 (10½-ounce) can crushed tomatoes
- 1 (1-pound, 12-ounce) can crushed tomatoes
- 1 large green pepper, cut into strips
- 12 ounces thin noodles, cooked, drained

Dredge beef with flour; brown in skillet with vegetable oil. Remove from heat; place beef in a large ovenproof casserole; add next 8 ingredients; cover. Bake at 300 degrees for 2½ hours. Remove from oven; stir in cooked noodles.

BEEF RING WITH BARBECUE SAUCE

1½ pounds ground chuck
¾ cup quick-cooking oats
1 cup evaporated milk
3 tablespoons onion, finely chopped
2 tablespoons Worcestershire sauce
3 tablespoons vinegar
2 tablespoons sugar
1 cup ketchup
½ cup water
6 tablespoons onion, finely chopped

Mix together ground chuck, oats, evaporated milk and 3 tablespoons onion. Pack into an 8-inch ring mold and bake 10 minutes. Remove to a larger pan.

Combine remaining ingredients to form the sauce. Pour sauce over beef ring. Bake at 350 degrees for approximately 1½ hours. Baste frequently with sauce during baking time.

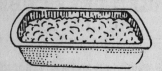

BROILED SCALLOPS
Serves 3

1½ pounds scallops
6 tablespoons butter
½ teaspoon salt
⅛ teaspoon black pepper
⅛ teaspoon dry mustard

Wash; clean the scallops; pick them over for shells; season with the mixture of above seasonings. Place in drip-pan tray, with wire grill removed. Dot with butter. Broil at medium heat on 2nd shelf for 5 minutes. Turn the scallops with a broad spatula and broil for 2–3 minutes.

Melt additional butter to serve with the scallops.

FILET MIGNON TETA-A-TETA
Valentine's Dinner for 2

4 tablespoons butter
2 tablespoons shallots, minced
1 clove garlic, whole
1 tablespoon Worcestershire sauce
1 teaspoon soy sauce
2 (6-ounce each) Filets Mignons
3 ounces brandy
1 tablespoon cashew nuts, coarsely chopped

Heat 2 tablespoons butter in skillet; add shallots and garlic; sauté over medium heat for 5 minutes. Remove and discard garlic. Increase heat to high, add Worcestershire sauce and soy sauce; place filets in pan. Let cook 3 minutes on each side, turning once for slightly rare. Transfer filets to warm dish. Deglaze pan with brandy and then ignite with a match (be careful of flames). Remove pan from heat, swirl in remaining butter to thicken sauce. Pour over filets and top with cashew nuts. Serve immediately.

SPANISH RICE STEAKS
Serves 4

4 cube steaks
1 cup all-purpose flour
1/2 cup vegetable oil
Salt and pepper to taste
1 onion, sliced
1 (5 ounce) can Spanish rice
1/4 teaspoon sugar
2 teaspoons parsley flakes

Coat steaks with flour. In skillet, brown steaks in oil. Transfer to lightly greased 9 inch square baking dish. Season with salt and pepper; set aside. Saute onions slices; add Spanish rice and sugar; mix well. Spoon rice mixture over steaks; sprinkle with parsley flakes.

FRUITED POT ROAST

4 pounds chuck roast or pot roast
2 tablespoons margarine
1-1/2 teaspoons salt
1/8 teaspoon pepper
1 cup apple juice
1 cup dried apricots
1 cup pitted prunes
1 cup tart apples, pared and sliced
2 cinnamon sticks, or 1/4 teaspoon ground cinnamon

Brown meat in margarine. Pour off the drippings. Season with salt and pepper. Cover and simmer in Dutch oven (or bake at 350 degrees) for 2-2-1/2 hours, or until tender.

Turn meat over and add fruit. Continue cooking for 30 minutes or until apples are tender. Serve on a warm platter, surrounded by the fruit.

MOCK STROGANOFF
Serves 6

1/4 cup onion, chopped
1 tablespoon margarine, melted
2 tablespoons oil, any kind (except olive oil)
Salt to taste
3 cups cubed, cooked beef
1 can (10-3/4 ounces) condensed tomato soup
1 can (3 or 4 ounces) chopped mushrooms
1 (8 ounce) can peas, drained
1 teaspoon sugar
1 cup dairy sour cream
Hot cooked and buttered noodles of your choice

Saute onion in oil and margarine in a large frying pan; add beef and brown lightly. Stir in tomato soup, mushrooms, peas, sugar, and salt. Cover mixture, simmer 20 minutes to blend flavors. Stir in sour cream; heat just to boiling point (Don't let sauce boil, as sour cream may curdle). Serve over buttered hot noodles.

HERBED SEAFOOD PIE

1 pound fish fillets (ocean perch, haddock or cod)
1 cup water
1/8 teaspoon salt
1 teaspoon dried tarragon
1 teaspoon dried chervil
4 tablespoons butter or margarine
2-1/2 tablespoons celery, minced
2-1/2 tablespoons onion, minced
4 tablespoons all-purpose flour
2 cups half-and-half cream
1/4 teaspoon dry mustard
1 tablespoon pimiento, chopped
Pastry for two-crust (9-inch) pie, unbaked

In a skillet, place fish fillets, water, salt, tarragon, and chervil. Bring water to a boil; reduce heat; cover and simmer 7 minutes. Remove fish gently; drain; cool and flake; set aside. Sauté celery and onion in butter; stir in flour; add half-and-half and dry mustard. Cook until thickened. Remove from heat; stir in flaked fish and pimiento. Spoon mixture into pastry-lined 9-inch pie pan; cover with top crust; seal and flute edges. Cut steam vent in top crust. Bake at 375 degrees for 35-40 minutes for a golden top. Before cutting, allow pie to rest for 15 minutes.

FISH DIVAN
Serves 5

1 (16-ounce) package frozen fish fillets
2 (10-ounce) packages frozen broccoli spears
1 teaspoon salt
1 (10-3/4 ounce) can condensed cream of chicken soup
1/2 cup milk
1 (3-ounce) can French fried onions

Cut frozen fish crosswise into five equal parts (let stand at room temperature 10 minutes before cutting). Rinse frozen broccoli under running cold water to separate; drain. (If broccoli stems are more than 1/2 inch in diameter, cut lengthwise into halves.) Place fish in center of ungreased 9x13x2-inch baking dish. Arrange broccoli around fish. Sprinkle fish and broccoli with salt. Mix soup and milk; pour over top. Bake uncovered in 350-degree oven until fish flakes easily with fork, about 30 minutes. Sprinkle with onions; bake 5 minutes longer.

STIR-FRIED TUNA
Serves 4

2 cans (6-1/2 ounce each) water-packed tuna
3 tablespoons salad oil
1 red or green pepper, seeded and cut into 1/2-inch cubes
8 green onions, cut into 1/2-inch slices
1 clove garlic, minced
1 cup celery, sliced 1/2-inch diagonally
2 cups snow peas
1 (8-ounce) can water chestnuts, drained and sliced
Seasoning Sauce (recipe follows)

Seasoning Sauce: (Mix together)

1 tablespoon salad oil
1 tablespoon cornstarch
3 tablespoons soy sauce
3 tablespoons water
3 tablespoons sugar
1 tablespoon white vinegar
1/4 teaspoon ground ginger

Drain tuna. Break into chunks; set aside. Heat oil in wide frying pan. Add pepper, onions, and garlic. Stir-fry for 15 seconds. Add celery, snow peas, and water chestnuts. Stir-fry for 1 minute or until vegetables are brightly colored.

Stir in Seasoning Sauce. Cook over high heat, tossing and stirring until sauce is slightly thickened. Add tuna, mixing well. Serve over hot rice.

BARBECUED SHRIMP & PINEAPPLE KABOBS
serves 5-6

1 cup bottled Italian dressing
1/2 cup chili sauce
1 tablespoon lemon juice
Pepper to taste
1-1/2 pounds medium shrimp, peeled, deveined and dried well
1 onion, cut into 2-inch pieces
1 large green pepper, cut into 2-inch pieces
1/4 fresh pineapple, cut into 2-inch pieces; place with
1 box cherry tomatoes
Orange and lemon slices

In 2-quart bowl, mix dressing, chili sauce, lemon juice, and pepper. Add shrimp and stir to coat well. Cover and refigerate overnight. Drop onion and green pepper into boiling water for about 1/2 minute. Drain and dry thoroughly. Alternate shrimp, onion green pepper, pineapple, tomatoes, and orange and lemon slices on skewers. Brush with marinade. Place on barbecue and cook on one side. Turn and cook other side until shrimp is pink and tender, about 10 to 15 minutes.

LEMON PERCH
Serves 4

1/4 cup butter
2 tablespoons lemon juice
1/2 teaspoon salt
1/4 teaspoon dill weed
1 pound perch fillets

Melt butter in skillet; stir in lemon juice and seasonings. Place fish in skillet, skin side down; cook 4-5 minutes over medium heat. Turn; continue cooking until fish flakes easily with fork. Serve butter mixture over fish.

LASAGNA
Serves 8

1 pound ground beef
1 cup chopped onion
1-2 teaspoons garlic powder
2 teaspoons oregano
2 cans tomato soup
1/2 cup water
2 teaspoons vinegar
9 lasagna noodles, cooked and drained
1 cup grated mozzarella cheese
5 slices mozzarella cheese
1 cup cream-style cottage cheese or grated Parmesan cheese

In skillet, brown beef, onion, garlic, oregano. Add soup, water, and vinegar. Cook over low heat 30 minutes.

Arrange alternate layers of cooked noodles, grated cheeses, and meat sauce in a 9 x 13" pan. Top with mozzarella slices.

Bake at 350 degrees for 35 minutes. Let set 15 minutes for easier cutting.

Serve with warm garlic French bread and tossed salad.

PARTY LIVER PLATE
Makes 1-1/2 cups

1 pound liver (chicken, calf, beef or pork)
1/2 pound lard (butter or chicken fat)
2 tablespoons minced onion
1/2 bay leaf
1/2 teaspoon thyme
1 teaspoon salt
1/4 teaspoon pepper

Put liver through grinder twice, using finest knife. Add lard and seasonings, mix well and put through grinder again. Pat firmly into small bowls. Cover with foil, fasten tightly, and steam over hot water for 1-1/2 hours. Remove foil, cool and chill. Serve with crackers, Melba toast or assorted chips, if desired.
NOTE: A small peeled clove of garlic may be ground with the liver.

BACON CHEESEBURGERS

2 pounds ground beef
8 slices crisp bacon, crumbled
1/2 cup Cheddar cheese, shredded
1 teaspoon seasoned salt
1/2 cup onion, chopped
1 teaspoon parsley flakes

Mix ground beef with remaining ingredients; shape into patties. Grill until done.

BEEF TURNOVERS
Makes 20

1/2 pound ground beef
1 small onion, finely chopped
1 teaspoon cornstarch
1/4 teaspoon salt
3 tablespoons ketchup
1 medium egg
1 tablespoon water
2 rolls, (7-1/2 ounce each) refrigerated biscuits, ten per roll
Sesame seeds

In skillet, cook ground beef and onion until beef is browned, drain off all fat. Stir cornstarch and salt into beef mixture. Stir in ketchup, cook until mixture is slightly thickened. Remove from heat and cool well. Heat oven to 400 degrees. Lightly grease two large baking sheets. In cup, beat together egg and water. To shape each turnover, press a biscuit into a 3-1/2 inch round. Brush with some egg mixture. Place a tablespoon of meat mixture in center. Fold in half, press biscuits around unfolded edge to seal. Place on baking sheet; brush turnovers with egg mixture. Pierce each one with fork on top of surface. Sprinkle each one with sesame seeds. Bake 10-12 minutes, or until golden brown. These are nice for children's school box lunches.

BEEF PINWHEELS ITALIANA

1-1/2 pounds ground chuck
1 teaspoon salt
1/8 teaspoon pepper
3/4 teaspoon oregano
1/4 cup evaporated milk
1 egg, beaten
1/2 cup green pepper, chopped
1/4 cup onion, chopped
2/3 cup soft bread crumbs
1/2 pound Mozzarella cheese, shredded

Combine all ingredients except cheese. Pat on wax paper into 12-inch squares; sprinkle with cheese, patting down a little. Roll meat into a roll. Seal edges. Refrigerate overnight. Cut into 12 slices. Broil 12 to 15 minutes 6 inches from heat source, turning once. Garnish with small mushrooms if desired.

This looks good and is a pleasant change from pizza meatloaf — even the kids like this.

INSIDE-OUT RAVIOLIS

1 pound ground beef
1/2 cup chopped onion
Garlic salt to taste
10 ounce package frozen spinach
1 quart Ragu sauce or you own spaghetti sauce
1/2 teaspoon salt
2 cups shells (small), cooked and drained
1/2 cup Cheddar cheese, grated
1/2 cup Parmesan cheese, grated
1/2 cup bread crumbs
2 well beaten eggs
1/4 cup oil

Brown beef, onion and garlic salt. Add salt and simmer. Cook spinach, following package directions. Drain. Add salt to sauce. Combine spinach, shells, cheeses, bread crumbs, eggs and oil.

Spread in a 9 x 12 x 2" baking dish. Top with sauce. Bake at 350 degrees for 30 minutes. Let stand 10 minutes before serving.

TOMATO KRAUT AND FRANKS
Serves 4

1 (16 ounce) can sauerkraut
1/2 teaspoon pepper
1 (4 ounce) can mushrooms
1 medium onion, thinly sliced
1 cup tomato juice
8 frankfurters, in 1-inch pieces

Drain sauerkraut; rinse with cold water, drain again. Grease or spray 1-1/2-quart casserole. Mix sauerkraut, mushrooms, onions, and frankfurters. Put in casserole, sprinkle with pepper and pour tomato juice over all. Cover and bake at 350 degrees 45 minutes. Then uncover and bake 15 minutes longer.

RAISIN SAUCE FOR HAM

This is wonderful sauce over canned or boned ham.

Mix 1/2 cup brown sugar, 1 teaspoon dry mustard, 2 tablespoons cornstarch. Slowly add 2 tablespoons vinegar. Then add 1/4 teaspoon grated lemon peel, 2 tablespoons lemon juice, and 1-1/2 cups water. Use medium saucepan. Cook over low heat, stirring constantly until thick. Add 1/2 cup raisins and 2 tablespoons butter. Serve hot over ham.

EASTER BAKED HAM

Heat oven to 325 degrees. Place whole ham, fat side up, on a rack in a shallow pan. Insert meat thermometer in center of thick part; making sure thermometer tip does not touch bone. Do not cover; roast ham to an internal temperature of 160 degrees. Picnic or shoulder hams should be baked to an internal temperature of 170 degrees.

Half an hour before ham is done,

Place a little piece of aluminum foil over ham so the top doesn't get tough. The sides are left open. Turn occasionally, once or twice during cooking time. Bake at 350 degrees for 3-5 hours depending on size of ham. I cook a 3 pound for 3-4 hours.

HAM ROLLS
Serves 4

2 tablespoons soft butter
1-1/2 teaspoons prepared mustard
1 cup ground ham
2 cups all-purpose flour
4 teaspoons baking powder
1/2 teaspoon salt
1/4 cup shortening or lard
3/4 cup milk

Combine butter and mustard with the ground ham; set aside. Sift together flour, baking powder, and salt. Cut in shortening until mixture resembles fine crumbs. Add the milk to make a soft dough. Roll out 1/4-inch thick and spread with the ham mixture. Roll up like a jelly roll and cut into 1-1/2 inch slices. Place cut side down in a greased baking pan. Bake in a 425 degree oven for 15-20 minutes.

FRANK-MACARONI SKILLET
Serves 4

2-1/2 cups water
8 ounce can tomato sauce
1 envelope spaghetti sauce mix
1 cup uncooked macaroni
4 or 5 franks, cut into 1-inch pieces
1-1/2 teaspoons Worcestershire sauce

In large saucepan, combine water, tomato sauce and spaghetti sauce mix. Bring to boiling; stir in macaroni; cover and cook over low heat until macaroni is tender, about 15 to 20 minutes, stirring frequently. Stir in franks and Worcestershire sauce; heat through.

HAM STRIPS IN CHILI-TOMATO SAUCE

1/2 cup vegetable oil
2 cups green pepper, chopped
2 cups celery, chopped
1 cup onion, chopped
1 clove garlic, minced
2-15 ounce cans tomato sauce
1/2 teaspoon chili powder
4 cups cooked ham, cut into strips
1/2 cup tomato juice
1-8 ounce jar Picante sauce

Heat oil in skillet. Add green peppers, celery, onion and garlic. Saute until tender, about 8 minutes (do not brown). Stir in tomato sauce and chili powder; cook until mixture comes to a boil, about 2 minutes. Reduce heat to low and simmer, uncovered, 20 minutes. Stir in ham, tomato juice and Picante sauce. Cover; simmer 5 minutes or until heated thoroughly. Serve over rice, noodles or spaghetti.

CRANBERRY BURGUNDY GLAZED HAM
Serves 20-25

1 (10-14 pounds) bone-in, fully-cooked ham
Whole cloves
1 (16 ounce) can whole cranberry sauce
1 cup brown sugar
1/2 cup burgundy
2 teaspoons prepared mustard

Place ham, fat side up, in shallow roasting pan. Score fat in diamond pattern; stud with cloves. Insert meat thermometer. Bake in 325 degree oven for 2-1/2 to 3 hours, or until meat thermometer registers 130 degrees.

In saucepan, stir together cranberry sauce, brown sugar, burgundy, and mustard; simmer 5 minutes, uncovered. During last 30 minutes baking time for ham, spoon half of cranberry glaze over it. Pass remaining as a sauce. Makes 3 cups sauce.

JELLIED TURKEY OR CHICKEN LOAF

Serves 4

2 cups diced turkey or chicken
2-1/4 tablespoons powdered gelatin
3-1/2 cups turkey or chicken stock
1 cup mayonnaise
1 teaspoon onion juice
1/2 teaspoon lemon juice
2 cups diced celery or chopped cabbage
3 hard-cooked eggs, sliced
1 teaspoon salt
2 teaspoons pimiento
Parsley or watercress

Soften gelatin in little of the stock and dissolve in remainder that has been heated. Chill in refrigerator. When begins to thicken, stir in mayonnaise; add remaining ingredients, which have also been chilled. Place in loaf pan; return to refrigerator to chill and stiffen. Unmold; garnish with parsley or watercress.

HOLIDAY TURKEY-HAM ROLL-UPS

Serves 4

5 cups cabbage, cooked, chopped, and drained
1 cup Swiss cheese, shredded
8 slices cooked turkey ham
1/4 cup onion, minced
3 tablespoons butter or margarine
3 tablespoons flour
1-1/2 cups sweet milk
2 teaspoons Dijon mustard
1 tablespoon parsley, chopped
1/4 cup bread crumbs

Combine cabbage and 1/2 cup cheese; spoon 3 tablespoonfuls onto each ham slice; roll up; place seam side down in a greased baking dish. Sauté onions in 2 tablespoons butter; blend in flour; add milk and mustard; boil gently, stirring constantly. Add remaining 1/2 cup cheese and the parsley; pour over turkey ham rolls. Melt remaining 1 tablespoon butter; combine with bread crumbs; sprinkle over cheese sauce. Bake at 375 degrees, uncovered, for 25-30 minutes.

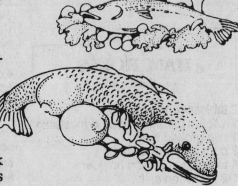

PHYLLO TURKEY PUFFS

Serves 6

2 tablespoons butter or margarine
2 tablespoons flour
2 cups chicken broth
3/4 cup milk
2 eggs, beaten lightly
1 tablespoon Parmesan cheese, grated
3 ounces cream cheese
1/4 teaspoon pepper
1/4 teaspoon nutmeg
2 cups turkey, cooked and cubed
1/2 cup butter, melted
12 sheets frozen phyllo dough, thawed

In saucepan melt butter; add flour gradually. Stir in broth and milk; cook over medium heat; stir until thickened. Remove from heat; beat mixture into eggs, then return egg mixture to pan. Add cheeses, pepper, nutmeg, and turkey. Brush inside of muffin cups with melted butter; set aside. Stack 12 sheets of phyllo dough together; brush each with butter; cut into 6 pieces. Line muffin cups with phyllo; fill with turkey filling. Fold corners of pastry over filling to cover; brush with melted butter. Bake at 375 degrees for 25-30 minutes or until puffed and golden. Let stand in pan 5 minutes before removing.

SEAFOOD LOAF

1 (1 pound) can salmon
1 (10-1/2 ounce) can cream of celery soup
1 cup fine dry bread crumbs
2 eggs, slightly beaten
1/2 cup chopped onion
1 tablespoon lemon juice

Drain salmon, reserving 1/4 cup liquid. Remove skin and bones from salmon; flake. Thoroughly mix salmon liquid and remaining ingredients. Pack into a well greased 9x5x3 inch loaf pan. Bake at 375 degrees for 1 hour or until browned. Cool loaf in pan for 10 minutes; loosen from sides of pan and turn out on serving platter. Garnish with parsley, lemon, and orange slices.

FRENCH-STYLE SALMON MEAL

Serves 6

1 can (7-3/4 ounces) salmon
2 hard-boiled eggs, diced
2 tablespoons finely chopped celery
2 green onions, chopped
2 tablespoons cocktail sauce
2 tablespoons mayonnaise
12 slices bread
3 eggs, slightly beaten
1/2 cup milk
1/4 teaspoon salt
1-1/4 cups crushed potato chips
Butter

Drain salmon, reserving liquid. Flake salmon and combine with hard-boiled eggs, celery, onion, cocktail sauce and mayonnaise. Spread filling on 6 slices of bread. Top with remaining slices. Combine eggs, reserved salmon liquid, milk and salt. Dip salmon sandwiches in egg mixture, then in crushed chips. Brown sandwiches on both sides in small amount of butter on hot griddle.

64

STUFFED CORNISH GAME HENS

Serves 8

4 Cornish game hens
1/2 cup chopped mushrooms
1/2 cup chopped onions
6 tablespoons minced parsley
3/4 pound hot Italian sausage meat
1 teaspoon minced garlic
1 egg, beaten
1/2 cup bread crumbs from fresh Italian bread
2 tablespoons butter

Saute onion, garlic, and mushrooms until soft. Add sausage meat and saute until no longer pink. Remove from heat; stir in parsley and bread crumbs; let cool. Add egg. Stuff each hen with 1/4 of the stuffing. Baste hens with a mixture of one stick unsalted, melted butter and 1 cup Sauterne wine. Bake in a preheated 350 degree oven for 1-1/2 to 2 hours, until brown, basting often.

HOT CHICKEN DISH

1 - 7 ounce box croutons
2 pounds chicken; skinned, boned, cut into chunks
1 onion, chopped
3 stalks celery, chopped
1 small green pepper, chopped
1/2 cup margarine
1 can cream of chicken soup
1 can cream of celery soup
1 can of water

Saute onion, celery, and green pepper in the margarine. Add the soups and water to pan; stir. Heat until hot. In a greased 9 x 13 inch pan, arrange chicken chunks. Then pour over the croutons, the mixture of sauted ingredients and soups. Cover with foil and bake in a 350 degree oven for 1 hour. Remove foil; bake an additional 30 minutes.

CHICKEN AND MUSHROOMS WITH MUENSTER CHEESE

4 whole chicken breasts, boned and skinned
3 eggs
1/2 cup Italian flavored bread crumbs
6 tablespoons butter
10-3/4-ounces chicken broth
2 teaspoons lemon juice
6 ounces sliced Muenster cheese
8 ounces fresh mushrooms

Cut chicken breasts into bite-size pieces. Soak several hours or overnight in 3 beaten eggs. Preheat oven to 350 degrees. Roll chicken pieces in bread crumbs; sauté with sliced mushrooms in margarine for 10 to 15 minutes. Place in casserole. Pour chicken broth over chicken and mushrooms. Sprinkle with lemon juice. Cover with sliced Muenster cheese. Bake uncovered for 30 to 40 minutes.

CHICK-A-DEE DIPPERS

1 large chicken breast, boneless and skinned
1-1/2 slices white bread
1 egg yolk
1 tablespoon minced parsley
1 tablespoon grated onion
1/2 teaspoon salt
1/4 teaspoon pepper
1/4 teaspoon ground cumin
1/8 teaspoon garlic powder
1/8 teaspoon ground tumeric
1/3 cup all-purpose flour
Vegetable oil

Cut chicken into 1-inch pieces and put chicken and bread slices into fine blade food grinder until finely ground. Place into bowl and mix with egg yolk, parsley, onion, salt, pepper, cumin, garlic powder and tumeric. Cover and refrigerate for 30 minutes. Shape mixture into balls (1 rounded teaspoon each) and roll in flour to coat. Pour 1 inch oil in a 2-quart saucepan. Heat to 350 degrees. Fry 6 balls at a time until golden (3-4 minutes). Drain on paper towel. Keep warm in 200 degree oven until ready to use.

Dipping Sauce:
1/2 cup mayonnaise
1/4 cup chili sauce
2 tablespoons peach jam
2 tablespoons dry onion soup mix

Cook all ingredients until hot, but not boiling.

CREOLE CHICKEN NUGGETS

1 small onion, grated
1/2 cup plain dry bread crumbs
1-1/2 teaspoons chili powder
1 teaspoon ground cumin
2-4 drops hot pepper sauce
1 teaspoon dried thyme
1 teaspoon garlic powder
2 pounds boneless chicken breasts, cut into 1-inch pieces
Oil

Combine first 7 ingredients. Dip chicken in mixture, coating well. Heat oil in skillet. Cook chicken until tender and golden; drain on paper towels.

CHICKEN HASH

A slow pot recipe

3 cups cooked chicken, chopped
2 small onions, chopped
2 small raw potatoes, chopped
2 large carrots, chopped
2 eggs
1 teaspoon salt
3 tablespoons parsley, chopped
1/2 teaspoon poultry seasoning
1-1/2 cups chicken gravy

In food grinder, chop chicken, onion, potato and carrots. Mix well with remaining ingredients. Place in slow pot; cook on low for 8 to 10 hours.

CHICKEN AND NOODLES ROMANOFF

2 packages wide noodles
1 cup diced cooked chicken (large pieces)
1 pint white sauce made with chicken stock or broth
1 cup mushrooms
2 tablespoons butter
1/2 cup chopped pimiento (optional)
Salt and pepper to taste

While noodles are cooking according to package directions, sauté mushroom slices in butter; adding pimiento just before done. Combine sauce, mushrooms, pimiento, and chicken. Simmer together over low heat. Drain cooked noodles; butter them and mix with other ingredients; salt and pepper to taste. Pour into greased casserole. Place in 350 degree oven for 20 minutes. Serve hot.

1890 CHICKEN AND MACARONI SUPPER
Serves 4

8 ounces macaroni
Boiling salted water
4 cups cooked chicken, cut into bite-size pieces
1/4 cup butter or margarine
Salt and pepper to taste
1 cup chicken broth
1 cup half and half
Parsley sprigs as garnish

Cook macaroni in boiling salted water until almost tender, about 12 minutes; drain. Place 1/3 of macaroni on bottom of 2-quart lightly-greased casserole. Top with 1/2 the chicken pieces; dot chicken with 1/2 the butter or margarine, salt and pepper and 1/2 the chicken broth. Repeat layers, ending with remaining 1/3 of macaroni on top. Pour cream over all; bake at 350 degrees for 20-30 minutes, or until bubbly.

mixture; roll up as for jelly roll. Pinch ends of dough together; place on lightly greased jelly roll pan. Brush roll lightly with melted butter.

CHICKEN RICE PILAF
Serves 4-6

2/3 cup long grain rice
2/3 cup broken thin spaghetti
1/3 cup olive oil
3 cups chicken broth
1 cup fresh or frozen broccoli florets
1/4 teaspoon thyme, crushed
1 cup cooked chicken, (cut in julienne strips)
1/2 cup sliced green onion (scallions)
1/4 cup chopped walnuts
1/4 cup diced red pepper

In saucepan, sauté rice and spaghetti in oil until golden, stirring often. Add chicken broth and bring to boil. Add broccoli and thyme. Cover; simmer 15 minutes or until rice is tender, stirring occasionally. Add remaining ingredients and cook through.

CHICKEN 'N BISCUIT TRIANGLES
Makes 16 biscuits

1-1/2 cups all-purpose flour
1/4 teaspoon salt
4 teaspoons baking powder
1/4 teaspoon nutmeg
2 tablespoons shortening
1 cup cooked potatoes, mashed
3/4 cup cooked chicken, chopped finely
1 egg
1/4 cup sweet milk
Melted butter or margarine
1 tablespoon parsley, minced

Combine first 4 ingredients; cut in shortening; add mashed potatoes and chicken. Mix egg with milk; add to flour mixture; stir until just blended. Knead dough lightly; pat to 3/4 inch thickness. Cut into 3-inch squares, then into triangles. Place on a greased baking sheet; bake at 375 degrees for 10 minutes. Brush with melted butter; sprinkle with parsley; bake 5 additional minutes.

COUNTRY CHICKEN ROLL
Serves 6

Filling:
2 tablespoons shortening
2 tablespoons flour
1 cup chicken stock
1/4 teaspoon salt
1/8 teaspoon pepper
2 cups cooked chicken, chopped

Dough for roll:
3 cups buttermilk biscuit mix
2 tablespoons parsley, minced
2 tablespoons melted butter for brushing

Melt shortening; remove from heat. Add flour; stir to a smooth paste. Add chicken stock gradually, stirring constantly; cook until thick. Add salt, pepper, and cooked chicken. Set aside to cool. Prepare biscuit mix according to package directions. Roll dough to about 1/3 inch thick; add parsley; spread dough with chicken

CHICKEN DUMPLINGS
From 1904
Serves 6

3 cups flour
1 teaspoon baking powder
1/2 teaspoon salt
3 eggs, beaten
1/4 cup milk

Mix all ingredients well; pour out onto well-floured board. With rolling pin, roll out 1/2 batter at a time. Cut into 1" squares. Drop one at a time into 2 quarts boiling chicken broth in a 4-quart Dutch oven. Cook 20 minutes.

Micro-
MAGIC

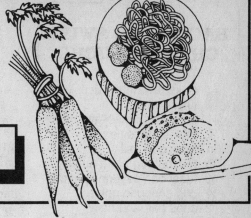

TUNA VEGETABLE CHOWDER

1½ cups water
1 medium potato, diced
2 tablespoons chopped onion
¼ cup diced carrot
¾ teaspoon salt
¼ teaspoon celery salt
Dash pepper
1 teaspoon chopped chives
1 teaspoon Worcestershire sauce
⅔ cup fresh *or* frozen corn
1 (6½-ounce) can tuna, drained
1 cup half-and-half

In 2-quart container combine water, potato, onion, carrot, salt, celery salt, pepper, chives and Worcestershire sauce. Cover and microwave on HIGH for 7–15 minutes, or until vegetables are just about tender. Add corn; cover and return to microwave; heat for 5–8 minutes on HIGH, or until corn is tender. Stir in tuna and cream; cover and microwave for 2–4 minutes until heated through

SHRIMP STIR-FRY

1 head bok choy, sliced (about 8 cups)
1 large red pepper, chopped
1 tablespoon cooking oil
2 cloves garlic, minced
8 drops hot pepper sauce
1 teaspoon sesame seed
12 ounces uncooked fresh shrimp, well-drained
1 tablespoon water
2 teaspoons cornstarch

Combine bok choy and red pepper in a 2-quart bowl; microwave on HIGH, uncovered, for 5–6 minutes; stir once or twice; set aside. Combine oil, garlic, hot pepper sauce and sesame seed in casserole; microwave on HIGH, uncovered, for 2–2½ minutes, stir in shrimp; microwave on HIGH, uncovered, for 2–2½ minutes until shrimp are pink; stir once. Combine water and cornstarch in a 1-cup glass measure; mix well. Drain juices from vegetables and from shrimp into measure; blend well. Microwave on HIGH, uncovered, for 1–1½ minutes, or until mixture boils and thickens. Add to shrimp along with vegetables; toss lightly to coat. Microwave on HIGH, uncovered, for 1–2 minutes, or until heated through.

FISH CREOLE

1 pound sole or orange roughy fillets
1 (8-ounce) can tomato sauce
1 (2.5-ounce) jar sliced mushrooms
½ green pepper, diced
¼ teaspoon garlic powder
¼ teaspoon oregano
3 green onions, sliced
1 stalk celery, diagonally sliced
3 tablespoons water
1 teaspoon instant chicken bouillon

Rinse fish and pat dry. Arrange in 3-quart oblong baking dish with thicker portions toward outside of dish. Combine remaining ingredients in a 4-cup glass measure; pour evenly over fish. Cover with plastic wrap; microwave on HIGH for 8–10 minutes, or until fish flakes easily. Let stand 5 minutes.

SALMON STEAKS

2 (8-ounce) salmon steaks
1 tablespoon butter
½ tablespoon lime juice
1 green onion, chopped
⅛ teaspoon ground pepper
⅛ teaspoon dill weed

Place salmon steaks on microwave-safe plate; place a paper towel over top of steaks and microwave on HIGH for 3–3½ minutes. Set aside. Combine butter, lime juice, onion, dill weed and pepper in small dish; microwave on HIGH for 30–45 seconds until melted. Pour over salmon. Garnish with lime slices.

BACON AND SWISS CHEESE QUICHE

1 (9-inch) single crust pie shell
½ pound bacon (9–11 strips)
2 tablespoons flour
¼ teaspoon salt
½ teaspoon ground nutmeg
⅛ teaspoon cayenne pepper
¼ cup chopped onion
2 cups half-and-half
4 eggs
⅓ cup grated Swiss cheese
   Paprika
   Parsley flakes

Microwave pie shell in a glass pie plate on HIGH for 5–7 minutes; rotate ½ turn after 2½ minutes. Cool. Arrange bacon in single layer on microwave bacon rack; top with paper towels. Microwave on HIGH for 9 minutes, or until crisp. Cut into bite-sized pieces and sprinkle over bottom of crust.

In a 1½-quart casserole combine flour, salt, nutmeg, cayenne and onion; whisk in half-and-half to blend well. Microwave on HIGH for 4–6 minutes, whisking every minute until hot and thick. Meanwhile in small bowl beat eggs to blend; add about ¼ of half-and-half mixture to eggs and whisk well. Then add mixture back to warm half-and-half; microwave on MEDIUM HIGH (70 percent) for 3–5 minutes. Pour into pie shell. Distribute cheese evenly over top, then sprinkle with paprika and parsley; microwave at MEDIUM (50 percent) for 6–9 minutes. Let stand 15 minutes.

SAUSAGE WEDGES

½ pound bulk pork sausage
1 cup (4 ounces) shredded cheddar cheese

or American
2 tablespoons diced onion
¾ cup milk
4 eggs, beaten
1 teaspoon dried parsley
2 tablespoons butter

Crumble sausage in a 9-inch pie plate. Cover with paper towel and microwave for 3–4 minutes on HIGH. Drain off fat; sprinkle cheese over sausage; stir in onion. In a medium bowl combine milk and eggs; add parsley and butter. Pour over sausage; cover with plastic wrap and microwave 4 minutes on HIGH. Stir; cover and microwave for 6–8 minutes on MEDIUM (50 percent). Let stand, covered, 5 minutes.

PORK STIR-FRY

1 pound boneless pork, cut into thin strips
2 cloves garlic, minced
2 tablespoons soy sauce
2 tablespoons sherry
¼ cup apple juice
1 tablespoon cornstarch
3 green onions, sliced
2 cups broccoli pieces
1 cup shredded carrots
   Dash pepper
2 cups fresh bean sprouts

Combine pork, garlic, soy sauce and sherry in a 2-quart casserole. Stir to coat evenly; let stand 10 minutes. Blend together apple juice and cornstarch; stir into pork mixture. Cover with casserole lid. Microwave on HIGH for 4–5 minutes; stir once. Add onion, broccoli, carrots and pepper; do not stir; cover, microwave for 3–4 minutes, or until vegetables are tender-crisp. Add sprouts; cover and microwave for 1½–2 minutes. Toss to mix.

HEARTY MINESTRONE
Serves 6–8

5 cups water
1 can condensed beef bouillon
5 teaspoons instant beef bouillon granules
1 clove garlic, finely minced
1 small onion, finely chopped
1 (16-ounce) can tomatoes, undrained
1 cup broken spaghetti pieces, uncooked
1 teaspoon salt
⅛ teaspoon pepper
¼ teaspoon oregano
¼ teaspoon basil
1 cup frozen peas
1 (16-ounce) can kidney beans, undrained
1–2 cups cooked beef, cubed

Combine water, bouillon, garlic, onion, tomatoes, spaghetti, beef, salt, pepper, oregano and basil in 3-quart casserole. Cover and microwave on HIGH for 22–30 minutes, or until spaghetti is tender. Add peas and beans; cover and return to microwave to cook for 8 more min-

RICE PILAF

1 cup regular rice, long grain
1 cup pearl barley
¼ cup butter
8 green onions, chopped
3 cubes beef bouillon
4 cups water
½ pound fresh mushrooms, sliced
2 large cloves garlic
1 teaspoon salt

Combine rice, barley and melted butter; microwave for 5 minutes on HIGH; stir twice. Add remaining ingredients; cover and microwave on HIGH for 6 minutes, then 16–18 minutes on 70 percent power.

LOW COUNTRY EGG PIE

- 4 slices firm-textured white bread, no crusts
- 1 cup milk
- ⅔ cup half-and-half
- 1 cup coarsely shredded sharp cheddar cheese
- ¼ cup grated Parmesan cheese
- 2 tablespoons finely grated onion
- 3 eggs, lightly beaten
- 2 tablespoons Dijon mustard
- ½ teaspoon salt
- ¼ teaspoon ground hot red pepper
- ⅛ teaspoon white pepper
- 1 tablespoon *each* parsley flakes and paprika
- 2 hard-cooked eggs, peeled and coarsely chopped

Soak bread in milk and half-and-half for 5 minutes. Combine with cheeses, onion, eggs, mustard, salt, hot red pepper and white pepper; fold in hard-cooked eggs. Spoon into 9-inch round, 1½-quart casserole; sprinkle with paprika and parsley. Microwave, uncovered, on MEDIUM (50 percent) for 18–21 minutes. Rotate casserole every 4 minutes, or until set. Cover pie with foil and let stand 5–7 minutes; cut into wedges and serve warm.

EGGS VERDI

- ½ cup butter *or* margarine
- 1 tablespoon lemon juice
- ⅛ teaspoon ground red pepper
- 3 large egg yolks, beaten
- 1 (12-ounce) package frozen spinach soufflé, thawed
- 4 large eggs
- 2 English muffins, split and toasted

In a 1-quart bowl combine butter,

¼ cup water, lemon juice and pepper; microwave, uncovered, on HIGH for 2½ minutes or until boiling. With a wire whisk beat in egg yolks a little at a time. Cook, uncovered, on HIGH for 15 seconds (will be thin). Let stand 5 minutes; stir twice.

Place soufflé in custard cups divided evenly; microwave on HIGH for 4 minutes; stir once. Crack an egg into each cup over soufflé mixture; with wooden pick puncture yolk. Cover the cups with waxed paper; microwave on HIGH for 3–4 minutes. Rearrange the cups in oven after 2 minutes. Let stand, covered, for 3 minutes. Reheat sauce on HIGH for 1 minute. Run spatula around edge of soufflé mix in each cup; turn out each onto a muffin half. Spoon sauce over. Serve immediately.

PLAN AHEAD BRUNCH

Serves 9

1 package (12 ounces) frozen hash brown potatoes
6 eggs
1/3 cup whipping or light cream
1 cup (4 ounces) shredded Cheddar cheese
2 tablespoons chopped chives
1/4 teaspoon salt
Dash of pepper
1 cup (4 ounces) diced ham, or Canadian bacon

Place potatoes in 8-inch square baking dish; cover with plastic wrap and microwave on HIGH 6-7 minutes until steaming, stir once. Combine eggs, cream, chives, salt, pepper, cheese, and ham. Add mixture to potatoes, cover with waxed paper, and microwave 12 minutes at MEDIUM (50%) stirring twice. Then finish cooking for 3-4 minutes on HIGH or until set. Let stand 5 minutes, cut into squares.

FRUIT DELIGHT

Prepare this ahead of time to allow flavors to develop.

- 1 (20-ounce) can pineapple chunks, juice pack
- 2 (11-ounce) cans mandarin orange sections, drained
- ½ to 1 cup seedless grapes, halved
- 2 kiwis, halved lengthwise and sliced
- ½ cup orange juice
- ¼ cup honey
- 1 tablespoon lemon juice

Drain pineapple; reserve juice. In a large bowl combine pineapple, mandarin oranges, grapes and kiwi. Combine pineapple liquid, orange juice, honey and lemon juice. Pour over fruit. Cover and chill until ready to serve.

CARROTS WITH VINEGAR

- 1½ pounds carrots, peeled and cut into ½-inch cubes
- ¼ cup minced onion
- 3 tablespoons red wine vinegar
- 1 bay leaf
- ¼ teaspoon salt
- Dash pepper

Mix carrots and onion in 2-quart casserole. Add vinegar and bay leaf; cover with lid and microwave on HIGH for 10 minutes; stir at halftime. Stir and cover with paper towel; microwave on HIGH for 5 minutes, until almost all liquid evaporates and carrots are tender. Add salt and pepper to taste. Let stand covered for 3 minutes.

VEGETABLE STIR-FRY

1 tablespoon oil
1 clove garlic, minced
1 small onion, sliced
1 cup sliced mushrooms
2 cups sliced cauliflower pieces
¾ cup thinly sliced carrot
½ cup sliced green pepper
  pieces
3 tablespoons teriyaki sauce
½ tablespoon cornstarch
3 tablespoons cashews *or*
  peanuts

Combine oil, garlic, onion and mushrooms in a microwave casserole. Microwave on HIGH, uncovered, for 1½–2 minutes; stir in cauliflower, carrot and green pepper; cover with lid. Microwave for 3½–4 minutes. Stir once. Combine teriyaki sauce and cornstarch in 1-cup glass measure. Drain juices from vegetables into cup and mix well. Microwave on HIGH, uncovered, for 1–1½ minutes; stir once. Pour over vegetables; sprinkle with nuts; toss lightly.

ORANGE ASPARAGUS

1½ pounds fresh asparagus
1 tablespoon water
1 tablespoon honey
2 teaspoons cornstarch
½ cup orange juice
1 tablespoon margarine

Snap off tough ends of asparagus spears; place in a 10 x 6-inch pan; add water; cover with plastic wrap and vent. Microwave on HIGH for 5–6 minutes; drain and set aside. Combine honey, cornstarch and orange juice in a 1-cup measure; microwave on HIGH, uncovered, for 1–1½ minutes; stir once. Stir in margarine; spoon sauce over asparagus.

SHALIMAR SALAD

4 stalks broccoli
1 large head cauliflower
2 bell peppers, thinly sliced
1 can water chestnuts,
  drained and sliced
½ pound fresh mushrooms,
  cut in large pieces
1 (8-ounce) jar Indian chutney
3 tablespoons curry powder
1½ to 2 cups mayonnaise
1 cup chopped pecans

Break broccoli florets into bite-size pieces, discarding heavy stalks. Microwave fon HIGH or 2 minutes; rinse immediately in cold water; drain and repeat with cauliflower. Mix broccoli and cauliflower with peppers, water chestnuts and mushrooms. Cover and refrigerate.

To make dressing: Thoroughly mix chutney, mayonnaise and curry powder; refrigerate. One hour before serving, toss vegetables well with the dressing. Refrigerate until needed. Just before serving, sprinkle with nuts.

SURPRISE SLAW

Combine in large bowl:
4 cups shredded cabbage
1 cup finely chopped celery
1 green pepper, chopped
1 medium onion, chopped

Combine for dressing:
½ cup mayonnaise
½ cup sour cream
½ teaspoon salt
⅛ teaspoon pepper
½ cup dry-roasted peanuts,
  chopped
1 tablespoon butter
¼ cup Parmesan cheese

Brown in microwave on HIGH for 3–6 minutes; stir twice. Add ¼ cup grated Parmesan cheese; sprinkle on top of slaw mixture.

CORN-ON-THE-COB
Serves 4

4 medium ears of corn (in husk)
8 paper towel sheets

For each ear, hold 2 connected paper towel sheets under running water until soaked, but not dripping. Squeeze gently to remove excess water. Spread paper towel sheets flat on counter. Place corn (in husk) lengthwise in center of 2 connected paper towel sheets. Fold one long side over corn. Fold both ends toward center. Roll up over corn. Place loose edge of packet down on microwave-safe platter. Microwave on HIGH for 9 to 15 minutes, or until tender, rearranging ears once. Let stand for two minutes. Remove and discard paper towels. If desired, place corn in husks on edge of grill to keep warm, turning ears once or twice.

SUPREME RICE CASSEROLE

1 stick butter, cut into pieces
1⅓ cups uncooked instant rice
1 can onion soup
⅓ pound fresh mushrooms,
  sliced, *or* 1 (4-ounce) can
½ teaspoon pepper

Combine all ingredients in baking dish; cover tightly and microwave 5 minutes on HIGH. Stir and microwave 5 additional minutes on 50 percent power. Let stand several minutes before serving.

MICROWAVE POTATOES

Peel and dice 3 or 4 large potatoes. Place in microwave casserole dish; dot with 1/2 stick margarine. Return to microwave and cook 3-5 minutes more, or until potatoes are done. Season with salt, pepper, and parsley flakes.

CELERY WITH CARROTS

A microwave recipe
Serves 4

6 sticks celery, cleaned and cut into julienne (match stick size) strips
1/2 pound carrots, scraped and cut into julienne (match stick size) strips
2 tablespoons butter
1 tablespoon snipped chives
1 teaspoon marjoram
Dash salt
Dash pepper
1 teaspoon chopped parsley

The total weight of the vegetables should be about 12 ounces. Arrange the celery and carrots in 3-3/4 cup oval or round casserole dish. Flake butter over vegetables. Sprinkle with chopped chives and marjoram; season well with salt and pepper. Spoon over 2 tablespoons water. Cover with plastic wrap and pierce. Microwave on HIGH for 10 minutes. Vegetables should be stirred half way through cooking, to make sure they cook evenly. Allow to stand 5 minutes, covered. Sprinkle with parsley before serving. Total Microwave cooking time: 10 minutes.

BAKED CUSTARD

2 cups milk
4 eggs, beaten
1/3 cup sugar
1 teaspoon vanilla
Dash of salt
Dash ground nutmeg

In a 4-cup glass measure, heat milk on HIGH for 4 minutes until very hot, but not boiling. Meanwhile, combine beaten eggs, sugar, vanilla and a dash of salt. Beat until well-blended; gradually add hot milk to beaten egg mixture; beat well. Divide egg mixture evenly between 6 (6-ounce) cups. Place in a 13 x 9 x 2-inch baking dish; sprinkle with nutmeg.

Pour about ½ cup boiling water around cups in dish; cover with waxed paper. Microwave on medium power (50 percent) for 8½ minutes; rearrange cups every 3 minutes. Remove any that are soft-set. Rearrange the remaining custards in dish; microwave on medium power (50 percent) for 5 minutes. Let stand 10 minutes.

MOCHA CREAM PUDDING

⅔ cup sugar
2 tablespoons cornstarch
¼ teaspoon salt
1⅔ cups milk
1½ (1-ounce) squares unsweetened chocolate
1 egg, beaten
2 tablespoons butter *or* margarine
1 teaspoon instant coffee crystals
1 teaspoon vanilla

In a 1½-quart bowl combine sugar, cornstarch and salt. Stir in milk and chocolate; mix well; microwave on HIGH for 6 minutes, stirring after 3 minutes, then every minute.

Gradually stir small amount of the hot milk mixture into the beaten egg; return all to bowl and mix well; microwave on HIGH for 30 seconds; stir after 14 seconds; add butter, coffee crystals and vanilla. Stir until butter melts. Cover with waxed paper. Cool, then chill.

BREAD PUDDING

¼ cup butter *or* margarine
4 slices bread, cubed
½ cup sugar
2 tablespoons lemon juice
1 cup milk
3 eggs
Cinnamon

Microwave butter on HIGH in a 1-quart casserole for about 1 minute;

add bread, sugar and lemon juice; toss to lightly mix. Combine milk and eggs; beat until smooth; pour over bread mixture. Sprinkle with cinnamon. Place casserole in an 8-inch square glass baking dish; add 1 cup warm water to baking dish. Microwave on HIGH, uncovered, for 11–13 minutes, or until center is just about set. Serve with Rum Custard Sauce.

Rum Custard Sauce:
1½ cups milk
½ cup light cream
⅓ cup sugar
⅛ teaspoon salt
3 large eggs, lightly beaten
3 tablespoons rum

Combine milk, cream, sugar and salt in a 2-quart glass measure. Place in microwave and cook for 4 minutes on 70 percent power. Stir ½ cup milk mixture into eggs; gradually stir eggs into milk mixture and microwave on 50 percent power for 2½ minutes.

Stir, then microwave for 2½ minutes on 30 percent power. Let stand until cooled; stir in rum. Serve over Bread Pudding.

PEANUT BUTTER PIECES

2 sticks butter
1 pound powdered sugar
1 cup graham cracker crumbs
1 cup peanut butter
1 (12 ounce) package chocolate chips

Place butter in large bowl and microwave on HIGH for 2-3 minutes. When butter is melted, add sugar, crumbs, and peanut butter. Mix until smooth; press into 8x8 dish; microwave on HIGH for 2 minutes. Put chocolate chips in large bowl and microwave 50% for 3-4 minutes; stir several times while cooking.

When melted, spread over peanut butter layer; chill. Cut into squares and store in airtight container.

MEXICAN CHOCOLATE CAKE

- 1 package microwave chocolate cake mix with pan
- ⅔ cup water
- ⅓ cup oil
- 1 egg
- 1 teaspoon cinnamon

Topping:
- 1 (6-ounce) package (1 cup) semisweet chocolate chips
- ¼ cup amaretto *or* 2 teaspoons almond extract *and*
- 2 tablespoons water
- ½ cup whipping cream
- 1½ teaspoons confectioners' sugar
- ½ teaspoon vanilla
- ¼ cup sliced almonds

Using solid shortening, grease a 7-inch round pan. In a medium bowl, combine all cake ingredients. Beat with a spoon for about 75 strokes; pour into a prepared pan; microwave on HIGH for 6½ minutes. Cake is done when it pulls away from sides of pan. If cake is not done, add additional time in 30-second intervals. Immediately invert onto serving plate. Cool completely.

In small microwave-safe bowl, combine chocolate chips and amaretto; microwave on MEDIUM (50 percent) power for 1½–2½ minutes; stir once partway through cooking, beating until smooth. Cool 20 minutes; spread on top of cake.

In small bowl, beat whipping cream until soft peaks form. Blend in confectioners' sugar and vanilla; beat until stiff peaks form. Spread over chocolate mixture; top with almonds. Store in refrigerator.

FROZEN DELIGHT

- 2 tablespoons butter *or* margarine

- 1½ cups chocolate cookie crumbs
- ½ cup sliced almonds
- ½ teaspoon cooking oil
- ½ gallon vanilla ice cream
- ¼ cup flaked coconut
- 1 teaspoon almond extract
- ½ cup grated semisweet chocolate (3 ounces)

Microwave butter on HIGH in a 12 x 8-inch dish for 45 seconds. Stir in crumbs until well-mixed; press into the bottom of dish. Microwave on HIGH, uncovered, for 1½–2 minutes; set aside to cool. Combine almonds and oil in a small dish; stir and microwave on HIGH, uncovered, for 2½–3 minutes; stir 3 times. When cool, chop half of the almonds finely; set aside. Microwave the ice cream on HIGH for 45–60 seconds in an uncovered container to soften. Place in mixing bowl; add coconut and extract; then add chocolate and chopped almonds; mix. Spoon into crust; sprinkle with remaining almonds. Cover and freeze until firm.

GOLDEN SPICE MARBLE CAKE
Serves 6

- 1 package microwave yellow cake mix
- ⅔ cup buttermilk
- ⅓ cup oil
- 1 egg
- 1 tablespoon molasses
- ½ teaspoon cinnamon
- ¼ teaspoon nutmeg

Frosting:
- 1 cup confectioners' sugar
- 1 tablespoon margarine *or* butter
- ½ teaspoon lemon juice
- 1–2 tablespoons milk

Use solid shortening; grease a 7-inch round pan. In a medium bowl, combine all cake ingredients; beat with a spoon until well-blended. Pour half of batter (about 1 cup) into second bowl. Stir in molasses, cinnamon and nutmeg. Spoon yellow and spice batter alternately into prepared pan. Pull knife through batter in wide curves; turn pan and repeat for marble effect.

Microwave on HIGH for 5 minutes. Cake is done when it pulls away from the sides of the pan. If any additional time is necessary, add it in 30-second intervals. Immediately invert onto serving plate. In a small bowl combine confectioners' sugar, margarine and lemon juice; gradually add milk until desired spreading consistency.

ELEGANT KRISPIE BARS

- 6 ounces white chocolate coating
- 1 cup peanut butter
- 4 cups rice cereal
- 1 cup salted peanuts

Combine coating and peanut butter in a 2-quart bowl and microwave on HIGH for 2½–3 minutes until coating is melted; stir twice. Add cereal and peanuts. Press into 13 x 9-inch baking dish. Refrigerate until set, about 1 hour. Cut into squares.

CHOCOLATE CHIP BARS

- ½ cup butter
- ¾ cup brown sugar
- 1 egg
- 1 tablespoon milk
- 1 teaspoon vanilla
- 1¼ cups flour
- ½ teaspoon baking powder
- ⅛ teaspoon salt
- 1 (6-ounce) package chocolate chips, divided
- ½ cup nuts (optional)

Mix all together, using only half of the chips in the batter. The other half goes on top. Using an 8- or 9-inch square dish, microwave on HIGH for 6½ minutes.

PEANUT BUTTER BARS

⅓ cup creamy *or* chunky
   peanut butter
⅓ cup light brown sugar
1 egg
1 teaspoon vanilla
2 tablespoons milk
⅔ cup flour
¼ teaspoon baking soda
¼ cup chopped peanuts
   (optional)
2 milk chocolate bars

Beat peanut butter with sugar, egg, vanilla and milk. Mix flour with baking soda and add to peanut butter mixture. Beat until smooth; add peanuts. Spread in greased 8-inch square dish. Microwave, uncovered, on MEDIUM HIGH (70 percent) for 5½–6 minutes; rotate dish after 3 minutes.

Let stand, uncovered, for 5 minutes. Let cool. Place 2 milk chocolate bars on top while it is standing; swirl for a quick frosting.

APPLESAUCE-RAISIN BARS

Makes 32 bars

¼ cup margarine
⅔ cup brown sugar, packed
1 egg
1 cup applesauce
1 cup flour
½ teaspoon baking soda
½ teaspoon salt
½ teaspoon ground cinnamon
¼ teaspoon ground nutmeg
⅛ teaspoon ground cloves
½ cup raisins
   Confectioners' sugar

Microwave the margarine on HIGH for 15–30 seconds, or until soft. Blend in brown sugar; beat in egg and applesauce. Stir in remaining ingredients, except raisins and confectioners' sugar; beat until smooth. Stir in raisins. Pour into 12 x 8-inch baking dish greased on bottom only. Microwave on HIGH, uncovered, for 9–10 minutes, or until no longer doughy. Cool. Sprinkle with confectioners' sugar. Cut into bars. The applesauce adds a moist texture to these spicy bars.

MILK CHOCOLATE ALMOND BARS

½ cup butter *or* margarine, softened
½ cup dark brown sugar, firmly packed
1¼ cups flour
¼ teaspoon salt
1 (6-ounce) package milk chocolate morsels
½ cup chopped almonds

Combine butter and sugar until creamy. Sift flour and salt together and blend into butter and sugar mixture. Press evenly into 13 x 9 x 2-inch baking dish. Microwave on HIGH for 4–5 minutes. Rotate the dish after 2 minutes. Sprinkle milk chocolate morsels over top and return to microwave for 1 minute on HIGH. Spread evenly over top; sprinkle with chopped almonds. Cool before cutting.

APRI-ORANGE SAUCE

Makes 2 cups

1/2 cup apricot jam
1 tablespoon cornstarch
1/2 cup orange juice
1/8 teaspoon ground cloves

Combine jam, cornstarch, and orange juice in a 2-cup glass measure; mix well. Microwave on HIGH, uncovered, 2 to 2-1/2 minutes or until mixture boils and thickens; stir once. Stir in cloves.

SWEET POTATO SOUFFLÉ

1 (18-ounce) can sweet potatoes
1/4 cup granulated sugar
1/4 cup dark brown sugar
1/4 cup margarine, melted
2 eggs
3/4 cup evaporated milk
1/2 teaspoon cinnamon
1/2 teaspoon nutmeg
1/4 teaspoon vanilla

Topping:
6 tablespoons margarine, melted
1/2 cup brown sugar
1/2 cup walnuts, chopped
1 cup crushed crackers, Ritz® or
   Townhouse®

Combine potatoes with next 8 ingredients and mix well. Pour into a 2-quart casserole and microwave on 70% for 13-16 minutes. Rotate dish once, if necessary. Combine topping ingredients and spread over potatoes. Microwave on 70% for 2-4 more minutes.

SOUPER CHEESE POTATOES

4 large potatoes, peeled and cubed
1/4 cup water
1/2 can condensed Cheddar cheese
   soup
1/2 cup sour cream
1/2 cup half-and-half
1 tablespoon snipped chives
1/2 teaspoon garlic salt
1/2 cup (2 ounces) shredded
   Cheddar cheese
Paprika
1 teaspoon parsley
1/8 teaspoon pepper

Combine potatoes and water in a casserole; cover with lid and microwave on HIGH for 12-14 minutes; stir once. Stir in soup, sour cream, half-and-half, chives, and garlic salt. Microwave on HIGH for 4-5 minutes, uncovered; stir once. Sprinkle with cheese and paprika. Let stand, covered, about 5 minutes or until cheese is melted. Sprinkle with paprika, parsley, and pepper.

PARMESAN POTATO SLICES

1 small onion, chopped
1/2 cup chopped celery
2 tablespoons butter or margarine
3 medium unpeeled potatoes, cleaned
1/2 teaspoon garlic salt
Dash pepper
1/4 cup Parmesan cheese, or to taste
1/4 teaspoon poultry seasoning
1/2 teaspoon dried parsley flakes
Paprika

Combine onion, celery, and butter in an 8-inch square baking dish. Cover with waxed paper. Microwave on HIGH 2-1/2 to 3 minutes or until vegetables are just about tender. Thinly slice potatoes into baking dish; mix lightly. Cover and microwave on HIGH 10-12 minutes or until potatoes are tender; stir once. Add garlic salt, pepper, cheese, seasonings; mix lightly. Sprinkle with paprika. Microwave on HIGH for 1-2 minutes, uncovered.

LIME-THYME POTATOES

1/4 cup melted margarine or butter
1 teaspoon grated lime peel
1 tablespoon lime juice
1 teaspoon dried thyme leaves
3 medium baking potatoes
1/4 cup grated Parmesan cheese
Paprika, salt and pepper

In a pie plate combine butter, thyme leaves, lime peel, and juice. Cut each potato lengthwise into eighths; toss in butter mixture. Arrange skin side down on paper-towel-covered plate; sprinkle with cheese, paprika, salt, and pepper. Microwave on HIGH for 13 minutes, covered with waxed paper; rotate dish halfway through.

SESAME-SPRINKLED BRUS-SELS SPROUTS
Serves 4

1 pound brussels sprouts
1 tablespoon water
2 tablespoons butter or margarine
2 teaspoons sesame seed
1 tablespoon soy sauce
1 teaspoon sesame oil
1/8 teaspoon lemon pepper

Combine brussels sprouts and water in a 1-quart casserole; cover; microwave on HIGH for 8-9 minutes or until tender. Drain and set aside. Place butter and sesame seeds in uncovered small glass dish and microwave on HIGH for 3-4 minutes, until toasted; stir twice. Mix in the soy sauce and sesame oil; spoon over the brussels sprouts; sprinkle with lemon pepper. Mix lightly.

PEA PODS ORIENTAL

1 (10-ounce) package frozen pea pods
1 tablespoon oil
1 tablespoon soy sauce

Remove wrapping from box of frozen pea pods. Place box on paper towel in microwave. Microwave on HIGH 3-4 minutes, or until heated through. Place in a bowl; toss lightly with oil and soy sauce. Microwave on HIGH 1-2 more minutes. These are served tender crisp. Do not overcook. Leftovers can be refrigerated and tossed into a salad for another use.

BROCCOLI AND MUSHROOMS

1 pound fresh mushrooms
1 pound fresh broccoli flowerets
1/4 cup hot water
2 cups Italian dressing

In a 3-quart casserole combine broccoli and water; cover and microwave for 1 minute on HIGH. Drain and rinse in cold water. In a bowl or plastic bag combine broccoli, mushrooms, and dressing.

Refrigerate at least 8 hours. If using a bowl stir several times, with a bag just turn bag over several times. Remove vegetables to serving platter with slotted spoon.

CHEESE-STUFFED MUSHROOMS

10 medium large mushrooms
1 tablespoon butter or margarine
1 (3-ounce) package cream cheese
2 tablespoons Parmesan cheese
1/8 teaspoon garlic salt
1/8 teaspoon hot pepper sauce
Paprika

Remove stems from mushrooms by gently twisting them. Place caps, open side up, on microwave-safe plate; set aside. Chop stems; combine stems and butter in a 1-quart casserole. Microwave (HIGH), uncovered, 2-3 minutes or until tender. Add cheeses; mix until softened and creamy. Stir in garlic salt and pepper sauce. Spoon cheese mixture into each cap, mounding mixture. Microwave (HIGH), uncovered, 2-3 minutes or until mushrooms are heated through. Sprinkle with paprika and/or parsley flakes.

PITA CHIPS
Makes 24

1 tablespoon margarine
Dash garlic powder
Dash paprika
1 pocket-bread pita round

Microwave the margarine on HIGH for 30 seconds or until melted. Stir in garlic powder and paprika. Cut pocket bread in half horizontally. Brush inner side with margarine; cut rounds into strips. Place on paper-towel-lined plate. Microwave on HIGH, uncovered, for 1 min. 30 seconds to 1 min. 45 seconds, or until bread is crisp. Serve plain or with favorite dip. (10 calories each)

MICROWAVE TOMATOES

4 large ripe tomatoes
3/4 cup mayonnaise
1/4-1/2 teaspoon curry powder
One-half of a 6-ounce package ranch dressing

Halve the tomatoes and arrange in a circle, cut side up, in a 9-inch pie plate. Mix remaining ingredients and spread over the top of the tomatoes. Microwave for 3-5 minutes on HIGH, turn around halfway through the cooking time. Do not cover. Let stand one minute.

SCALLOPED CORN MICROWAVE

1 (17-ounce) can whole kernel corn
1 (17-ounce) can cream style corn
1/2 cup Ritz Cracker crumbs
1 (5-ounce) can evaporated milk
1 egg, slightly beaten
1/8 teaspoon dry mustard
1 tablespoon dry onion flakes (or 1/4 cup chopped onion, sauted in butter)
1 (2-ounce) jar chopped pimiento
3 tablespoons grated Parmesan cheese
3 tablespoons margarine, cut into small pieces
1 teaspoon paprika

Combine all ingredients, except cheese, butter, and paprika; mix well. Put into a greased 1-1/2 quart casserole. Place cheese on top of casserole and dot with butter. Cover and microwave 10 minutes on Level 8 or until set. Let stand, covered, 3-5 minutes. Sprinkle with paprika before serving.

HOT CHEESE DIP

1/4 green pepper (finely chopped)
1/2 bunch green onions (finely chopped)
1-5 ounce jar of sharp Old English cheese
1- 8 ounce jar Cheese Whiz
1-7 ounce can minced clams, drained
Garlic powder to taste

Combine all ingredients in a 1-1/2 quart glass casserole dish. Heat uncovered on full power for 2 minutes; stir after one minute. Serve hot with corn chips. This is a very tasty cheese dip!

PUMPKIN SOUP
Serves 5-6

1 can chicken broth
3 cups water
1 tablespoon chicken bouillon or granules
1 small onion, chopped
1/2 cup chopped celery
1/2 cup chopped carrot
1 can (16-ounce) pumpkin
1/3 cup dry white wine (optional)
2 tablespoons butter
1/4 teaspoon thyme
Dash pepper
1/8 teaspoon garlic powder
Sour Cream

Combine chicken broth, water, bouillon, onion, celery, and carrots in 2-quart casserole; cover; microwave 15-30 minutes or until vegetables are tender. Let stand 10 minutes. Transfer vegetable mixture to food processor or blender. Process at medium or until smooth; add pumpkin; process until smooth. Return mixture to casserole; stir in wine, butter, salt, thyme, and garlic powder. Microwave on HIGH, uncovered, for 5-8 minutes, or until heated through, stirring 2 or 3 times. Serve in bowls; top with a spoonful of sour cream.

ICED FRESH TOMATO SOUP

2 tablespoons vegetable oil
6 medium tomatoes, chopped
1/4 cup catsup
1 tablespoon dry dillweed
Dash of Tabasco sauce
1 cup chopped onion
1 (10-ounce) can beef broth
3 cups crushed ice
1 teaspoon salt
1/2 cup heavy cream

Place oil, onion, and tomatoes in 8-cup measure, microwave on HIGH 2-3 minutes to make onion tender. Stir in beef broth and catsup. Microwave on HIGH for 2 minutes, cool slightly, and pour into blender and process until smooth. Return to 8-cup measure; stir in ice and seasonings. Chill until cold. Whip cream, and top each bowl of soup with it.

TACO PORK STRIPS
Serves 4

1 boneless pork chop 1/2 inch thick
2 teaspoons taco breading

Cut pork chop in 1/2-inch thick strips. Coat strips with breading; place in dish; cover with plastic wrap. Microwave on 30% power or MEDIUM LOW or 2 minutes. Turn strips over and rearrange; cover; microwave 2-1/2 minutes on MEDIUM LOW (30%).

Taco Breading:

1/2 cup cornflake crumbs
1-1/2 tablespoons taco seasoning mix

Combine. Makes 1/2 cup for enough for 4 chops.

BACON STICKS
Makes 10

10 thin bread sticks (any flavor)
5 slices of bacon (cut lengthwise)
1/2 cup Parmesan cheese

Dredge one side of bacon strip in cheese. With cheese side out, roll bacon around bread stick diagonally.
Place sticks on microwave dish or paper plate lined with paper towels. Microwave on HIGH 4-1/2 - 6 minutes. When done, roll again in cheese.

ULTIMATE NACHOS
Serves 4

Paper towel
24 large tortilla chips
1 cup shredded Monterey Jack,
  Cheddar or Colby cheese
6-7 tablespoons canned refried
  beans
2 tablespoons chopped onions,
  optional
1 medium tomato, chopped
1-2 cups shredded lettuce
1/4 cup sour cream, optional
1/4 cup sliced black olives
1 tablespoon jalapeño pepper,
  fresh or canned, optional
Taco sauce

Place towel on microwave-safe plate; arrange tortilla chips on the paper towel-lined plate. Spread chips with refried beans; top with shredded cheese and chopped onions. Microwave 2-5 minutes at 50% (medium). Before serving, after cheese has melted, top with shredded lettuce, chopped tomato, olives, jalapeño pepper, taco sauce, and small dollops of sour cream.

OUTRAGEOUS SPINACH DIP

1 (10-ounce) box frozen chopped
  spinach
1 (8-ounce) can water chestnuts,
  finely chopped
1-1/2 cups sour cream
1 cup mayonnaise
1 package dried vegetable soup
  mix
2 green onions, finely chopped
1/4 teaspoon garlic powder
1/2 teaspoon seasoning salt

Remove paper from box of spinach; place box on paper towel in microwave oven. Microwave on HIGH for 6 minutes. In mixing bowl combine remaining ingredients; drain and squeeze spinach before adding to cream mixture. Refrigerate for 2 hours before serving. Serving suggestion: Take a round un-sliced loaf of pumpernickel bread and cut a circle in the top and remove. Gently pull bread from inside to be later used to dip. When ready to serve, pour dip into bread.

PUMPERNICKEL SURPRISE MUFFINS

1 cup milk
1/3 cup oil
1 egg
2 tablespoons molasses
3/4 cup whole wheat or white flour
1/2 cup rye flour
1/4 cup packed brown sugar
1/4 cup unsweetened cocoa powder
2 teaspoons baking powder
1 teaspoon caraway seeds
1/2 teaspoon salt
1 (3-ounce) package cream cheese
1/2 teaspoon grated orange rind

Beat together milk, oil, egg, and molasses in 2-cup measure. Combine flours, brown sugar, cocoa, baking powder, caraway seeds, and salt in a bowl. Add milk mixture; stir just until moistened. Cut cream cheese into 12 equal cubes; roll grated orange rind in as you roll into a ball. Line the muffin cups with paper liners; spoon a little batter into each cup, filling 1/4 full. Place a cream cheese ball in the center of each muffin. Top with remaining batter; fill 3/4 full. Microwave, uncovered, on HIGH for 2 to 2-1/2 minutes for 6 muffins.

VEGETABLE CORN MUFFINS

Makes 12 muffins
(Microwave - Diabetes Exchange)

1 cup all-purpose white flour
1/2 cup cornmeal
1 tablespoon sugar
1 tablespoon baking powder
1/2 teaspoon salt
3/4 teaspoon Italian seasoning
1/8 teaspoon garlic powder
2 eggs, beaten
1 tablespoon vegetable oil
1/2 cup corn, drained
1/3 cup skim milk
1/3 cup chopped green pepper
1/4 cup finely chopped onion

Combine all ingredients in mixing bowl. Stir just until blended. Line each muffin or custard cup with 2 paper liners. Fill 1/2 full. Microwave on HIGH as directed below or until top springs back when touched, rotating and rearranging after 1/2 the time.

Cooking time:
1 muffin = 1/4 to 3/4 minutes
2 muffins = 1/2 to 2 minutes
4 muffins = 1 to 2-1/2 minutes
6 muffins = 2 to 4-1/2 minutes

OATMEAL APPLE MUFFINS

1/4 cup water
1/2 cup quick cooking oats
3 tablespoons butter or margarine
2 tablespoons oil
1 egg
1/2 cup packed brown sugar
1/2 cup whole wheat or white flour
1 teaspoon baking powder
1/4 teaspoon salt
1/2 teaspoon cinnamon
1/4 teaspoon nutmeg
3/4 cup chopped apple

Topping:
1 tablespoon butter or margarine
2 tablespoons brown sugar
1 tablespoon flour
1 tablespoon chopped nuts
1/4 teaspoon cinnamon

Microwave water in mixing bowl for 2-3 minutes or until boiling. Stir in oats; let stand 5 minutes. Add butter and oil; stir until butter is melted. Beat in egg and brown sugar; add flour, baking powder, salt, cinnamon, nutmeg; stir until moistened; stir in apple.

Line 12 microwave-safe muffin cups with paper liners; spoon batter into cups, filling 2/3 full. Combine topping ingredients in small bowl; mix with fork until crumbly; spoon mixture evenly onto muffin batter. Microwave on HIGH, uncovered, 2 to 2-1/2 minutes. Repeat with remaining muffins.

FROSTY PUMPKIN PRALINE PIE

Crust:
1/4 cup butter or margarine
1-1/4 cups graham cracker crumbs
2 tablespoons sugar

Praline pieces:
1/4 cup firmly packed brown sugar
1/4 cup sliced or slivered almonds
1 tablespoon butter or margarine
1 teaspoon water

Filling:
1 cup canned pumpkin
1/2 cup firmly packed brown sugar
1/4 cup milk
1 teaspoon cinnamon
1/2 teaspoon nutmeg
1/4 teaspoon ginger
1/4 teaspoon salt
1 pint (2 cups) vanilla ice cream

Topping:
1 cup whipping cream
2 tablespoons sugar
1 teaspoon vanilla

In bowl microwave butter on HIGH 1/2-1 minute or until melted; stir in crumbs and sugar until combined. Press mixture into bottom and up sides of a 9-inch pie plate; microwave uncovered 1-1/2 to 2-1/2 minutes or until heated through. Rotate twice, if necessary. Cool.

In an 8-inch round glass baking dish, combine all ingredients for praline pieces; microwave on HIGH, uncovered, 2-3 minutes or until bubbly and nuts are lightly toasted, stirring several times. Cool; break into pieces.

Combine in glass mixing bowl, all ingredients for filling, except ice cream. Microwave on HIGH for 3-4 minutes, uncovered; stir once. Stir in ice cream; let stand until ice cream can be easily mixed in. Pour into crust. Freeze until firm. Beat cream until thickened; beat in sugar and vanilla. Spread over pie; sprinkle with praline pieces. Freeze until served. You can use crushed gingersnaps for cracker crumbs.

SPECIAL CHOCOLATE PIE

Yield 1-9 inch pie

24 large marshmallows
1/2 cup of half & half
1-6 ounce package of semi-sweet chocolate chips (it must be real chocolate, not the food type)
2 tablespoons creme de cocao
2 tablespoons Kahlua
1 cup whipping cream
1-9 inch chocolate wafer crust; (recipe on page 50)

Microwave marshmallows, milk (half & half), and chocolate, in a 3 quart casserole at MEDIUM, 3-4 minutes; stir and cool slightly. Add the creme de cocao and Kahlua to the half & half mixture. Chill 20-30 minutes. Whip the cream until stiff. Fold into chocolate mixture. Pour filling into the chocolate wafer crust and freeze. Remove from freezer 5-10 minutes before serving.

ONE MINUTE CHOCOLATE WAFER PIE CRUST

Makes one pie crust

7 tablespoons butter
1-1/2 cups chocolate wafers crushed crumbs
2 tablespoons walnuts, crushed crumbs

Microwave butter in a 9 inch glass pie plate at HIGH for 1 minute. Stir in the wafer and walnut crumbs. Press mixture evenly in the pie plate. Chill, pour pie filling into shell and freeze.

LO -CAL COCOA

1 cup nonfat dry milk powder
2 teaspoons unsweetened cocoa

2 - 4 packets Equal

Combine the dry milk and cocoa. Store at room temp. Makes enough for 4 cups of cocoa. Fill mug with 3/4 cup water. Microwave on HIGH for 1 minute or until hot. Stir in 1/4 cup Cocoa mix and 1/2 - 1 packet of Equal

MICROWAVE APRICOT CRISP

Serves 4

1-14 ounce can apricot pie filling
1 tablespoon sugar
2 oranges, grated rind and juice
1/4 cup soft margarine
3/4 cup raw oats
1/3 cup light brown sugar
3 tablespoons flour
4 gingersnaps, crushed

Mix together pie filling, sugar, orange rind, and juice in a shallow, oven-proof dish. Combine margarine, oats, brown sugar, and flour, until crumbly. Spoon evenly over fruit mixture and sprinkle with the crumbs. Place in microwave and cook about 10 minutes or until fruit juices begin to bubble through crisp crust.

Serve warm with whipped cream.

SEASONED SEEDS

1 cup pumpkin seeds
1 tablespoon butter or margarine
1/2 teaspoon Worcestershire sauce
1/4 teaspoon garlic salt
1/4 teaspoon onion salt or seasoned salt

Remove membrane from seeds. If seeds are washed, pat dry. Place in a 9-inch glass pie plate; add remaining ingredients; microwave on HIGH for 8-10 minutes until lightly toasted, stirring 4-5 times. Cooking time will depend on size of seeds and moistness.

CORN MUFFINS

1/2 cup buttermilk
3 tablespoons oil
1 egg
3/4 cup cornmeal
1/2 cup whole wheat or white flour
3 tablespoons sugar
2 tablespoons baking powder
1/2 teaspoon soda
1/2 teaspoon salt
1 (4-ounce) can green chilies
1 cup fresh or canned corn, drained
1/2 teaspoon dried minced onion
1 teaspoon jalapeno peppers
   (optional)

Beat together buttermilk, oil, and egg in a 2-cup measure. Place cornmeal, flour, sugar, baking powder, and soda and salt in mixing bowl. Add buttermilk mixture; stir just until moistened. Mix in chilies, corn, minced onions, and jalapeno peppers. Line muffin cups with paper liners; spoon batter into cups, fill 3/4 full. Microwave 6 muffins at a time on HIGH, uncovered, 2 to 2-1/2 minutes.

CARAMEL TOPPED RICE CUSTARD

(Microwave Method)

Combine caramels and 1/4 cup milk in 2-cup glass measure. Cook on HIGH (maximum power) 2 minutes, or until caramels melt, stirring every minute. Pour equal amounts into 6 buttered cups. Spoon 1/3 cup rice into each cup. Blend remaining ingredients; pour evenly into each cup. Place cups in shallow micro-proof dish, containing 1 inch water. Cook at 70% power for 15 minutes, or until almost set, rotating dish 1/4 turn every 5 minutes. Let stand 10 minutes. Loosen custard with knife and invert onto dessert plates. Garnish with chopped nuts or coconut, if desired. Serve warm.

CHOCOLATE AMARETTO MOUSSE

2 ounces cream cheese
2 tablespoons semisweet chocolate
   pieces
1/2 tablespoon Amaretto liqueur
1/2 cup whipping cream
2 tablespoons sugar

Combine cream cheese and chocolate pieces in 1-cup glass measure. Microwave on HIGH, uncovered, 30-45 seconds or until chocolate is soft. Stir to melt chocolate; blend in liqueur; set aside.

Beat cream and sugar until thick; fold in chocolate. Spoon into individual dishes. Refrigerate until set, about 2 hours. Top with shaved chocolate or chocolate jimmies.

CARAMEL NUT POPCORN CLUSTERS

1 (14-ounce) bag approximately 40
   caramel squares
2 tablespoons light cream
2 quarts popped popcorn, lightly
   salted
1 cup salted, roasted peanuts

Combine caramel squares and cream in small bowl. Microwave 2 minutes, 30 seconds to 3 minutes on MEDIUM HIGH, stirring several times or until caramel is smooth. In large bowl, mix popcorn and peanuts together, adding caramel sauce gradually. Stir until combined. Drop by spoonfuls onto wax paper. Let cool.

LEMONY BARBECUE SAUCE

Makes 1 cup

2 tablespoons butter or margarine
1/2 cup chopped onion
1 clove garlic, minced
1/2 cup catsup
1/4 cup lemon juice
2 tablespoons molasses
1 tablespoon Worcestershire sauce
1/4 teaspoon dry mustard
1/4 teaspoon salt
1/4 teaspoon pepper
1/4 teaspoon ground cumin
5 thin slices lemon, seeded and
   quartered

Place butter in a 1-1/2-quart casserole. Microwave on HIGH for 45 seconds or until melted. Add onion and garlic; cover with lid; microwave on HIGH for 2 minutes. Add remaining ingredients; cover and microwave on HIGH for 3-4 minutes; stir once. Use as a basting sauce for beef, pork, or chicken.

ALMOND VANILLA CUSTARD SAUCE

Makes 1 cup

1 egg, beaten
3/4 cup half-and-half
2 tablespoons sugar
1/2 teaspoon vanilla extract
1/4 teaspoon almond extract

Combine all ingredients in a 2-cup measure; mix well. Microwave on MEDIUM (50%) power for 4-7 minutes or until thickened. Stir with whisk after 2 minutes and every minute thereafter. Stir well; cover and chill. Serve over pound cake or fruit.

SWEET AND TANGY BARBECUE SAUCE

Makes 1-1/2 cups

1 cup chopped onion
3 cloves garlic, minced
2 tablespoons oil
1/2 cup brown sugar, packed
1/2 cup red wine vinegar
1/3 cup water
1 (6-ounce) can tomato paste
2 tablespoons soy sauce
1 teaspoon instant beef bouillon
1 teaspoon prepared mustard

Combine onion, garlic, and oil in 1-quart casserole; cover with lid. Microwave on HIGH for 2 to 2-1/2 minutes or until tender. Stir in remaining ingredients. Cover. Microwave on HIGH, 5-6 minutes. Sauce can be covered and refrigerated for up to 2 weeks.

BARBECUED LAMB SHANKS

Serves 4

12 thin lemon slices
4 lamb shanks (about 3-1/2 pounds)
Barbecue sauce
8 paper towel sheets

For each lamb shank, place 2 paper towel sheets, one on top of the other, on the counter. Place three lemon slices diagonally across center of paper towel sheets. Place lamb shank on lemon slices. Fold three corners toward center, covering lamb like an envelope. Roll up over remaining corner. Hold under running water until soaked, but not dripping. Place loose corner down on microwave-safe plate.

Microwave on HIGH for 5 minutes. Rotate plate half turn. Microwave on MEDIUM (50 per cent power) for 5 minutes per pound, rotating plate once. Remove and discard paper towel sheets. Brush lamb shanks with barbecue sauce. Place lamb on hot grill. Grill to desired doneness, 20 to 30 minutes, turning and brushing occasionally with barbecue sauce.

CRAB AND CORN BISQUE

8 servings

2 tablespoons butter or margarine
1 small onion, chopped
1 small red pepper, chopped
1 large celery stalk, chopped
1/4 teaspoon dried thyme leaves
1/8 teaspoon ground red pepper
1 can condensed cream of potato soup, undiluted
2 cups milk
1 (17-ounce) can cream-style corn
1 (12-ounce) package fish and crab blend (surimi)

In 3-quart casserole, melt butter on HIGH one minute; add chopped onion, pepper, celery, thyme and ground red pepper; cover with plastic wrap; turn back one corner to vent. Cook on HIGH for 5 minutes, stirring once. Stir in soup, milk, corn and surimi; cover and vent; microwave on HIGH for 7 minutes or until boiling.

CHEDDAR FISH BUNDLES

Serves 4

1-1/2 cups shredded cheddar cheese
1-1/2 cups fresh bread crumbs
2 tablespoons mayonnaise
2 teaspoons horseradish
1 pound sole fillets
1 tablespoon margarine, melted

Combine 1 cup cheese, crumbs, mayonnaise, and horseradish; mix lightly. Spoon mixture over fish; roll up; secure with wooden toothpicks. Place fish, seam side down, in baking dish, drizzling with margarine. Microwave on HIGH for 5-6 minutes or until fish flakes easily; turn dish after 3 minutes. Sprinkle with remaining cheese; microwave 1-1/2 to 2 minutes or until melted.

QUICK AND LIGHT FISH PLATTER

Serves 1

2 carrots, cut into 2 inch x 1/8 inch strips
1 stalk celery, cut into 1" slices
1 tablespoon water
Parsley flakes
1 tablespoon butter or margarine
4 to 6 ounces defrosted flounder fillets
2 teaspoons lemon juice
Paprika
1 tablespoon sliced green onion
2 tablespoons almonds, toasted

Place carrot strips around edge of a dinner plate; top with celery, water and parsley; dice 1 teaspoon of butter and place on vegetables. Cover with plastic wrap; turn back one edge to vent. Microwave on HIGH for 2 minutes. Uncover; place fish on center of plate. Top with lemon juice, remaining butter, paprika, and onion. Re-cover with plastic wrap; microwave on HIGH for 2 minutes. Let stand 2 minutes. Sprinkle with toasted almonds.

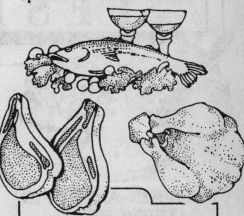

ITALIAN CHICKEN SUPREME

2 medium carrots, cut in thin strips
1 medium zucchini, cut in thin strips
1 medium onion, thinly sliced
2 whole boneless chicken breasts, skinned and cut in half (about 1 pound)
1 teaspoon Italian seasoning
4 pats butter
Salt and pepper

Divide carrots, zucchini, and onion evenly among the 4 paper towels. Place a pat of butter, salt, and pepper over assembled vegetables. Cover vegetables with boneless chicken breast. Sprinkle with Italian seasoning. Fold towel around chicken and vegetables to completely enclose. Moisten under running water. Place paper towel bundles in a round glass baking dish. Microwave on HIGH for 9-10 minutes, or until chicken is cooked. Remove from microwave and let stand 1 minute before serving.

Makes 4 servings of 1 chicken breast and 1/2 cup vegetables each.

For 2 servings: 6 minutes on HIGH
For 1 serving: 3 minutes , 30 seconds on HIGH
Calories per serving: 167

Pies

FESTIVE

PUMPKIN-APPLE PIE (TWO-CRUST)

A different kind of pie. May be made ahead of time and frozen.

- 4 cups raw pumpkin, cut in small, chunky pieces
- 2 cups sliced apples
- 1 cup sugar
- 1 teaspoon cinnamon
- 1 teaspoon nutmeg
- 1 teaspoon grated lemon rind *or* ½ teaspoon lemon extract
- ¼ cup butter

Combine all ingredients except butter and mix well. Put them into a 9-inch pie shell. Dot the top with butter and cover with top crust. Bake for 15 minutes in 400-degree oven; then reduce heat to 325 degrees and continue to bake for 45 additional minutes.

APPLE PIE

Makes 8 or 9-inch pie

Pastry for two-crust pie:
5 or 6 apples, pared and sliced
2/3 cup fructose

1/2 teaspoon nutmeg *and/or* 1/2 teaspoon cinnamon
1/4 cup cornstarch
2 tablespoons lemon juice (if desired for extra tartness)

Prepare pastry for 2-crust pie. Spray bottom and sides of pie pan and line with half rolled-out crust. Combine fructose, nutmeg *and/or* cinnamon, cornstarch, and mix well.

Pare and slice apples; add lemon juice, if desired. Stir fructose mixture into apples and arrange in pie crust. Cover with remaining rolled-out crust. Press edges together and flute in attractive manner. Bake at 400 degrees for approximately 45 minutes, or until well browned.

IMPOSSIBLE FRENCH APPLE PIE

6 cups sliced apples
1-1/4 teaspoons cinnamon
1/4 teaspoon nutmeg
1 cup sugar
3/4 cup milk
1/2 cup Bisquick
2 eggs
2 tablespoons softened butter
Streusel Topping (recipe follows)

Grease pie plate (10x1-1/2-inch). Mix apple and spices; turn into plate. Beat remaining ingredients, except streusel, until smooth, 15 seconds, in blender or 1 minute with mixer. Pour into plate over apples. Sprinkle with streusel. Bake at 350 degrees until knife comes out clean, 55-60 minutes.

Streusel Topping:
1 cup Bisquick
1/2 cup chopped nuts
1/3 cup brown sugar
3 tablespoons margarine

Mix all ingredients together until crumbly.

OZARK PIE

Serves 6

- ½ cup all-purpose flour
- 2 teaspoons baking powder
- ½ teaspoon salt
- 2 eggs
- 1 cup brown sugar, firmly packed
- 1 teaspoon vanilla
- 1 cup chopped walnuts
- 1 cup finely chopped apples
- 1 (9-inch) unbaked pie shell
  Whipped cream *or* ice cream for garnish
- ½ cup broken nuts

Mix flour, baking powder and salt. Beat eggs until light and lemon-colored. Beat in sugar gradually. Continue to beat until creamy. Stir in flour mixture, vanilla, nuts and apples; mix well. Spoon into pie shell. Bake at 450 degrees for 15 minutes; reduce heat to 350 degrees and bake 15 minutes longer, or until filling is set. Cool pie. Garnish with whipped cream or ice cream. Decorate with chopped nuts.

MINCE-APPLE PIE

1 (9-ounce) package instant condensed mincemeat
1/4 cup sugar
2 cups thinly sliced apples
1/4 teaspoon grated lemon peel
1 tablespoon lemon juice
1 teaspoon rum flavoring
Pastry for 9-inch 2-crust pie
Fluffy Hard Sauce (recipe follows)

Prepare mincemeat following
package directions, except use 1/4
cup sugar.

Combine mincemeat with apples,
lemon peel, lemon juice, and rum
flavoring. Line 9-inch pie plate with
pastry; pour in mincemeat mixture.
Adjust top crust and crimp edges. Cut
slits in top of upper crust for escape of
steam. Bake at 400 degrees for 40 to
45 minutes. Serve warm with Fluffy
Hard Sauce.

Fluffy Hard Sauce:
2 cups sifted confectioners' sugar
1/2 cup butter or margarine
1 egg yolk, beaten
1 teaspoon vanilla
1 egg white, stiffly beaten

Thoroughly cream together sifted
confectioners' sugar and butter (or
margarine). Stir in beaten egg yolk
and 1 teaspoon vanilla. Fold in stiffly
beaten egg white. Chill.

BROWN BAG
APPLE PIE
(no muss, no fuss)

9" unbaked pie shell
6 cups thinly sliced apples
1/2 cup light brown sugar, firmly
  packed
2 tablespoons cornstarch
1 teaspoon cinnamon
1/4 teaspoon mace
1/2 teaspoon nutmeg
2 tablespoons lemon juice

Put apples into a bowl; mix with
sugar, cornstarch, cinnamon, mace,
nutmeg and lemon juice. Place apple
mixture into pie shell; pat apples
down evenly.

Streusel Topping:
1/4 cup butter
1/4 cup flour
1/2 cup light brown sugar

Mix together until crumbs are the
size of peas. Sprinkle evenly over
apples; pat down around edges.

Slide pie into brown paper bag;
fold end under the pie; put on a
baking sheet. Bake at 350 degrees for
1 hour 10 minutes.

CRAZY CRUST
APPLE PIE
Serves 6

1 cup all-purpose flour
1 teaspoon baking powder
½ teaspoon salt
1 tablespoon sugar
1 egg
⅔ cup shortening
¼ cup water
1 (1-pound, 5 ounce) can apple
  pie filling
1 tablespoon lemon juice
½ teaspoon apple pie spice *or*
  cinnamon

In small mixer bowl, combine
flour, baking powder, salt, sugar,
egg, shortening and water. Blend
well; beat 2 minutes at medium
speed of mixer. Pour batter into a 9-
inch pie pan.

Combine pie filling, lemon juice
and spice; pour into center of batter.
Do not stir. Bake at 425 degrees for
45–50 minutes.

CARAMEL-NUT
APPLE PIE
Serves 8

1½ cups heavy cream,
  unwhipped

¾ cup brown sugar
⅓ cup butter
1 ounce sweet chocolate
1 cup chopped mixed nuts
1 deep-dish apple pie, baked
  and cooled

In heavy saucepan, combine
cream, brown sugar, butter and
chocolate. Bring to a boil and cook
over medium heat until mixture
lightly coats a spoon, about 15 minutes. Remove from heat and stir in
nuts. Set aside to cool slightly. Invert
cooled pie onto serving dish and
spoon caramel-nut mixture over top
so it runs down the sides. Chill thoroughly before serving.

HARVEST
WALNUT PIE
Serves 6–8

1 ready-prepared graham
  cracker crust
2 egg yolks
1 cup sugar
4 tablespoons flour
1 cup sour cream
½ teaspoon walnut extract *or*
  vanilla extract
¼ teaspoon lemon rind
½ cup walnuts, finely chopped

Topping:
2 egg whites
¼ teaspoon cream of tartar
1 cup brown sugar
½ cup walnuts, coarsely
  chopped
¼ teaspoon walnut extract

Mix egg yolks, sugar, flour, sour
cream, walnut extract, lemon rind
and walnuts together. Cook in the
top of a double boiler over boiling
water. Stir with wire whisk until
thickened and pour into pie shell.
For topping, beat egg whites with
cream of tartar until they form soft
peaks. Add brown sugar, walnuts
and extract. Spread over filling.
Bake at 325 degrees for 15 minutes,
or until brown.

LAYERED BANANA SPLIT PIE

1 pint vanilla ice cream, softened
1 (9-inch) graham cracker crust
  Chocolate Sauce (recipe follows)
1 cup chopped pecans, divided
½ pint chocolate ice cream, softened
1 (8-ounce) can crushed pineapple, drained
2 bananas, sliced
1 cup whipping cream
¼ cup sifted confectioners' sugar
1 tablespoon grated, unsweetened chocolate (optional)

Spread half of vanilla ice cream evenly over crust; cover and freeze until firm. Spread ⅓ of Chocolate Sauce over ice cream; sprinkle with ½ cup pecans. Cover and freeze until set.

Spread chocolate ice cream evenly over pie; cover and freeze until firm. Spoon half of remaining Chocolate Sauce over chocolate ice cream; top with pineapple; cover and freeze.

Spread remaining vanilla ice cream evenly over pie; cover and freeze until firm. Spread remaining Chocolate Sauce over ice cream; top with remaining ½ cup pecans and banana slices.

Beat whipping cream until foamy; gradually add confectioners' sugar, beating until soft peaks form. Spread whipped cream over pie; sprinkle with grated chocolate. Freeze. Let stand at room temperature 5 minutes before serving.

Chocolate Sauce:
½ cup semisweet chocolate morsels
1 (5.3-ounce) can evaporated milk
1 cup sifted confectioners' sugar
¼ cup margarine

Combine all ingredients in top of a double boiler; bring water to a boil. Reduce heat to low; cook 15–20 minutes, or until slightly thickened, stirring occasionally. Cool completely.

EXQUISITE BUTTERSCOTCH PIE

1 cup golden *or* dark raisins, chopped
1 cup brown sugar
6 tablespoons cornstarch
½ teaspoon salt
1½ cups milk
3 eggs, separated
¼ teaspoon cream of tartar
6 tablespoons sugar
2 tablespoons butter
2 teaspoons vanilla
1 cup sour cream
1 (9-inch) pie crust, baked

Combine sugar, cornstarch and salt. Add milk gradually. Cook on medium heat, stirring until slightly thickened. Then cook on low heat until very thick. Remove from heat, and carefully stir in beaten egg yolks. Return to heat for 5 minutes, stirring constantly. Remove from heat and add butter, vanilla and raisins. Cool somewhat, then stir in sour cream and place in baked crust. Cover with meringue made by beating egg whites with ¼ teaspoon cream of tartar to soft peaks and then adding gradually 6 tablespoons sugar. Brown in 350-degree oven for 10 minutes, or until lightly browned.

PUMPKIN ICE CREAM PIE

1 pint vanilla ice cream
2 cups pumpkin
½ cup sugar
½ teaspoon salt
1 teaspoon cinnamon
1 teaspoon cloves
1 teaspoon vanilla

Mix pumpkin, sugar, spices and vanilla. Fold mixture into ice cream, which has been softened. Pour into baked pie shell. Cover and freeze for 4 hours before serving.

FROZEN MOCHA PECAN PIE

Crust:
2 cups toasted pecans, finely chopped
5 tablespoons plus 1 teaspoon dark brown sugar
5 tablespoons cold butter, cut into small pieces
2 teaspoons dark rum

Filling:
6 ounces semisweet chocolate
½ teaspoon instant coffee powder
4 eggs, at room temperature
1 tablespoon dark rum
1 teaspoon vanilla
1½ cups heavy cream (reserve ½ cup for topping)

Garnish:
3 tablespoons shaved semisweet chocolate *or*
½ cup pecan halves

To prepare crust, blend ingredients in bowl until mixture holds together. Press into bottom and sides of a 9-inch pie pan. Freeze 1 hour.

To prepare filling, melt chocolate with coffee powder in top of double boiler over hot water. Remove from heat; whisk in eggs, rum and vanilla until smooth. Let cool; whip 1 cup of the cream until stiff; fold into chocolate mixture. Pour into crust and freeze.

One hour before serving transfer pie to refrigerator. Whip remaining ½ cup cream; dollop or pipe over pie. Sprinkle with chocolate shavings or ½ cup pecan halves.

DOUBLE-LOOK CAKE PIE

Top Part:
- ½ cup sugar
- ¼ cup margarine *or* shortening
- 1 egg
- ½ cup milk
- 1 cup flour
- 1 teaspoon baking powder
- ½ teaspoon vanilla

Lower Part:
- ½ cup sugar
- ⅓ cup hot water
- ¼ cup cocoa
- ¼ teaspoon vanilla

For top part, cream shortening, sugar and egg. Add milk alternately with sifted flour and baking powder; add vanilla. Set aside.

For lower part, combine sugar and cocoa. Add hot water and vanilla. Pour into an unbaked pie crust, then pour top part over lower part. Bake 40 minutes in 350-degree oven. Serve as you like, warm or cold, topped or plain.

BON-BON PIE

- 15 chocolate creme-filled cookies
- 2 tablespoons melted butter
- 1 pint ice cream, softened
- 24 Bon-Bon brand ice cream nuggets
  - Sweetened whipped cream
  - Chocolate syrup

Crush cookies; combine with butter. Press into a buttered 8-inch pie plate. Bake in moderate 350-degree oven for 8–10 minutes. Cool. Spoon ice cream into pie shell. Cover surface of ice cream with Bon-Bon brand ice cream nuggets; gently press down into ice cream. Freeze. Before serving, cover pie with whipped cream and drizzel with chocolate syrup. Pre-made chocolate pie shell may be used-just eliminate cookies and butter.

FUDGE PIE

- ¼ cup butter
- 1 (13-ounce) can evaporated milk
- 3 eggs, separated
- ½ cup brown sugar, packed
- 1 teaspoon vanilla
- ½ cup chopped pecans
- 2 tablespoons semisweet chocolate pieces
  - Pinch of salt
- 1 (9-inch) prepared chocolate crumb crust

Combine butter, evaporated milk, egg yolks and brown sugar. Cook in double boiler over boiling water, stirring constantly, until thick. Add vanilla and nuts; remove from heat. Add chocolate and stir until melted. Set aside. Beat egg whites with salt until stiff. Fold into cooled chocolate mixture and pour into pie shell. Freeze until firm.

STRAWBERRY CHIFFON PIE
Serves 6–8

- 1 (9-inch) baked pastry shell
  - Strawberry Chiffon Filling (recipe follows)

Pour filling into pastry shell and refrigerate until firm, about 3–4 hours. Garnish with sweetened whipped cream, if desired.

Strawberry Chiffon Filling:
- ½ cup sugar, divided
- 1 envelope (1 tablespoon) unflavored gelatin
- ¼ teaspoon salt
- ½ cup water
- 1 (10-ounce) package frozen strawberries, thawed and mashed
- 1 teaspoon grated orange rind
- 3–5 drops red food coloring, optional
- 2 egg whites
- ½ cup whipping cream, whipped

Combine ¼ cup sugar, gelatin and salt in saucepan. Stir to blend; add water. Stir over low heat for 3–4 minutes until gelatin is dissolved. Remove from heat; pour into a bowl; stir in strawberries, orange rind and food coloring. Refrigerate until slightly thicker than consistency of unbeaten egg whites. Beat egg whites until soft peaks form; gradually add ¼ cup sugar and beat until stiff peaks form. Fold beaten egg whites, then whipped cream into mixture.

PEACH PRALINE PIE
Serves 6

- 4 cups sliced *or* canned peaches
- ⅔ to ¾ cup sugar
- 1½ tablespoons quick-cooking tapioca
- 1 teaspoon lemon juice
  - Pastry for 1-crust, 9-inch pie
  - Praline Crumb Topping (recipe follows)

Combine peaches, sugar, tapioca and lemon juice. Roll pastry to ⅛-inch thickness. Line a 9-inch pie pan. Trim pastry 1 inch larger than pan and fold edge to form a standing rim. Flute or shape as desired. Sprinkle ⅓ of Praline Crumb Topping over bottom of pie shell. Fill with peach mixture and sprinkle with remaining topping. Bake at 425 degrees for 45 minutes, or until syrup boils in heavy bubbles that do not burst. Serve warm.

Praline Crumb Topping:
- ¼ cup flour
- 3 tablespoons butter *or* margarine
- ½ cup brown sugar, firmly packed
- ½ cup pecans, chopped

Combine flour, butter and brown sugar until crumbs are size of peas. Add pecans.

BLUEBERRY PEACH SOUR CREAM PIE

- 1 (9-inch) unbaked pie shell
- 1½ cups sour cream
- 2 large eggs
- ¼ cup flour
- ¾ cup sugar
- 1 teaspoon vanilla
- ½ teaspoon cinnamon
- 3 cups peaches, peeled and sliced
- 2½ cups blueberries
- 1 teaspoon lemon juice

Topping:
- ¾ cup brown sugar
- ½ cup flour
- 2 teaspoons cinnamon
- ½ cup walnut pieces
- ½ cup butter

In large bowl, combine sour cream, eggs, flour, sugar, vanilla, cinnamon, peaches, blueberries and lemon juice. Pour into pie shell and bake at 350 degrees for 50 minutes.

Topping:
In medium bowl, mix together brown sugar, flour, cinnamon, walnut pieces and butter. Remove pie from oven, and place topping on pie. Bake 10 minutes longer.

GOLDEN COCONUT PEACH PIE

- 4½ cups fresh peaches, sliced
- ½ cup sugar
- 3 tablespoons flour
- ¼ teaspoon nutmeg
- ⅛ teaspoon salt
- ¼ cup orange juice
- 1 (9-inch) unbaked pie shell
- 2 tablespoons butter
- 2 cups flaked coconut
- ½ cup evaporated milk
- 1 egg, beaten
- ¼ to ½ cup sugar
- ¼ teaspoon almond extract

Mix together peaches, sugar, flour, nutmeg, salt and orange juice; pour mixture into pie shell. Dot with butter; bake at 450 degrees for 15 minutes. Meanwhile, combine coconut, milk, egg, sugar and almond extract.. Pour over hot peach mixture. Reduce heat to 350 degrees and bake until coconut is toasted, about 30 minutes. Chill pie, unless eaten at once. So delicious!

SOUTHERN CHOCOLATE PECAN PIE

- 1 (4-ounce) package Baker's German Sweet Chocolate
- 3 tablespoon butter *or* margarine
- 1 teaspoon *instant* coffee
- ⅓ cup sugar
- 1 cup light corn syrup
- 3 eggs, slightly beaten
- 1 teaspoon vanilla
- 1 cup coarsely chopped pecans
- 1 (9-inch) unbaked pie shell
  Coffee-Flavored Topping
  (recipe follows)

Melt chocolate with butter in saucepan on very *low* heat, stirring constantly until smooth. Stir in coffee. Remove from heat. Combine sugar and syrup in saucepan. Bring to a boil over *high* heat, stirring until sugar is dissolved. Reduce heat and boil gently for 2 minutes, stirring occasionally. Remove from heat; add chocolate mixture. Pour slowly over eggs, stirring constantly. Stir in vanilla and pecans; pour into pie shell. Bake at 375 degrees for 45–50 minutes, or until filling is completely puffed across top. Cool. Garnish with Coffee-Flavored Topping and pecan halves, if desired.

Coffee-Flavored Topping:
- 1 teaspoon instant coffee
- 1 tablespoon sugar
- ¼ teaspoon vanilla
- ½ cup heavy cream

Combine ingredients in small bowl. Beat until soft peaks form.

HAWAIIAN CREAM PIE

- 2½ cups flaked coconut, toasted
- ⅓ cup butter *or* margarine, melted
- 1 (8-ounce) package cream cheese, softened
- 1 (14-ounce) can Eagle Brand sweetened condensed milk (not evaporated)
- 1 (6-ounce) can frozen pineapple-orange juice concentrate, thawed
- 1 (8-ounce) can crushed pineapple, well-drained
- 1 tablespoon grated orange rind
- 1 cup (½ pint) whipping cream, whipped
  Orange and pineapple slices

Combine coconut and margarine. Press firmly on bottom and up sides to rim of 9-inch pie plate. Chill. Meanwhile, in large mixer bowl beat cheese until fluffy. Gradually beat in sweetened condensed milk, then juice concentrate, until smooth. Stir in crushed pineapple and rind. Fold in whipped cream. Pour into prepared crust. Chill or freeze for 6 hours, or until firm. Garnish with orange and pineapple slices. Refrigerate.

OATMEAL PIE

- ¾ cup dark corn syrup
- ¾ cup sugar
- ¾ cup quick oatmeal
- ½ cup coconut
- ½ cup butter
- 2 eggs, well-beaten
- 1 (9-inch) unbaked pastry shell

Mix all ingredients together and put in an unbaked pie shell. Bake 45–50 minutes in a 350-degree oven.

LUSCIOUS LEMON MERINGUE PIE

- 1 (9-inch) baked pie shell
- 1½ cups sugar
- 6 tablespoons cornstarch
- 1¼ cups cold water
- ½ cup lemon juice
  Grated rind of 2 lemons
- 3 egg yolks, slightly beaten

Meringue:
- 3 egg whites
- ⅛ teaspoon cream of tartar
- ½ cup sugar

For filling, combine sugar and cornstarch in saucepan; stir in water, lemon juice and grated rind. Cook over low heat, stirring constantly, until thickened. Beat a small amount of hot mixture into egg yolks. Stir egg yolks into hot mixture and cook 2–3 minutes, stirring constantly. Remove from heat; cool. Pour into cooled pie shell.

For meringue, beat egg whites with cream of tartar until frothy; add sugar gradually, beating well. Lather meringue on top of pie and brown at 325 degrees for 10 minutes. Cool at room temperature.

PINEAPPLE CHEESE PIE

- ⅓ cup sugar
- 1 tablespoon cornstarch
- 1 (8¼-ounce) can crushed pineapple undrained
- 1 (9-inch) unbaked pastry shell
- 1 (8-ounce) package cream cheese
- ½ cup sugar
- ½ teaspoon salt
- ½ cup milk
- 2 eggs
- ½ teaspoon vanilla
- ¼ cup chopped pecans

In saucepan, combine sugar and cornstarch; gradually add pineapple. Cook, stirring constantly, until clear and thickened. Cool; spread onto bottom of pastry shell. Combine softened cream cheese, sugar and salt, mixing until well-blended. Blend in milk, eggs and vanilla. Pour over pineapple mixture; sprinkle with nuts. Bake at 400 degrees for 15 minutes. Garnish with pineapple slices; cut in half, add maraschino cherry halves, if desired.

LEMON MOUSSE PIE

- 2 envelopes unflavored gelatin
- ½ cup water
- 6 large eggs, separated (at room temperature)
- 1 cup sugar
- ¼ cup fresh lemon juice
- 1½ teaspoons grated lemon peel
- 1 cup whipping cream
- 1 (9-inch) baked pie shell

Sprinkle gelatin over water in small pan. Let stand 5 minutes. Heat over medium heat, stirring until gelatin is dissolved, 3–4 minutes.

Beat egg yolks and sugar in bowl until pale and thick. Beat in dissolved gelatin, lemon juice and peel. Beat egg whites in separate bowl until stiff. Fold into lemon mixture with rubber spatula. Pour cream into another bowl and beat until stiff. Fold cream into lemon mixture. Mound in pie shell. Refrigerate at least 3 hours or overnight.

SOUR CREAM PEAR PIE
Serves 8

- 2 cups peeled, diced ripe pears
- ½ cup sugar
- 1 egg, beaten
- 1 tablespoon flour
- 1 cup dairy sour cream
- 1 teaspoon vanilla
  Dash salt
- 1 unbaked 9-inch pastry shell

Crumb Topping:
- ½ cup sugar
- ⅓ cup flour
- ¼ cup butter, softened

Combine pears, sugar, egg, flour, sour cream, vanilla and salt; blend gently. Spoon into unbaked pie shell. Bake at 350 degrees for 25 minutes. Combine all of the topping ingredients until well-mixed. Sprinkle on top of pie; return to oven for 30 more minutes.

BLUEBERRY PIE

- ¼ cup Minute tapioca
- 1 (9-inch) double-crust unbaked pie shell
- 3 (12-ounce) packages frozen blueberries, defrosted, drained (reserve juice)
- ¼ cup cornstarch
- 1½ cups sugar, plus 1 tablespoon, divided
- 1 tablespoon butter
- 1 tablespoon cinnamon
- 2 tablespoons grated orange peel
- 1 tablespoon milk

In medium saucepan, mix tapioca with juice from defrosted blueberries. Let sit 5 minutes. In a small bowl, stir together cornstarch and 1½ cups sugar. Mix until cornstarch is no longer lumpy. Add to tapioca mixture. Over medium heat, heat until thickened, stirring constantly. Stir in blueberries, butter, cinnamon and orange peel. Heat about 10 minutes Pour into an unbaked 9-inch pie shell. Top with top crust; crimp edges, vent top with 5 cuts. Brush top with milk; sprinkle on 1 tablespoon sugar. Bake at 425 degrees for 45 minutes.

This recipe did win the top prize for pies at the Michigan State Fair, 1990.

RAISIN CUSTARD PIE

9 inch baked pie shell
1 cup raisins
1 cup water
2/3 cup sugar
1-1/2 heaping tablespoons flour
Pinch of salt
3 egg yolks
3 egg whites
2-3/4 cups milk
1 tablespoon butter
1 teaspoon vanilla
6 tablespoons sugar

Boil raisins in water for 5-10 minutes; drain well. Mix sugar, flour, egg yolks, salt, and milk and add to raisins; cook until thickened. Add butter and vanilla. Pour into pie shell. Whip egg whites until stiff an gradually add the 6 tablespoons sugar. Put onto filling and brown in 350 degree oven.

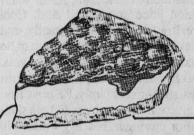

TROPICAL LEMON-COCONUT PIE
Serves 8

1 cup sugar
7 tablespoons butter *or* margarine
3 eggs, beaten
2 lemons, juice and grated rind
1 (9-inch) pie shell, baked
1¼ tablespoons cornstarch
3 tablespoons sugar
1 cup milk
¼ teaspoon salt
1¼ teaspoons lemon extract
⅓ cup flaked coconut

In a saucepan cream sugar and butter; stir in eggs, lemon juice and ½ of the lemon rind; cook gently until thickened. Pour into baked pie shell; cool. In a small saucepan combine next 5 ingredients; cook until thickened; stir in coconut. Pour over chilled lemon mixture in pie shell; garnish with remaining lemon rind.

POLAR BEAR PIE
Serves 8–10

1 apple, peeled, cored and finely chopped
1 egg
¼ cup all-purpose flour
½ cup sugar
1½ teaspoons baking powder
½ cup ground pecans
1 quart vanilla ice cream
1 cup toffee pieces
Chocolate Sauce (recipe follows)

Mix apple, egg, flour, sugar, baking powder and pecans well by hand. Pour into an 8-inch round, well-greased cake pan. Bake at 350 degrees for 20–25 minutes. Cool. Fill with vanilla ice cream. Top with toffee pieces. Drizzle with Chocolate Sauce or chocolate syrup.

Chocolate Sauce:

2 squares semisweet chocolate, melted
4 tablespoons sweetened *condensed* milk
1 tablespoon creme de cacao

Combine ingredients in top of double boiler. Cook until thickened.

MINT CHOCOLATE PIE

1 (9-inch) chocolate crumb crust
1 quart mint chocolate chip ice cream
1 jar hot fudge topping
1 (4-ounce) container whipped topping

Fill crumb crust with 1½ cups softened ice cream. Freeze to harden. Spread ¾ cup hot fudge topping on hardened ice cream. Freeze. Repeat with second layer using 1½ cups ice cream. Spread with whipped topping and serve frozen. Garnish with chocolate curls.

BUTTERMILK COCONUT PIE

1½ cups sugar
2 tablespoons flour
1 stick margarine, melted
3 eggs, beaten
½ cup buttermilk
1 teaspoon vanilla
1 (7-ounce) can flaked coconut
1 (9-inch) deep-dish pie crust, unbaked

Preheat oven to 350 degrees. Mix flour and sugar. Add eggs, margarine, buttermilk, vanilla and ⅔ of coconut. Mix well; pour into 9-inch pie crust. Sprinkle remaining coconut over top. Bake 1 hour. Place cookie sheet under pie to catch drips.

PEANUT BUTTER CREAM CHEESE PIE

1 (8-ounce) package cream cheese, softened
1 cup peanut butter
½ cup bitter cocoa
½ cup softened butter
2 teaspoons vanilla
2 cups Cool Whip
1 cup sugar
1 (9-inch) baked pie shell *or* graham cracker pie shell
Whipped topping, cocoa, chocolate syrup

Beat together cream cheese, peanut butter, sugar, cocoa, butter and vanilla. Add Cool Whip. Mix well. Pour into baked pie shell or graham cracker pie shell. Top with fluted decoration of whipped topping mixed with cocoa and drizzle chocolate syrup over pie in a string pattern.

ORANGE WHIMSY
Serves 6–8

An easy way to make orange sherbet pie!

Crust:
- 1¾ cups graham cracker crumbs
- ¼ cup melted butter
- 2 tablespoons sugar

Filling:
- 2 (8-ounce) packages softened cream cheese
- 1 (7-ounce) jar marshmallow creme
- 1 cup orange sherbet
- 2 cups whipped topping

Combine crust ingredients and pat into 1 (9-inch) pie plate. Beat cream cheese on high speed of electric mixer until smooth and fluffy. Stir in marshmallow creme, sherbet and topping. Pour into crust and freeze until firm. Top with additional topping.

BUTTERMILK LEMON PIE

- 1 (9-inch) unbaked pie shell
- 2 cups granulated sugar
- 3 tablespoons all-purpose flour
- ¼ teaspoon nutmeg
- ¼ cup melted butter *or* margarine
- 3 eggs, lightly beaten
- 1 cup buttermilk
  Juice of 1 lemon (¼ cup)
- 1 teaspoon vanilla

Combine sugar, flour and nutmeg; add butter; beat until creamy. Stir in eggs, buttermilk, lemon juice and vanilla. Bake in a 400-degree oven for 10 minutes. Reduce to 325 degrees and bake 30 minutes longer. Different and delicious!

BROWN SUGAR PIE

- Pastry for 2-crust pie
- ½ cup white sugar
- ¼ cup brown sugar
- 3 tablespoons flour
- ¼ to ½ teaspoon cinnamon
- ⅛ teaspoon salt
- 5 cups fresh peaches, peeled and sliced
- 1 tablespoon lemon juice
- ¼ teaspoon almond extract
- 2 tablespoons butter *or* margarine

Combine sugar, flour, cinnamon and salt. Sprinkle peaches with lemon juice and add almond extract. Add sugar/flour mixture to peaches; mix gently. Turn into pastry-lined pie pan. Dot with butter. Add top crust and cut vents in pastry. Bake at 425 degrees for about 35–45 minutes, or until juice bubbles in vents and crust is golden brown.

FRESH PINEAPPLE PIE
Serves 6–8

- 1 medium-size pineapple
- 2 eggs
- 1½ cups sugar
- 2 tablespoons flour
- 1 tablespoon *each* grated lemon peel and lemon juice
  Pastry for 2-crust (9-inch) pie

Trim peel from pineapple; core. Cut fruit in bite-size chunks (about 3 cups). Beat eggs with sugar, flour, grated lemon peel and lemon juice; blend with pineapple. Line a 9-inch pie pan with pastry; fill with pineapple mixture. Cover with pastry to make top crust and seal rim; slash top. Bake in a 425-degree oven for about 45 minutes, or until crust is brown. Cool before serving.

QUICK AND EASY COCONUT CUSTARD PIE

- 1½ cups coconut
- 3 eggs
- 1½ cups sugar
- 1 large can evaporated milk
- 1 deep-dish frozen pie shell, unbaked

Mix all ingredients together. Pour into unbaked pie shell. Bake at 350 degrees for 35 minutes.

LIKE ICE CREAM PIE

- 1 (3-ounce) package cream cheese
- 2 tablespoons sugar
- ½ cup milk
- 1 cup *or* 1 (6-ounce) package Bits of Brickle
- 1 (8-ounce) container whipped topping
- 1 (9-inch) graham cracker crust

Smoothly blend first 3 ingredients. Add the Bits of Brickle; fold in topping. Pile into crust. *Refrigerate several hours before serving.*
A fast and easy winner!

IMPOSSIBLE PIE

- 4 eggs
- 1¼ cups sugar
- 2 cups milk
- 1 teaspoon vanilla
- 1 cup coconut
- ½ stick butter *or* margarine, melted
- ½ cup self-rising flour

Mix all ingredients and blend well. Pour into a 9½-inch ungreased pie plate. Bake at 350 degrees for 30 minutes.
You may omit coconut and have an egg custard pie, if you prefer.

QUICKIE CHOCOLATE COOL PIE

2 cups milk
1½ cups vanilla ice cream
2 (3-ounce) packages instant chocolate pudding
1 baked 9-inch pie crust
Cool Whip, if desired

Blend milk and ice cream in large bowl. Add pudding mix and beat on low speed for 1 minute. Pour into the cooled crust and chill for 1 hour. Serve topped with Cool Whip, if desired.

LAYERED PECAN CREAM PIE

Serves 8

1 (10-inch) unbaked pastry shell
1 (8-ounce) package cream cheese, softened
⅓ cup sugar
1 egg
1 teaspoon lemon flavoring
¼ teaspoon salt
1¼ cups chopped pecans
3 eggs
1 cup dark corn syrup
¼ cup sugar
1 teaspoon vanilla

Combine cream cheese, sugar, 1 egg, lemon flavoring and salt; blend until smooth and creamy. Spread in pastry shell; sprinkle with pecans. Combine remaining ingredients; beat until well-blended. Pour over cream cheese mixture and pecans. Preheat oven to 375 degrees. Bake for 35 minutes, or until center is firm to touch.

GREEN LIMEADE PIE

1 envelope unflavored gelatin
¼ cup sugar
½ cup cold water
4 egg yolks, beaten
1 (6-ounce) can frozen limeade concentrate
4 egg whites
¼ cup sugar
½ cup whipping cream, whipped
1 (9-inch) baked pastry shell, cooled

In saucepan combine gelatin, ¼ cup sugar, water and egg yolks. Cook and stir over hot, not boiling, water until mixture is slightly thick. Remove from heat. Stir in concentrate. Chill, stirring occasionally, until mixture mounds slightly when spooned. Beat egg whites until soft peaks form. Gradually add remaining ¼ cup sugar, beating to stiff peaks. Fold in gelatin mixture, then whipped cream. Add few drops green food coloring, if desired. Pile into pastry shell. Chill until firm.

CHERRY TOP-OVER BANANA PIE

Makes 1 (9-inch) pie

1 (9-inch) baked pie shell
1 (16-ounce) can pitted red tart cherries
1 cup sugar
3 tablespoons cornstarch
1 tablespoon butter *or* margarine
½ teaspoon cinnamon
¼ teaspoon cloves
1 teaspoon almond extract
2 medium-size bananas

In saucepan, mix cherries with liquid, sugar and cornstarch. Cook; stir constantly until mixture thickens and boils. Boil 1 minute; stir in butter; cool. Stir in cinnamon, cloves and almond extract. Slice bananas in layers into baked pie shell; pour filling over banana slices; chill until set.

BRANDY ALEXANDER PIE

2 cups cold milk
2 tablespoons brandy
2 tablespoons creme de cacao liqueur
1 envelope whipped topping mix
1 (16-ounce) package vanilla *instant* pudding
1 (9-inch) baked pie shell
Chocolate curls for garnish, if desired

Combine milk, brandy, creme de cacao whipped topping mix and pudding in a deep, narrow-bottom bowl with an electric mixer. Beat at low speed until blended. Gradually increase speed and beat until mixture forms soft peaks, about 3–6 minutes. Spoon into baked shell. Chill 3 hours.

LEMON CHEESE PIE

4 eggs
¼ teaspoon salt
½ cup heavy cream
Grated rind of 1 lemon
4 tablespoons fresh lemon juice
1 teaspoon vanilla
¼ cup sugar
1 (8-ounce) package cream cheese
Pinch of nutmeg
1 (9-inch) unbaked pie shell

Topping:
4 tablespoons chopped walnuts
4 tablespoons sugar

Blend all ingredients, except topping, in blender. Pour into unbaked pie shell. Bake at 425 degrees for 10 minutes, or until just set. Sprinkle topping mixture over pie. Bake another 10–12 minutes, or until done. Serve warm or cold.

OUT OF THIS WORLD PIE
Makes 2 pies

2 (9-inch) baked pie shells
1 can cherry pie filling
¾ cup sugar
1 large can crushed pineapple with juice
1 tablespoon cornstarch
1 teaspoon red food coloring
1 (3-ounce) package raspberry gelatin
6 medium-firm bananas, sliced
1 cup chopped nuts
Whipped topping

In saucepan, combine pineapple and juice, cornstarch, cherry pie filling, sugar and food coloring. Cook on low heat until thickened. Remove from heat. Add dry gelatin; cool. Then stir in bananas and nuts. Pour into 2 crusts. Top with whipped topping. Refrigerate.

CHOCOLATE BOURBON PECAN PIE

1 (9- or 10-inch) unbaked pie shell
¾ cup pecans
4 eggs
1 cup sugar
1 cup corn syrup
¼ cup bourbon
1 tablespoon vanilla extract
3 (1-ounce) squares chocolate, melted
2 tablespoons melted butter

Preheat oven to 350 degrees. Bake pie shell until golden, about 10 minutes. Add pecans to pie shell. Combine remaining ingredients; pour into pie shell. Bake 45 minutes to 1 hour until done.

PEANUT BUTTER PIE
Serves 8

3 eggs
1 cup sugar
1 cup light or dark corn syrup
⅓ cup peanut butter
½ teaspoon vanilla
1 unbaked pie shell

Preheat oven to 400 degrees. Mix the first 5 ingredients until well-blended, approximately 5 minutes. Pour into the pie shell and bake at 400 degrees for 15 minutes. Reduce heat to 325 degrees; bake until filling seems set, for about 30 or 35 minutes more.

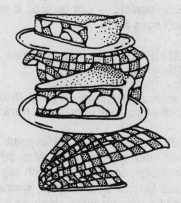

BLACKBERRY PIE

Pastry for 2-crust pie
4 cups fresh or frozen blackberries
3 tablespoons flour
1 cup sugar
1 tablespoon lemon juice
1 tablespoon butter

Place 1 crust in pie pan; chill. Combine blackberries, flour, sugar and lemon juice; spoon into pie shell. Dot with butter. Cover with second pastry crust. Cut steam vents. Bake at 450 degrees for 15 minutes. Reduce oven temperature to 350 degrees. Bake 30–40 longer, or until crust is brown.

SOUR CREAM RAISIN PIE

2 eggs, beaten
1½ cups commercial sour cream
1 cup sugar
2 tablespoons all-purpose flour
1 teaspoon vanilla extract
½ cup golden raisins
½ cup chopped Brazil nuts
1 (9-inch) unbaked pastry shell

Combine eggs, sour cream, sugar, flour and vanilla; beat at medium speed of electric mixer until blended. Stir in raisins and Brazil nuts. Pour mixture into pastry shell. Bake at 400 degrees for 10 minutes; reduce heat to 350 degrees, and bake an additional 30 minutes, or until set.

MEAT AND POTATO PIE

1 pound hamburger
1/3 cup chopped onion
1/2 cup chopped green pepper
1 egg
1/4 cup dry bread crumbs
Dash salt and black pepper
2 cups mashed potatoes
2 tablespoons milk
1 tablespoon parsley
1 tablespoon butter
1/3 cup grated cheese

Combine meat, green pepper, onion, egg, bread crumbs and seasonings. Mix lightly. Press meat mixture onto bottom and sides of a 9-inch pie plate. Bake at 350 degrees for 20 minutes. Drain excess fat from meat shell. Mash hot potatoes with milk and butter. Stir in cheese and parsley. Fill hot meat shell with potato mixture. Continue baking 15 minutes more.

DUTCH APPLE PIE
Serves 8

1 "Graham Cracker Ready Crust"
1 large egg yolk, slightly beaten
5-1/2 cups fresh sliced, cored, peeled cooking apples
1 tablespoon lemon juice (omit if apples are tart)
1/2 cup sugar
1/4 cup light brown sugar, firmly packed
3 tablespoons all-purpose flour
1/4 teaspoon salt
1/2 teaspoon cinnamon
1/4 teaspoon ground nutmeg
3/4 cup all-purpose flour
1/4 cup granulated sugar
1/4 cup brown sugar, packed
1/3 cup butter or margarine, room temperature

Preheat oven to 375 degrees. Brush bottom and sides of crust evenly with egg yolk. Bake on baking sheet about 5 minutes until lightly brown. Remove from oven. Combine sliced apples, lemon juice. 1/2 cup sugar, 1/4 cup brown sugar, 3 tablespoons flour, salt, cinnamon, and nutmeg. Mix well and spoon into crust. Mix remaining flour, sugars, and butter with fork until crumbly. Sprinkle mixture evenly over apples. Bake on baking sheet until topping is golden and filling is bubbling, about 50 minutes. Cool on wire rack. Serve at room temperature.

CARAMEL-PECAN APPLE PIE

Pastry for double-crust, 9-inch pie
6 cups apples, peeled, thinly sliced
3/4 cup sugar
2 tablespoons flour
1/4 teaspoon salt
2 tablespoons margarine
1/3 cup commercial caramel ice cream topping
2 teaspoons chopped pecans

Roll half of pastry onto a lightly-floured surface to 1/8 inch thickness. Fit into a 9-inch pie plate. Combine apples, sugar, flour, and salt; toss gently to coat. Spread in pie shell. Dot with margarine.

Roll out remaining pastry and place over filling. Cut several slits in top crust. Bake pie at 425 degrees for 35-40 minutes. Remove from oven; immediately drizzle caramel topping over pie. Sprinkle with pecans.

BERNICE PASSINO'S BLACKBERRY PIE

Do not confuse with blueberry or huckleberry. These look a little like raspberries and have seeds and a whitish core. Frozen without sugar — which is not needed if you freeze them yourself — can be used if you don't have fresh.

3 GENEROUS cups blackberries
1 Generous cups sugar
3 level tablespoons flour
1 recipe of nice, flaky pie crust. (It'll be flaky if you use enough shortening)

Sprinkle about a tablespoon of flour over bottom crust. Mix other two tablespoons of flour with sugar. Place berries in the crust; sprinkle with flour-sugar mixture; shake a bit so some of mixture works down through the berries. Dot with pieces of margarine. Add top crust; sprinkle sugar over crust before baking. Bake at 350 degrees for one hour or until nicely browned.

FRESH BLUEBERRY GLACE PIE

1 (9-inch) baked pie shell, cooled
4 cups fresh blueberries, divided
1 cup sugar
3 tablespoons cornstarch
1/4 cup salt
1/4 cup water
1/4 teaspoon cinnamon
1 tablespoon butter

Line cooled pie shell with 2 cups well drained blueberries. Cook re-maining 2 cups berries with sugar, cornstarch, salt, and water over medium heat; add cinnamon and butter and cool slightly. Pour over berries in pie shell. Chill until served. Store in refrigerator any leftover pie.

Most blueberry pie recipes you see are all cooked blueberry pies. This pie is great, so delicious, and one of my favorites. You are eating fresh blueberries in this pie, instead of other pies where all the berries are cooked.

BLUEBERRY CREAM CHEESE PIE

1 (9-inch) baked pie shell
1 (3-ounce) package cream cheese, softened
1/2 cup confectioners' sugar
3/4 teaspoon vanilla
1/2 pint whipping cream
2 cups blueberry pie filling

Mix cheese, sugar, and vanilla. Whip cream; add to cheese mixture. Pour into baked pie shell. Cover top of pie with blueberry pie filling. Chill over night before serving.

CRANBERRY PIE

1 (3 ounce) package raspberry gelatin
1 (3 ounce) package cream cheese
2 tablespoons milk
1 (16 ounce) can whole cranberry sauce
1 (9-inch) pie shell, baked

Prepare gelatin using 1 cup boiling water, stirring until dissolved. Add 1/2 cold water. Place in refrigerator until it begins to thicken, about 1 to 1-1/2 hours. Soften cream cheese with milk and spread into baked pie shell. After gelatin has begun to thicken, whip until fluffy. Stir whole cranberry sauce to break apart; fold into gelatin mixture. Pour into cream cheese lined pie shell and refrigerate until set. Serve with whipped cream.

CHERRY JUBILEE PIE

Serves 6 to 8

1 pound can cherry pie filling
9-inch unbaked pie shell
8-ounce package cream cheese, cubed
2 eggs
1/2 cup sugar
1 teaspoon vanilla extract
1/4 teaspoon almond extract
1 cup dairy sour cream
Nutmeg, optional

Pour cherry pie filling into pie shell; bake at 375 degrees for 15 minutes. Process cream cheese, eggs, sugar and extracts for 30 seconds or until smooth. Pour over hot cherry pie and spread evenly. Bake at 350 degrees for 30 minutes. Cool on rack. Spread sour cream over top. Sprinkle lightly with nutmeg, if desired.

SPEEDY LEMON PIE

Have ready:
1 baked 9 inch pie shell
1 quart vanilla ice cream, softened
1 - 6 ounce can frozen lemonade concentrate, thawed
2 very thinly sliced lemons
Method:
In a blender combine the ice cream and lemonade until smooth. Pour into baked pie shell. Freeze until firm, (about 1-1/2 hours).

Let stand 10 minutes before serving; then garnish with lemon slices.

3-LAYER LEMON MERINGUE PIE

Serves 6 to 8

1-1/3 cups sugar
1/2 cup flour
1/8 teaspoon salt

2 cups water
1/3 cup lemon juice
3 eggs, separated
3 drops yellow food coloring
1 teaspoon grated lemon rind
1 tablespoon butter
6 tablespoons sugar
1/4 teaspoon cream of tartar
Baked 9-inch pie shell

Combine 1-1/3 cups sugar, flour and salt in saucepan; gradually add water and lemon juice. Cook over medium heat until thick, stirring constantly. Stir a small amount of hot mixture into beaten egg yolks and stir back into hot mixture. Cook, stirring for 2 minutes. Remove from heat, add food coloring, lemon rind and butter. Beat egg whites and cream of tartar until frothy. Gradually add sugar, beating until stiff, glossy peaks form. Reserve 1 cup filling and pour remainder into pie shell. Fold 1/4 cup meringue into reserved filling and spread evenly over filling in pie. Top with meringue, sealing edges. Bake at 400 degrees for 8 - 10 minutes until golden. Cool on rack.

PEACH SILK PIE

3/4 cup all-purpose flour
1/4 teaspoon salt
1 teaspoon baking powder
1 egg
1/2 cup milk
3 tablespoons butter, melted
6-ounce box French vanilla pudding
2 cups canned or frozen peaches, drained
8-ounce package cream cheese
1/2 cup sugar
4 tablespoons peach juice
1 teaspoon mace
1 tablespoon sugar

Combine first 7 ingredients; blend well. Pour into large deep pie plate; arrange peaches on crust. Beat cream cheese, sugar and remaining peach juice until smooth. Pour over peaches. combine sugar and mace; sprinkle over top. Bake at 375 degrees for 45 to 50 minutes.

FRESH FRENCH PEAR PIE

6 cups thinly sliced fresh pears
2 tablespoons fresh lemon juice
1/3 cup corn syrup
1/3 cup sugar
1/2 teaspoon ginger
1 (9 inch) unbaked pie shell
1/3 cup shortening
1/4 cup brown sugar
1 cup sifted all-purpose flour

Combine pears, lemon juice, syrup and ginger; pour into pie shell. Mix together shortening, sugar, and flour. Spread over pear mixture. Bake at 350 degrees for 45 minutes, or until pears are tender.

BLUE RIBBON SOUR CREAM RAISIN PIE

1 whole egg, plus 3 egg yolks
1 cup sugar
1/4 teaspoon salt
3/4 teaspoon cinnamon
1/4 teaspoon nutmeg
1/4 teaspoon cloves
1 cup sour cream
1 cup raisins
1 unbaked 9-inch pie shell

Meringue:
3 egg whites
6 tablespoons sugar
1/2 teaspoon vanilla

Beat egg and yolks until fluffy; add sugar, salt, and spices. Continue beating, while adding sour cream. Beat well. Stir in raisins; pour into pie shell. Bake at 450 degrees for 10 minutes. Reduce heat to 350 degrees; bake 30 minutes more. Prepare meringue and spread over hot pie, being sure to seal edges. Bake at 450 degrees for 10-12 minutes until golden.

ICE CREAM SUNDAE PIE

1 Ready Crust Chocolate flavored pie crust
1 quart ice cream
1 (12-ounce) jar chocolate fudge topping
Whipped cream
Maraschino cherries
Walnuts

Allow ice cream to soften or stir with spoon until pliable. Spoon into pie crust. Cover and freeze until firm, about 3 hours. Serve pie wedges with fudge topping, whipped cream, and cherries. Add nuts, if desired.

CUSTARD PIE

4 slightly beaten eggs
1/2 cup sugar
1/4 teaspoon salt
1/2 teaspoon vanilla
2-1/2 cups scalded milk
9" unbaked pastry shell
Nutmeg or 1/2 cup flaked coconut

Blend eggs, sugar, salt and vanilla. Gradually stir in milk. Pour into pastry shell. Sprinkle lightly with nutmeg or coconut. Bake in moderate oven at 350 degrees for 35 to 40 minutes, or until knife inserted halfway between center and edge comes out clean. Cool on rack, then chill.

CARROT CUSTARD PIE

1/2 cup sugar
2/3 cup milk
1 teaspoon vanilla
1 tablespoon cornstarch
1-1/2 cups mashed, cooked carrots
1 unbaked 9 inch pie shell
2 eggs, beaten
1 tablespoon lemon juice
1/4 teaspoon cinnamon

Combine sugar and cornstarch. Add eggs, milk, carrots, lemon juice, and vanilla. Mix well; pour into pie shell. Sprinkle with cinnamon. Bake at 375 degrees for 45 minutes or until custard is set. Serve warm or cooled. "Really delicious!"

CARAMEL CUSTARD PIE

3 cups milk, scalded
1/3 cup caramelized syrup (below)
4 eggs, well beaten
1/3 cup sugar
1/2 teaspoon salt
1 teaspoon vanilla
Baked 10-inch pie shell

Blend together milk and caramelized syrup. Combine beaten eggs, sugar, salt, and vanilla. Slowly stir egg mixture into milk. Bake in a buttered 10-inch pie plate in a 350 degree oven for 40 minutes, or until a knife inserted in center comes out clean. Cool. Loosen edges of custard carefully with spatula. Shake gently to loosen bottom. Slide custard from pie plate into cooled pie shell.

Caramelized Syrup:
2 cups sugar
1 cup boiling water

Pour sugar into heavy skillet that heats uniformly. Melt over low heat, stirring constantly with wooden spoon to prevent scorching; the lumps will melt away.

When sugar becomes a clear brown syrup, remove from heat. Stir in boiling water slowly so that it does not splatter. Return to low heat, and stir until syrup is smooth again. Cool. (What you don't use can be put into a clean pint jar and stored in refrigerator for several weeks.)

OLD-FASHIONED VANILLA CUSTARD PIE
Serves 6

1 (9 inch) pie shell, unbaked
3 eggs
4 tablespoons granulated sugar
1/8 teaspoon salt
3 cups scalding hot milk
1-1/4 teaspoons vanilla extract
1/4 teaspoon freshly grated nutmeg

Beat eggs until thoroughly mixed and bubbly. Add sugar and salt; mix well. Add 3 tablespoons of the scalding hot milk to egg mixture; mix well. Add egg mixture to the milk; stir in vanilla. Beat gently until all is evenly mixed; pour into unbaked shell. Bake 400 degrees for 12 minutes; reduce heat to 350 degrees and bake 25 minutes or until tested done in middle. Remove from oven; cool; refrigerate at least 2 hours before cutting.

PEANUT BUTTER CREAM CHEESE PIE

Pecan crust:
1-1/2 cups pecans, toasted and finely chopped
1/2 cup sugar
1/4 cup butter
1/4 teaspoon cinnamon

To make crust: Mix together all crust ingredients and press into a 9 inch metal pie pan. Freeze.

Topping:
1/2 cup fudge ice cream topping
Filling:
1 cup whipping cream
1-1/4 cups powdered sugar (divided)
1 tablespoon vanilla
1 (8 ounce) package cream cheese at room temperature
1 cup creamy peanut butter
2 tablespoons butter

To make filling: Beat cream with 1/4 cup powdered sugar and vanilla, until stiff peaks form; set aside. In another bowl, beat remaining 1 cup powdered sugar, cream cheese, peanut butter, and butter until fluffy. Fold in half the whipped cream mixture. Spoon cream cheese mixture into reserved crust. Cover and chill 2 hours. Spread fudge topping on pie, leaving a 1 inch border. Rebeat reserved whipped cream mixture and spoon around border. Chill 1 hour.

PEANUT BUTTER PIE

1 cup "chunky" peanut butter
1 (8 ounce) package cream cheese at room temperature
3/4 cup sugar
2 tablespoons melted butter
1 cup whipping cream, whipped
1 tablespoon vanilla
1 prepared graham cracker crust
1/3 cup melted hot fudge topping

Cream together peanut butter, cream cheese, and sugar. Add butter and vanilla; blend. Fold in whipped cream until well blended. Pour into a graham cracker crust; chill 4-5 hours or until set. Drizzle top with hot fudge topping. Chill anywhere from 30 minutes longer to overnight.

This is very rich! It will serve several, because you only need a tiny slice.

DEER MEAT PIE

1 pound ground venison (2 cups)
1-1/2 teaspoons salt of less
1/2 teaspoon pepper or less
1 cup drained canned tomatos
1/2 cup grated or shredded American cheese
1 tablespoon chopped parsley (optional)
1 tablespoon chopped onion or more
1/2 teaspoon dried basil (optional)

Combine ground venison, salt and pepper; spread in 9-inch pie pan, bringing meat up the sides. Cover with drained tomatos. Sprinkle with cheese, parsley, onion and basil. Bake at 375 degrees for 20 to 25 minutes. Pour off fat; cut in wedges and serve hot. Ground beef can be substituted for the venison.

MERRY MINCE PIE

1 cup sugar
1/2 teaspoon salt
1/2 teaspoon cinnamon
1/4 teaspoon cloves
1/4 teaspoon ginger
1-1/2 cups finely chopped pared apples
1 cup raisins
1/2 cup jellied cranberry sauce
1/3 cup chopped walnuts
1 teaspoon grated orange peel
1/2 teaspoon grated lemon peel
1/4 cup lemon juice
4 tablespoons butter
Pastry for 2-crust pie

Combine sugar, salt, and spices. Add next seven ingredients; mix well. Pour into pastry-lined 9 inch pie plate. Dot with butter. Apply top crust; cut slits, and crimp edges. Bake in 400 degree oven for 35 minutes. Serve warm.

APPLESAUCE PECAN PIE

1 unbaked pie shell
2 tablespoons butter
1 cup light brown sugar
1/4 teaspoon cinnamon
3/4 cup dark corn syrup
1/2 cup applesauce
1 cup chopped pecans
3 eggs, beaten

Combine butter, sugar, and cinnamon. Add syrup, applesauce, pecans, and eggs. Blend well. Pour into pie shell. Bake in a 400 degree oven for 15 minutes. Reduce heat to 325 degrees and bake for 25-30 additional minutes. Delicious!

BLACK WALNUT PIE

1 cup black walnut halves
2 eggs, slightly beaten
1 cup dark corn syrup
1 teaspoon vanilla
1 tablespoon melted butter
1 cup white sugar
1/8 teaspoon salt
1 unbaked 9-inch pie shell

Mix ingredients, adding black walnuts last. Pour into unbaked pie shell and bake in conventional oven at 400 degrees for 15 minutes. Reduce temperature to 300 degrees and bake about 30 minutes more or until a toothpick inserted in the center comes out clean. Serve warm or cold. Enjoy!

CHOCOLATE CHIP WALNUT PIE

2 eggs
1/2 cup flour
1/2 cup sugar
1/2 cup packed brown sugar
1 cup butter, melted, cooled to room temperature
1 (6 ounce) package chocolate chips
1 cup chopped walnuts
1 (9 inch) unbaked pie shell

Beat eggs in large bowl until foamy. Beat in flour, granulated and brown sugars until well blended. Blend in melted butter. Fold in chocolate chips and walnuts. Spoon into unbaked pie shell. Bake at 325 degrees for 1 hour or until knife inserted in center comes out clean.

Do not overbake. Serve warm.

DATE-NUT PIE

1-9 inch pie shell
1 cup boiling water
2-8 ounce packages chopped dates
2 eggs
1-1/2 cups dairy sour cream
1 cup brown sugar - packed
1 cup coarsely chopped walnuts
1 tablespoon grated orange peel
2 tablespoons orange juice
1/4 teaspoon salt
3/4 teaspoon nutmeg

Prepare pie shell. Refrigerate until ready to fill. Pour water over dates in a medium bowl; let stand 10 minutes and drain. In a large bowl with rotary beater, beat eggs until fluffy. Blend in remaining ingredients, except dates. The final step, stir in dates.

Pour into unbaked pie shell. Bake at 375 degrees for 45-50 minutes or until filling is set in center when pie is gently shaken.

CHILLED CANTALOPE CREAM PIE
Serves 8

1 9-inch pie shell, baked
2 tablespoons cornstarch
2 tablespoons cold water
1/2 fresh lemon rind, grated
2 tablespoons fresh lemon juice
1/2 cup sugar
2 eggs, separated
1 cup boiling water
1-1/2 teaspoons unflavored gelatin
3 cups cantaloupe, diced
Vanilla ice cream

In a saucepan mix cornstarch with cold water. Stir in lemon rind, lemon juice, sugar, egg yolks, and gelatin; beat together; add boiling water. Cook until thickened; refrigerate until cool. Fold in diced cantaloupe and stiffly beaten egg whites; turn mixture into baked pie shell. Chill pie several hours until set. Cut into wedges, top with vanilla ice cream, and serve.

CREAMY COCONUT PIE

1 (3-ounce) package cream cheese, softened
2 tablespoons sugar
1/2 cup milk
1-1/3 cups Angel Flake coconut
1 (8-ounce) container frozen whipped topping, thawed
1/2 teaspoon almond extract, optional
1 (8-inch) graham cracker crust, prepared

Combine cream cheese, sugar, milk, and coconut in electric blender for 30 seconds. Fold into topping and add extract. Spoon into crust. Freeze until firm, about 4 hours. Sprinkle with additional coconut. Let stand at room temperature, 5 minutes before cutting. Store any leftover pie in freezer.

PINEAPPLE CREAM PIE

3/4 cup sugar
1/4 cup flour
1/4 teaspoon salt
2 cups milk
3 egg yolks
2 tablespoons butter or margarine
1 cup crushed pineapple
1 teaspoon vanilla

Preheat oven to 325 degrees. Combine sugar, flour, and salt. Add milk gradually, then slightly beaten egg yolks. Add butter. Cook over low heat until thickened. Add pineapple and vanilla. Pour into a 9-inch baked pie crust. Top with meringue; bake 20-25 minutes at 325 degrees.

RASPBERRY BAVARIAN PIE

1 (10-ounce) package frozen raspberries
1 (3-ounce) package lemon gelatin
1 (3-ounce) package strawberry gelatin
1 (8-ounce) container whipped topping
1 chocolate-flavored pie crust, prepared

Combine raspberries with 1 cup water. Heat to boiling, crushing berries with spoon or wooden pestle to extract juice. Strain and measure juice. Add enough additional hot water to make 3 cups liquid. Pour over gelatin and stir until gelatin dissolves. Chill until thickened. If gelatin mixture becomes too hard, microwave for 10 seconds on full power or until softened. Beat with rotary beater until foamy. Gently fold whipped topping into gelatin mixture. Turn into pie crust. Chill until firm, at least 4 hours.

RHUBARB ORANGE CREAM PIE

1 (9-inch) unbaked pastry shell
3 eggs, separated
1-1/4 cups sugar, divided
1/4 cup butter, softened
3 tablespoons frozen orange juice concentrate, thawed, undiluted
1/4 cup flour
1/4 teaspoon salt
2-1/2 cups rhubarb, cut into 1/2-inch pieces
1/3 cup chopped pecans

Prepare pastry shell; set aside. Beat egg whites until stiff, but not dry. Add 1/4 cup sugar gradually, beating until whites are stiff and glossy; set aside. Beat butter, orange juice concentrate, and egg yolks until well blended. Add remaining cup sugar, flour, and salt. Stir in rhubarb, then gently fold in egg white meringue. Pour into prepared shell. Sprinkle top with nuts. Place pie on bottom rack of oven; bake at 375 degrees for 15 minutes. Reduce temperature to 325 degrees, bake 45 minutes longer.

This is an innovative, delicious rhubarb pie that makes its own meringue topping as it bakes.

PECAN-CHEESE PIE
Serves 8-10

1 unbaked (10-inch) pie shell
4 eggs
1 (8-ounce) package cream cheese, room temperature
1/3 cup sugar
2 teaspoons vanilla
1-1/4 cups coarsely chopped pecans
1 cup light corn syrup
1/4 cup sugar
1/4 teaspoon salt

In large bowl, at medium speed, beat together until smooth the cream cheese, 1 egg, 1 teaspoon vanilla, and 1/3 cup sugar. Spread over bottom of pie shell and top with pecans. In a clean large bowl, at medium speed, beat remaining eggs until frothy. Add corn syrup, salt, 1/4 cup sugar, and 1 teaspoon vanilla; beat until well blended. Gently pour mixture over pecans. Bake in a pre-heated 375 degree oven until done, 40 minutes.

This will become one of your favorite pies!!

MOM'S CHEESE PIE

Crust:
1 cup sifted flour
1/2 teaspoon baking powder
2 tablespoons sugar
4 tablespoons shortening
1 egg, beaten

Note: Crust dough forms a ball. Do not roll out crust; press into 10-inch lightly greased glass pie plate.

Filling:
1 large and 1 small package cream cheese (11 ounces total)
7 heaping tablespoons sugar
2 heaping tablespoons flour
1 egg
Juice of half a lemon
1 teaspoon vanilla
2 cups milk (regular whole milk is best)

Have cheese, milk, egg and lemon at room temperature; mix together in large bowl. Pour into pie plate. Batter will be watery. Place carefully in oven. Bake in preheated 350 degree oven about 1 hour or until knife inserted in center comes out clean. Sprinkle with cinnamon.

PINA COLADA TOFU PIE

Tofu makes this a healthy dessert without sugar. Great for people on restricted diets.

1 pie crust (regular or graham cracker)
1 pound tofu cut-up and drained
1-1/2 tablespoons oil
1/3 cup plus 2 tablespoons honey
1-1/2 teaspoons cornstarch
1 teaspoon vanilla
1-1/4 cups drained crushed pineapple
3/4 cups shredded unsweetened coconut

Blend well all ingredients. Bake at 350 degrees for 20-30 minutes. Let cool to set.

SAWDUST PIE

1-1/4 cup white or brown sugar
1-1/2 cups chopped pecans
1-1/2 cups vanilla wafers or graham cracker crumbs
1-1/2 cups flaked coconut
1/2 teaspoon cinnamon
1/2 teaspoon nutmeg
7 egg whites, unbeaten
1 unbaked 9-inch pastry shell
1 sliced banana
Whipped cream

Combine the first seven ingredients in a large mixing bowl. Stir until just blended. Pour into pie shell and bake at 375 degrees for 35 minutes or until filling is set.

Presentation: Top each slice with a dollop of whipped cream and a slice of banana. Serve warm or at room temperature.

SHOO-FLY-PIE

Combine the following ingredients to make crumbs:

1/4 cup shortening
1-1/2 cups flour
1 cup brown sugar

Liquid filling:
3/4 teaspoon baking soda
1/8 teaspoon nutmeg
Dash of ginger
Dash of cinnamon
Dash of cloves
1/4 teaspoon salt
3/4 cup molasses
3/4 cup hot water

Mix well the baking soda, nutmeg, ginger, cinnamon, cloves, salt, and molasses. Add hot water. In an unbaked pie shell, place crumbs and liquid in alternate layers, with crumbs being on both bottom and top. Bake 15 minutes at 450 degrees; lower heat to 350 degrees and bake for an additional 20 minutes.

TRANSPARENT PIE

4 egg yolks
3/4 cup sugar
1 stick butter
1 cup evaporated milk
1 teaspoon vanilla
1 partially baked pie shell
8 tablespoons of sugar (additional)

Beat together egg yolks and sugar. Place in medium saucepan over low heat. Melt butter in egg mixture, stirring constantly. Remove from heat as soon as butter melts. Add evaporated milk and vanilla. Pour into crust and bake for 15 minutes at 400 degrees. Then reduce heat and bake until custard is set. Cover pie with meringue made form 4 egg whites and 8 tablespoons sugar. Return to oven to brown meringue. (Watch carefully)

BRAN PIE CRUST SHELLS
Makes two 8" or 9" shells

1/3 cup bran
2 cups sifted flour
1/2 teaspoon salt
2/3 cup shortening
6 tablespoons cold water

Crush bran into fine crumbs; mix with flour and salt. Cut in 1/3 cup of the shortening to the consistency of cornmeal. Cut in remaining shortening to the consistency of peas. Sprinkle cold water over top of mixture, a little at a time. Mixing with a fork until dough is just moist enough to hold together. Turn onto a sheet of waxed paper and shape the dough into a ball. Roll out according to directions.

COCONUT CREAM PIE

2 cups milk
1/2 cup granulated sugar
2 tablespoons all-purpose flour
2 tablespoons cornstarch
2 large eggs, separated
1 tablespoon butter
1/2 teaspoon salt
1-1/4 cups shredded coconut
1 teaspoon vanilla

Scald 1-1/2 cups milk in top of a double boiler. Combine sugar, flour, cornstarch, and salt. Stir in remaining 1/2 cup milk and egg yolks. Stir this flour mixture into hot milk; cook until thickened. Remove from heat. Add butter, vanilla, and 3/4 cup coconut. Allow mixture to cool, then pour into baked 9 inch pie shell. Cover with meringue and remaining coconut. Bake at 350 degrees 10-12 minutes, or until meringue browns lightly.

CRAZY PIE

1 cup flour
1 teaspoon baking powder
1/2 teaspoon salt
1 tablespoon sugar

Mix well the flour, baking powder, salt and sugar. Blend in:
2/3 cup butter-flavored shortening
3/4 cup water

Beat 2 minutes on medium speed with electric mixer. Pour batter into 9" pie pan. Do not spread. Pour favorite pie filling in center of batter. Do not stir. Bake 45-50 minutes in preheated 425 degree oven.

END OF THE LINE PIE

Serves 8

1 (4 ounce package) German Sweet Chocolate

1/4 cup butter
1 (13 ounce can) evaporated milk
1-1/3 cups flaked coconut
3 eggs, slightly beaten
1/2 cup sugar

In saucepan melt chocolate and butter. Gradually add milk and coconut. Combine eggs and sugar, and stir into chocolate mixture. Pour mixture into pie crust. Bake at 400 degrees for 45 minutes. Completely cool before cutting the individual servings.

FOURTH OF JULY PIE

1 (3-ounce) package lemon gelatin
2/3 cup boiling water
2 cups ice cubes
1 (8-ounce) container frozen whipped topping, thawed
1/2 cup sliced fresh strawberries
1/2 cup whole fresh blueberries
1 (9-inch) prepared graham cracker crumb crust

Dissolve gelatin in the boiling water, stirring about 3 minutes. Add ice cubes and stir constantly until gelatin is thickened, about 2 to 3 minutes. Remove any unmelted ice. Using a wire whip, blend in whipped topping and whip until smooth. Fold in strawberries and blueberries. Chill, if necessary, until mixture will mound. Spoon into pie shell. Chill about 2 hours.

HAWAIIAN CHESS PIE

3 eggs beaten
1/4 cup milk
1-1/2 cup sugar
2 tablespoons flour
2 teaspoons lemon juice
1/4 cup melted margarine
1 - 8 ounce can crushed pineapple, with juice
2/3 cup flaked coconut
1 - 9 inch deep dish unbaked pie shell

Combine eggs, milk, sugar, flour, lemon juice, and margarine. Beat until smooth. Add pineapple and coconut. Pour into pie shell. Bake at 350 degrees for 50-55 minutes or until center of pie is set. Cool and serve. Yummy!

MILLION DOLLAR PIE

1/3 cup lemon juice
1 can sweetened condensed milk
1 (No. 2 can) crushed pineapple, drained
1 (9 ounce) container frozen dessert topping, thawed
1 cup chopped nuts (reserve some for top to garnish)
1 (8 ounce) package cream cheese, softened
1 large (or 2 small) baked pastry or graham cracker shells.

Mix all ingredients together well and pour into pie shells. Sprinkle with reserved nuts and chill. Cut into small wedges.

NO-FOOL PIE

1 stick margarine
1 cup self-rising flour
3/4 cup sugar
3/4 cup milk
1 to 1-1/2 cups fruit, drained (blueberries, peaches, cherries, etc.)

Preheat oven to 350 degrees. Melt margarine in deep 8-inch cobbler pan while oven is preheating; set aside. Combine flour, sugar, and one-half of milk; stir until dry ingredients are moistened. Add remaining milk and stir until smooth. Pour batter over melted margarine. DO NOT MIX! Sprinkle drained fruit over top of this mixture. Do not stir to combine. Bake 30-40 minutes, or until lightly browned and center springs back when lightly touched with finger. Serve hot, with or without ice cream.

BANANA– SPLIT PIE

24 single graham crackers
6 tablespoons butter or margarine
1/4 cup sugar
30 large marshmallows
1 cup milk
1 (8-1/2 ounce) can crushed pine-
    apple, drained very dry
1 large banana, diced
1/3 cup pecans or walnuts, chopped
1 (2-ounce) package whipped
    topping mix
1/2 cup milk
1/2 teaspoon vanilla
8 maraschino cherries

Make a graham–cracker crust using finely crushed crackers, margarine or butter, and sugar. Line a 10-
inch pie plate, reserving 1/4 cup
crumbs for garnish. Bake in a 350–
degree oven for 10 minutes. Cool.
Melt marshmallows in milk over
boiling water. Cool to room temperature, stirring often. When crust and
marshmallows are cool, prepare topping mix according to package directions with 1/2 cup milk and flavoring;
fold into marshmallow mixture. Add
pineapple, banana and nuts. Spoon
into crust. Chill and garnish with
reserved crumbs and cherries. Chill
overnight.

brown sugar, salt, and vanilla in
bowl, using electric mixer at high
speed. Beat in egg yolks, one at a
time, beating well after each addition.
Beat in cooled chocolate. Beat egg
whites in another bowl until stiff
peaks form, using electric mixer at
high speed. Gradually beat in remaining 1/4 cup brown sugar. Beat until
stiff, glossy peaks form. Fold chocolate mixture into egg whites, then fold
in whipped cream. Pour mixture into
Chocolate Graham Crust, reserving
one-fourth of mixture for decorating.
Chill until filling sets slightly. With
tapered spoon, drop reserved mixture
in mounds over top of pie. Cover and
chill overnight.

Chocolate Graham Crust:

1-1/2 cups graham cracker crumbs
1/4 cup light brown sugar, packed
1/8 teaspoon ground nutmeg
1/3 cup melted butter or regular mar-
    garine
1 (1-ounce) square unsweetened
    chocolate, melted

Combine all ingredients and mix
until thoroughly blended. Press mixture into a 9-inch pie plate. Chill until
firm.

CARROT PIE

1 (9-inch) unbaked pie crust
2 cups cooked carrots (place in
    blender)
1 cup honey
3/4 cup undiluted evaporated milk
1/2 teaspoon salt
1 teaspoon cinnamon
1/2 teaspoon nutmeg
1/2 teaspoon ginger
Dash cloves
3 slightly beaten eggs

Allow pie crust to chill while
making filling. Combine all ingredients except eggs; fold in eggs. Pour
into the unbaked chilled pie crust.
Bake in a 400 degree oven for 40-45
minutes or until knife inserted comes
out clean. Remove from oven; cool
on rack for 30 minutes. Chill in refrigerator.

Great substitute for pumpkin pie.
Canned carrots may also be used.

CHOCOLATE
CHEESE PIE
Serves 6-8

Chocolate Graham Crust (recipe fol-
    lows)
1 (6-ounce) package semi-sweet
    chocolate pieces
1 (8-ounce) package cream cheese,
    softened
3/4 cup light brown sugar, packed
1/8 teaspoon salt
1 teaspoon vanilla
2 eggs, separated
1 cup heavy cream, whipped

Prepare Chocolate Graham Crust.
Melt chocolate pieces over hot
water, cool 10 minutes. Blend together cream cheese, 1/2 cup of the

ONION PIE
Serves 6

3 onions, peeled and sliced
1 tablespoon butter
3 eggs, beaten
1 pint of cream
Salt and pepper to taste
4 slices crisp fried bacon, crumbled
1/2 cup grated Cheddar cheese
Pastry for a double crust

Fry onions in butter until golden
brown. Beat eggs and cream together;
season, and add to onions. Line deep
dish pie plate with pastry. Pour in
creamed onions; sprinkle with bacon
and cheese. Cover with top crust.
Bake at 350 degrees for 1 hour or until
crust is golden.

MEATZA PIE

1 pound extra-lean ground beef
2/3 cup evaporated milk (or 1 small
    can)
1 teaspoon garlic salt
1/2 cup Kellogg's cornflake crumbs
1 cup shredded mozzarella cheese
2 tablespoons grated Parmesan
    cheese
1 (6-ounce) can tomato paste
1 (4-ounce) can mushrooms
1/4 teaspoon oregano

Combine meat, milk, crumbs, and
garlic salt together. Place meat mixture into a 9-inch pie plate. Pat into
bottom and up sides of plate. Spread
tomato paste over meat. (The meat is
the crust!) Sprinkle with cheese and
oregano. Drain mushrooms and arrange on top. Bake at 350 degrees for
25 minutes.

HOSPITALITY FRESH PINEAPPLE PIE

9-inch double-crust pastry
3-1/4 cups fresh bite-sized pineapple chunks
2 eggs
3/4 cup sugar
flour
1 teaspoon lemon rind
1/4 teaspoon cardamom
1/4 teaspoon nutmeg
1/2 teaspoon cinnamon

Roll out bottom crust; place in pie pan. Combine pineapple, eggs, sugar, flour, lemon rind, and spices; turn mixture into pie shell. Roll out pastry; cut into lattice strips. Arrange strips over filling; flute the edge; sprinkle strips with small amount of sugar. Bake at 400 degrees for 10 minutes; lower heat to 375 degrees for 40 to 45 minutes. Delicious chilled and served with a dollop of vanilla ice cream or whipped cream.

PEACH PIE
Serves 6-8

Pastry for 2-crust 9-inch pie
6 cups peeled and sliced peaches
   (about 2 pounds), or half
   peaches and half nectarines
1/2 cup sugar
3 tablespoons cornstarcn
Dash salt
1/2 teaspoon ground nutmeg
1/2 cup sour cream
Milk
Sugar

Roll out half of pastry Use to line bottom of 9-inch pie plate. Place peaches in pastry-lined pie plate (or alternate layers of peaches and nectarines if nectarines are used).

In small bowl, mix sugar, cornstarch, salt, nutmeg, and sour cream. Pour over peaches. Roll out remaining pastry and make lattice top. Brush pastry with milk and sprinkle with sugar. Bake at 425 degrees for 10 minutes. Reduce heat to 350 degrees. Continue baking 45-50 minutes longer. Cool on rack.

GLAZED PEACH PIE

1 graham cracker Ready-crust pie
   crust
4 cups unsweetened fresh or frozen
   peaches, drained thoroughly
3/4 cup sugar
1/2 teaspoon nutmeg, optional
1/4 cup flour
1/4 teaspoon salt
1 teaspoon lemon juice
1/4 teaspoon almond extract
1/4 cup peach preserves
1 egg yolk, beaten

Brush crust with beaten egg yolk. Bake on cookie sheet for 5 minutes at 375 degrees. Toss together in large bowl peaches, sugar, nutmeg (if desired), flour, salt, lemon juice, and almond extract. Pour into prepared pie shell. With spoon, arrange peaches in concentric circles evenly in pie shell. Bake at 375 degrees for 35 minutes. While baking, melt peach preserves in saucepan. If too thick, add drop of almond extract. Brush peach preserves over baked pie. Allow pie to cool. Serve with ice cream or whipped cream.

PEACH-PRALINE PIE

Unbaked 9-inch pie shell
4 cups sliced peaches
1/2 cup sugar
2 tablespoons tapioca
1/2 cup chopped pecans
1 teaspoon lemon juice
1/4 cup brown sugar, firmly packed
1/2 cup sifted flour
1/4 cup margarine

Combine peaches, sugar, tapioca, and lemon juice in bowl; let stand 15 minutes. Combine flour, brown sugar, and pecans in small bowl; cut in butter with fork or mix with fingers until crumbly. Sprinkle 1/3 of pecan mixture over bottom of pie shell; cover with peach mixture; sprinkle remaining pecan mixture over peaches. Bake in 425 degree oven 10

minutes; reduce heat to 350 degrees and bake 20 minutes longer.

STRAWBERRY PIE

1/2 cup water
1 envelope unflavored gelatin
1/2 cup sugar
1 (10-ounce) package frozen strawberries
Juice of 1/2 lemon
1 cup heavy cream, whipped
1 baked pie shell

Soak gelatin in cold water, then dissolve over boiling water. Add lemon juice, sugar, and strawberries, partially thawed. Stir with fork. Fold in whipped cream. Pour filling into baked pie shell; refrigerate for two or three hours before serving.

Easy, quick, never-fail, and delicious.

FRESH STRAWBERRY PIE

2 boxes strawberries
1 cup sugar
3 tablespoons cornstarch
1/4 cup water
1 tablespoon lemon juice
Pinch of salt
1 (9-inch) baked pie crust

Crush 1 cup berries. Add sugar, cornstarch, water and salt, if desired. Cook, stirring constantly, until clear. Remove from heat and add lemon juice. Arrange remaining berries in baked pie crust. Pour cooked mixture over berries and chill. Serve.

During the lazy, hazy strawberry months have you often wished you could have one of these berries in December? Have you frozen one, only to be disappointed, as it was often mushy and fit only for a cold cereal topping? Here is an ideal way to recapture that wonderful taste sensation. . .make this bread and freeze!

MYSTERY PECAN PIE

1 unbaked pie crust (9-inch)
1 (8-ounce) package cream cheese
1/3 cup sugar
1/4 cup sugar
4 eggs, divided
2 teaspoons vanilla, divided
1/4 teaspoon salt
1-1/4 cups pecan halves
1 cup corn syrup

Beat together the cream cheese, 1/3 cup sugar, 1 egg, 1 teaspoon vanilla, and salt in small bowl; set aside. Beat 3 eggs well; add the 1/4 cup sugar, corn syrup, and 1 teaspoon vanilla; blend well.

Spread cream cheese mixture in bottom of unbaked crust. Sprinkle pecans over cheese layer. Pour corn syrup mixture gently over top of pecans. Bake at 375 degrees for 40 minutes, or until center is firm to touch.

MOCK PECAN PIE

2/3 cup regular oats, uncooked
2/3 cup light corn syrup
2 eggs, beaten
2/3 cup sugar
1 teaspoon vanilla
1/4 teaspoon salt
2/3 cup melted butter or margarine, cooled
1 (8-inch) pie shell, unbaked

Combine oats, corn syrup, eggs, sugar, vanilla and salt, mixing well. Add melted butter and mix thoroughly. Pour into pastry shell and bake 1 hour at 350 degrees. Cool before serving.

BLENDER PECAN PIE

2 (8-inch) unbaked pie shells
3 eggs
1/2 cup heavy cream
1/2 cup dark corn syrup
1/8 teaspoon salt
1 cup granulated sugar
1 teaspoon vanilla
1 tablespoon sherry
2 tablespoons butter
1-1/2 cups chopped pecans

Put all ingredients into blender, except nuts. Blend 10 seconds or until well mixed. Stir in nuts. Pour into pie shells. Bake at 400 degrees for 30-35 minutes.

PECAN CRUNCH PIE

3 egg whites
1 cup sugar
1 teaspoon baking powder
1 teaspoon vanilla flavoring
1 cup crushed graham-cracker crumbs
1 cup chopped pecans

Beat egg whites until stiff. Combine sugar and baking powder; beat into egg whites. Add vanilla. Fold in graham-cracker crumbs, then pecans. Pour into a buttered 9-inch pie plate and bake at 350 degrees for 30 minutes or until done. Cool. Good served with vanilla ice cream or whipped cream.

PECAN FUDGE PIE

1 (9-inch) unbaked pastry shell
1 (4-ounce) package sweet chocolate
1/4 cup margarine or butter
1 (14-ounce) can condensed milk
2 eggs, slightly beaten
1/4 cup hot water
1 teaspoon vanilla
1/8 teaspoon salt
1/2 cup broken pecans

Preheat oven to 350 degrees. In heavy saucepan over low heat, melt chocolate and margarine. Remove from heat. In large mixing bowl combine remaining ingredients, except pecans. Add chocolate mixture.

Mix well and pour into crust. Top with pecans. Bake 35 to 40 minutes or until top is lightly browned.

PECAN PRALINE PIE

1/3 cup butter or margarine
1/3 cup brown sugar
1/2 cup chopped pecans
1 baked (9-inch) pastry shell
1 (5-ounce) package vanilla pie filling (not instant)
3 cups milk
1 envelope whipped topping

Heat butter, sugar, and nuts in pan until melted; spread on bottom of pie shell. Bake at 450 degrees for 5 minutes. Cool. Prepare pie filling with milk; cool 5 minutes, stirring occasionally. Measure 1 cup of pudding; cover with wax paper and chill. Pour remainder of filling into pie shell and chill. Prepare whipped topping as package directs. Fold 1-1/3 cups topping into reserved, chilled pudding and spread over filling in pie; chill. Garnish with remaining whipped topping and pecans.

CRUSTLESS DATE-PECAN PIE
Serves 6

2 eggs
1 cup sugar
Dash salt
1 teaspoon vanilla
1/2 cup soft bread crumbs
1 cup cut-up dates
1 cup coarsely chopped pecans
Vanilla ice cream or whipped cream

Beat eggs lightly in bowl. Add sugar, salt, vanilla, bread crumbs, dates, and pecans. Spoon mixture into buttered 8-inch pie pan and bake at 200 degrees for 40 minutes. Raise temperature to 250 degrees and continue to bake an additional 25 minutes or until top is firm. Cool; cut into wedges and serve with either ice cream or whipped cream.

STRAWBERRY DAIQUIRI PIE
Serves 6-8

9-inch graham cracker crust, baked and cooled
1 pint strawberries, hulled
3/4 cup sugar
1 (1 1/4 oz.) envelope unflavored gelatin
1/3 cup lime juice
1/3 cup light rum
1/2 pint whipping cream, whipped
Whole strawberries for garnish

In blender, combine hulled berries and sugar; process until berries are pureed. Set aside 15 minutes to let mixture soak and blend. In saucepan, stir gelatin into lime juice; let stand 5 minutes to soften. Stir over medium heat until gelatin dissolves. With blender running at medium speed, add gelatin mixture to pureed mixture; process until blended. Strain through fine sieve into bowl. Stir rum into mixture. Refrigerate, stirring often, until mixture begins to mound when spooned on top of itself. Fold in whipped cream. Spoon into crust. Freeze 4 hours. Decorate with whole berries.

CHOCOLATE MOUSSE PIE
Serves 6

1 (6-ounce) package semi-sweet chocolate bits
3 eggs
1 teaspoon vanilla extract
2 tablespoons cold coffee
1 (9-ounce) container frozen whipped topping, thawed
1 (9-inch) prepared graham cracker shell

Melt chocolate over hot (not boiling) water; add one whole slightly-beaten egg and beat well. Separate remaining two eggs and add yolks to chocolate, one at a time, beating well after each addition. Beat egg whites until stiff; carefully fold into chocolate. Then fold in half the topping, the vanilla, and cold coffee. Turn mixture into pie shell; spoon on remaining topping. Refrigerate for at least two hours or overnight. Freezes well.

CHOCOLATE MOUSSE PIE

1 (9-inch) pie crust, baked
1 cup chocolate chips
1 egg
2 egg yolks
1 teaspoon rum
2 egg whites
2 cups Cool Whip (divided in half)
1/2 square unsweetened chocolate

Melt chocolate chips over hot, *not boiling* water. Remove from heat and beat in the 1 whole egg and the 2 egg yolks, one at a time. Add rum. Beat 2 egg whites, until stiff peaks form. Fold together 1 cup Cool Whip and the egg yolk mixture and spoon onto the pie crust. Refrigerate until well chilled. Serve topped with the remaining 1 cup Cool Whip and shave the unsweetened chocolate over Cool Whip.

A light, delicious chocolate pie.

FRENCH SILK CHOCOLATE PIE

1 baked pie shell
3/4 cup sugar
1/2 cup butter
1 teaspoon vanilla
2 eggs
2 squares unsweetened chocolate

Melt chocolate over hot water and cool. Mix cooled chocolate, butter, and sugar; add one egg and beat 5 minutes; add the other egg and beat 5 minutes more; add vanilla and beat again. Place into a baked shell and serve with whipped cream. Eat heartily!

SOUTHERN CHOCOLATE PIE
Serves 8

1 (4-ounce) package German Sweet Chocolate
1/4 cup butter or margarine
1 (13-ounce) can evaporated milk
1 cup sugar
3 eggs
1 teaspoon vanilla
9-inch unbaked pie shell with high rim
1-1/4 cups flaked coconut
1/2 cup chopped pecans

Melt chocolate and butter over low heat. Remove from heat and blend in evaporated milk and sugar. Beat in eggs and vanilla. Pour into pie shell. Top with coconut and nuts. Bake at 375 degrees for 45-50 minutes or until top is puffed. Cool 4 hours.

GERMAN CHOCOLATE PIE

1 (4-ounce) German Sweet Chocolate bar
1/4 cup butter
1 (13-ounce) can evaporated milk
1-1/2 cups sugar
2 eggs
1 teaspoon vanilla
3 tablespoons cornstarch
Salt to taste
1 unbaked 9-inch pie shell
1/2 cup chopped pecans
1-1/3 cups coconut

Melt chocolate with butter over low heat, stirring until blended. Remove from heat, and gradually blend in milk. Mix sugar, cornstarch, and salt. Beat in eggs and vanilla. Gradually blend in chocolate mixture. Pour into pie shell. Sprinkle with coconut and pecans. Bake at 375 degrees for 45-50 minutes. Cool for 4 hours before serving.

The aroma, as this pie bakes, will fill the house and tickle the taste buds ahead of time.

CHOCOLATE CHIP PIE

1 cup sugar
1/2 cup flour
2 eggs, well beaten
1 stick margarine, melted
1 teaspoon vanilla
1 cup semi-sweet chocolate bits
3/4 cup pecans
1/2 cup coconut
1 unbaked deep dish pie shell

Blend flour, sugar, eggs, melted margarine, and vanilla. Stir in chocolate bits, pecans, and coconut. Pour mixture into unbaked pie shell. Bake at 350 degrees for 30-35 minutes until firm.

NUTTY CHOCOLATE PIE

3 eggs
1 cup light or dark corn syrup
1 cup coarsely-chopped walnuts
6 ounces (1 cup) semi-sweet
   chocolate morsels
1/2 cup sugar
2 tablespoons butter or margarine,
   melted
1 teaspoon vanilla extract
1 unbaked (9-inch) pie shell

Preheat oven to 350 degrees. In large bowl, beat eggs until well combined. Add corn syrup, walnuts, semi-sweet morsels, sugar, butter, and vanilla extract. Mix until well blended. Pour evenly into pie shell. Bake at 350 degrees for 50-60 minutes. Cool completely before serving.

FUDGE PIE

1 stick margarine, melted
1/4 cup cocoa
1/4 cup flour
1 cup sugar
1/4 teaspoon vanilla
2 eggs
1 unbaked pie shell

Mix all ingredients and pour into pie shell. Bake at 350 degrees for 25 minutes.

HERSHEY BAR PIE

1/2 cup milk
1 (4-ounce) Hershey bar with
   almonds
18 large marshmallows
1/2 pint heavy whipping cream
1 graham cracker crust

In top of double boiler melt Hershey bar, milk, and marshmallows. Whip the cream in bowl until stiff and fold this into chocolate mixture. Pour into crust and place in refrigerator to cool. When cool, place in freezer. Remove at dinner time and pie will be thawed for dessert. Keeps indefinitely in freezer.

GOLDEN APRICOT CREME PIE

1 (8-ounce) package cream cheese
1/4 cup sugar
1 cup heavy cream
1 teaspoon vanilla extract
1/8 teaspoon almond extract
1 (10-1/2 ounce) can apricot halves;
   drain, reserve juice
1 envelope unflavored gelatin
1 ready-made graham cracker pie
   shell
1/2 cup melted currant jelly

Beat cheese and sugar until light and fluffy. Slowly add cream; stir in vanilla and almond extracts. Drain apricot halves; reserve syrup. Soften gelatin in 1/2 cup of reserved apricot syrup; heat syrup mixture to dissolve gelatin. Stir gelatin mixture into cream cheese mixture; pour into pie shell; chill until set. Arrange apricot halves on top of pie in a decorative manner; spoon melted jelly over apricots. Rechill.

BANANA CREAM PIE

Crust:
10 graham crackers, crushed
4 tablespoons sugar
4 tablespoons melted butter

Mix ingredients; pack firmly into 9 inch pie pan. Refrigerate 15 minutes.

Filling:
1 cup cream, whipped
1 tablespoon powdered sugar
1/2 teaspoon vanilla
2 bananas, thinly sliced
Grated coconut
Combine filling ingredients. Just before serving, spoon into shell.

sprinkle with coconut.

BANANA CREAM CHEESE PIE

1 baked pie shell
3 medium bananas
1 (8-ounce) package cream cheese,
   room temperature
1 can sweetened condensed milk
1/2 cup lemon juice
1 tablespoon vanilla

Slice 2 bananas; place them in pie shell. Beat cream cheese until light and fluffy. Add milk gradually and continue beating until mixture is smooth. Stir in lemon juice and vanilla. Pour into pie shell; chill until filling is firm. About 1 hour before serving, slice remaining banana; arrange slices on top of pie filling.

101

ICE CREAM PARFAIT PIE

1 (3-ounce) package strawberry
  gelatin
1-1/4 cups hot water
1 pint vanilla ice cream
1 cup sliced strawberries
1 pie shell, baked
Whipped cream, optional

Dissolve gelatin in 1-1/4 cups hot water. Spoon in ice cream and stir until melted. Place in refrigerator until thickened. Let it set 15-25 minutes. Fold in strawberries. Turn filling into baked pie shell. Chill until firm, 30-60 minutes. Serve with whipped cream, if desired.

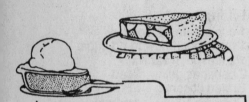

BLACK FOREST PIE

1 (9-inch) unbaked pie shell
3/4 cup sugar
1/3 cup unsweetened cocoa
2 tablespoons flour
1/4 cup margarine
1/3 cup milk
2 eggs, beaten
1 (21-ounce) can cherry pie filling
1 (9-ounce) container frozen whipped
  topping
1 (1-ounce) square unsweetened
  chocolate (coarsely grated)

In saucepan, combine sugar, cocoa, and flour; add margarine and milk. Cook until mixture begins to boil, stirring constantly. Remove from heat. Add small amount of hot mixture to eggs; return mixture to pan. Fold half the can of pie filling into mixture. Pour into crust-lined pan. Bake at 350 degrees for 35-45 minutes or until center is set but still shiny. Cool. Chill one hour. Combine 2 cups topping and grated chocolate; spread over pie. Place remaining pie filling around edge of pie. Cool.

AMISH VANILLA PIE

1/2 cup firmly packed brown sugar
1 tablespoon flour
1/4 cup dark corn syrup
1-1/2 teaspoons vanilla
1 egg, beaten
1 cup water
1 cup flour
1/2 cup firmly packed brown sugar
1/2 teaspoon cream of tartar
1/2 teaspoon baking soda
1/8 teaspoon salt
1/4 cup butter
1 unbaked 9-inch pie shell

Combine first 5 ingredients in 2-quart saucepan. Slowly stir in water. Cook over medium heat until mixture comes to a boil, stirring constantly. Let cool. Combine rest of ingredients (except pie shell) and mix until crumbly. Pour cooled mixture into pie shell and top with crumbs.

Bake at 350 degrees for 40 minutes or until golden brown.

HAWAIIAN WEDDING PIE

1 (9-inch) baked pie shell
1/2 cup sugar
1/3 cup cornstarch
1-1/2 cups milk
3 beaten egg yolks
1 tablespoon butter or margarine
1-1/2 teaspoons vanilla
1 small can crushed pineapple, well
  drained
1/2-3/4 cup coconut
Whipped cream for topping
Toasted coconut for garnish

Combine sugar, cornstarch, and milk; mix well. Add beaten egg yolks. Cook over medium heat, stirring constantly, until mixture begins to boil and is thickened. Remove from heat. Add butter, vanilla, crushed pineapple, and coconut, thoroughly combining all. Pour mixture into pie shell and chill. When chilled, cover top with whipped cream. Sprinkle with toasted coconut.

PENNSYLVANIA DUTCH SHOOFLY PIE

2 (8-inch) pastry shells, unbaked
2 cups flour
1 cup sugar
1 teaspoon baking powder
1 stick butter or margarine
1 cup dark molasses
1 teaspoon baking soda
1 cup boiling water
Pinch of salt
1 egg, beaten

Sift together flour, sugar, and baking powder. Cut in butter. In a separate bowl, mix molasses, baking soda, and water. Stir in salt, egg, and 2 cups of the flour-butter mixture. Pour into prepared pie shells and sprinkle with remaining crumbs. Bake at 375 degrees for 45 minutes.

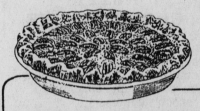

4TH OF JULY PIE

1 pint blueberries
20-25 strawberries, hulled
Whipped cream
1 (3-1/4 ounce) package regular
  vanilla pudding mix
2 cups milk
1 (8-ounce) package cream cheese,
  softened
1/2 teaspoon vanilla
1 8-inch graham-cracker pie crust

Combine pudding mix and 2 cups milk in saucepan. Bring to full boil over medium heat, stirring constantly. Remove from heat. Add cream cheese and stir until smooth. Add vanilla. Let mixture cool for 5 minutes, stirring twice. Pour pudding mixture into pie crust. Refrigerate 3 hours or overnight. Place strawberries in circle on outer edge of pie. Place one in center. Place blueberries over remaining pudding.

Serve chilled, with whipped cream on top.

GARDEN OF EDEN PIE

1 cup Carnation evaporated milk
1 tablespoon lemon juice
1 cup brown sugar
1/4 teaspoon salt
1/4 teaspoon cinnamon
1/8 teaspoon mace
1/2 teaspoon nutmeg
2 cups finely chopped apples
2 cups ground raisins
1 (9-inch) pie pastry shell, unbaked

Mix milk, juice, sugar, salt, and spices. Add fruits; pour into unbaked pie shell and bake in hot oven 450 degrees for 10 minutes to set crust; then reduce temperature to 325 degrees and bake an additional 40 minutes or until filling is set.

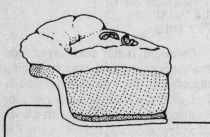

ORANGE COCONUT CHESS PIE

1 stick butter, at room temperature
2 cups sugar
5 eggs
1/2 cup thawed orange juice concentrate
1/3 cup water
1 tablespoon flour
1 tablespoon yellow cornmeal
1/2 cup coconut
2 unbaked 9-inch pie shells

Preheat oven to 350 degrees. Cream butter in large bowl with electric mixer. Gradually add sugar and beat well. Beat in eggs, one at a time. Combine orange juice concentrate and water; blend with butter mixture. Beat in flour and cornmeal. Fold in coconut. Divide mixture evenly between 2 pie crusts. Bake until golden—about 50-60 minutes. Let pie cool before serving.

ORANGESICLE PIE

1 (14-ounce) can Eagle Brand Sweetened Condensed Milk (not evaporated)
4 egg yolks
1/2 cup orange juice
1 tablespoon grated orange rind
1 (6-ounce) package graham cracker crumb crust
1 (3-ounce) package cream cheese, softened
1/3 cup confectioners' sugar
1/4 cup sour cream
1/4 teaspoon vanilla extract

Preheat oven to 325 degrees. In large bowl combine sweetened condensed milk, egg yolks, orange juice, and rind; mix well. Pour into crust. (Mixture will be thin). Bake 35 minutes or until knife inserted near center comes out clean. Meanwhile in small mixer bowl, combine remaining ingredients. Beat until smooth and well blended. Spread evenly on top of pie. Bake 10 additional minutes. Cool; chill thoroughly.

SHAKER SUGAR PIE

1 unbaked 9-inch pie shell
3/4 cup firmly-packed light brown sugar
1/4 cup flour
2 cups half-and-half
1 teaspoon vanilla extract
Few grains ground nutmeg
1/2 cup butter or margarine, softened

Prick pie shell and bake at 450 degrees for 5 minutes. Set aside. Reduce oven temperature to 350 degrees. Mix brown sugar with flour until blended. Spoon over bottom of partially-baked pie shell. Combine half-and-half, extract, and nutmeg; pour over sugar in pie shell. Dot with butter. Bake at 350 degrees for about 55 minutes, or until crust is lightly browned and filling is set.

A most delicious pie.

FRENCH COCONUT PIE

3 eggs, beaten well

Add:
1-1/2 cups sugar
1 stick margarine, melted
Pinch of salt
1 cup Angel Flake coconut
1 tablespoon lemon juice

Pour into unbaked pie shell; bake 1 hour at 325 degrees.

SOUTHERN MOLASSES CRUMB PIE

1 unbaked pie crust

Filling:
1/2 cup molasses
1 egg yolk

Add:
1/2 teaspoon soda dissolved in 3/4 cup boiling water. Mix.

Crumb portion:
3/4 cup flour
2 tablespoons shortening
1/2 teaspoon cinnamon
1/8 teaspoon nutmeg
1/8 teaspoon ginger
1/8 teaspoon cloves
1/2 cup brown sugar, well packed
1/4 teaspoon salt

To make the crumbs combine: flour, sugar, spices, and salt; then work in shortening. Put alternate layers of crumbs and filling into unbaked pie shell. Top with crumbs. Bake in hot oven 450 degrees until edges of crust begin to brown. Reduce heat to 375 degrees and bake until firm (about 20 minutes). Serve plain or with whipped cream.

HICKORY NUT PIE

3 eggs, slightly beaten
3/4 cup sugar
1 cup white Karo syrup
1 teaspoon vanilla
2 tablespoons butter or margarine
1 cup hickory nuts, chopped
1 unbaked pie shell

Mix eggs, sugar, syrup, vanilla, and margarine, adding nuts last. Pour into pie shell and bake in 400-degree oven for 10 minutes then reduce heat to 350 degrees and bake 40 additional minutes.

CUSTARD PIE

4 eggs, well beaten
6 tablespoons sugar
1 teaspoon vanilla
1/8 teaspoon salt
2 cups milk
1 (9-inch) pie shell
Nutmeg

Beat eggs; add sugar, milk, vanilla, and salt. Pour into unbaked pie shell. Sprinkle top with nutmeg.

Bake in a 425 degree oven for 10 minutes. Reduce heat to 350 degrees and bake 20 minutes longer.

RHUBARB ORANGE CUSTARD PIE

2 cups rhubarb, cut up

Cook until tender in about 1/2 cup water about 5-8 minutes.

1 cup sugar
2 tablespoons cornstarch
3 egg yolks
Juice of one large orange
1 teaspoon grated orange peel
Pinch salt

Mix together sugar, cornstarch, yolks, orange juice, orange peel and salt. Pour this mixture into hot rhubarb which has been cooked until tender. Cook until it thickens. Pour into a baked pie crust.

Meringue:
3 egg whites
6 tablespoons sugar
1/8 teaspoon cream of tartar
1/2 teaspoon vanilla

Beat egg whites until frothy. Add cream of tartar. When stiff, beat in sugar slowly. Continue beating until sugar is dissolved. Bake in 350-degree oven until lightly browned.

EARLY SPRING RHUBARB CUSTARD PIE

Filling:
1 unbaked 9-inch pie shell
4 cups rhubarb, cut into 1/4-inch slices
3/4 cup sugar
2 tablespoons flour
1-1/4 tablespoons fresh lemon juice
1/8 teaspoon salt

Topping:
3 eggs
1 cup whipping cream
2-1/4 tablespoons butter or margarine, melted
1/2 teaspoon nutmeg

In a bowl combine rhubarb, sugar, flour, fresh lemon juice, and salt. Mix well; turn into pie shell; bake 375 degrees for 25 minutes. Meanwhile beat eggs; stir in cream, butter, and nutmeg. Pour over hot rhubarb in pie shell; bake 10 minutes until top is golden. Chill in refrigerator at least 2 hours before serving.

EASY CARAMEL CUSTARD PIE

1 cup instant non-fat dry milk
1/2 cup sugar
1/4 teaspoon salt
1 cup cold water
2 teaspoons vanilla
3 eggs, beaten
1-1/2 cups boiling water
6 tablespoons brown sugar
Dash salt
1/4 teaspoon cinnamon
1 unbaked 9-inch pie shell

Preheat oven to 350 degrees. Sift dry ingredients together; add water and vanilla; mix until smooth. Stir in beaten eggs, then stir in boiling water. Combine brown sugar, cinnamon, and salt; sprinkle over bottom of unbaked pie shell. Pour in custard mixture. Bake 45-50 minutes, or until knife inserted comes out clean. Cool and serve.

JELLY PIE

1/2 cup butter
1/2 cup plum jelly
1/2 cup evaporated milk
1 teaspoon flour
2 eggs, beaten
1 teaspoon vanilla
1/2 cup sugar
Pinch of salt

Combine butter and sugar; add beaten eggs. Add all other remaining ingredients. Pour into an unbaked 8-inch pie shell. Bake at 350 degrees for 45 minutes. Cool. Cover with a layer of whipped cream; chill. Use any flavor jelly you like. This is an old-fashioned pie and is very good.

MACAROON PIE
Serves 8

16 saltine crackers, finely rolled (about 1/2 cup)
16 pitted dates, finely snipped
1/2 cup chopped pecans
3/4 cup granulated sugar
1/4 teaspoon baking powder
3 egg whites
Heavy cream, whipped

Blend first 4 ingredients. Add baking powder to egg whites and beat until stiff, but not dry. Fold into date mixture and spread in a well buttered 8-inch pie plate. Bake in a preheated 350 degree oven for about 25 minutes. Cool. Serve topped with whipped cream.

Salad
BOWL

YUM YUM SALAD

- 1 (3-ounce) package lime gelatin
- 1 (8-ounce) package cream cheese, softened
- 1 cup boiling water
- 1 cup whipping cream *or* 1 package whipped topping mix, prepared
- 1 small can crushed pineapple
- ½ cup chopped pecans
  Toasted coconut

Place gelatin, hot water and cream cheese in pan and stir over low heat until cheese is blended well into mixture. Remove from heat; add crushed pineapple and pecans. Place in refrigerator until it begins to thicken. Add whipped cream and let set until firm. Sprinkle with toasted coconut before serving.

GREEN AND WHITE VEGGIE SALAD

- 1 cup salad dressing
- ½ cup sour cream
- 1 tablespoon vinegar
- 1 tablespoon granulated sugar
- 1 small onion
- ⅛ teaspoon Worcestershire sauce
  Dash hot sauce
  Salt and pepper to taste

- 1 head cauliflower, pulled into florets
- 1 bunch broccoli, washed and cut up

Place the onion in food processor and process until finely chopped. Add remaining ingredients, except veggies, and process until well-blended. Pour over the broccoli and cauliflower.

CHEESE-LIME SALAD
Serves 10

- 3 cups boiling water
- 2 (3-ounce) packages lime-flavored gelatin
- 1 cup pineapple juice
- 1 teaspoon vinegar
- ½ teaspoon salt
- 2 cups creamed cottage cheese
- 1 teaspoon onion, finely chopped
- 1 teaspoon green pepper, finely chopped
- ½ cup cucumber, coarsely chopped
- ½ cup celery, coarsely chopped

Pour boiling water on gelatin in bowl; stir until gelatin is dissolved. Stir in pineapple juice, vinegar and salt. Pour 1 cup of the gelatin mixture into an 8-cup mold. Refrigerate until firm.

Refrigerate remaining mixture until slightly thickened, but not set; beat with beater until light and fluffy. Mix in remaining ingredients and pour on gelatin layer in mold. Refrigerate until firm. Unmold on serving plate.

SWEET AND SOUR PINEAPPLE COLESLAW

- 1 (1 pound, 4½-ounce) can crushed pineapple, drained
- 3 cups crisp cabbage, shredded
- ½ cup celery, chopped
- ¼ cup green pepper, chopped
- 1 cup miniature marshmallows
- ½ cup heavy cream
- 4 tablespoons wine vinegar
- ¼ teaspoon salt
- ⅛ teaspoon pepper

Combine first 5 ingredients. Beat cream until stiff; fold in vinegar, salt and pepper. Continue beating until well-blended; mix with salad; chill.

CELEBRATION SALAD
Makes 16 squares

- 1 large package raspberry gelatin
- 1 cup boiling water
- 1 (20-ounce) can pineapple, undrained
- 1 pint raspberry sherbet
- 2 cups vanilla ice cream, softened

Prepare gelatin in boiling water. Allow to cool before adding pineapple and sherbet. Fold in ice cream. Place in an 8 x 8-inch glass cake dish. Allow to set.

HARVEST CARROT SALAD

Serves 6–8

- 3 cups shredded carrots
- 1 (17-ounce) can apricot halves, drained and chopped
- ½ cup sliced celery
- ⅔ cup raisins
- ¼ cup chopped walnuts, toasted
- ½ cup salad dressing *or* mayonnaise

Combine all ingredients, tossing well. Cover and refrigerate before serving.

SPINACH SOUFFLÉ SALAD

- 1 (10-ounce) package frozen, chopped spinach
- 1 envelope unflavored gelatin
- ½ cup sugar
- ¾ teaspoon salt
- 1 cup cold water
- ¼ cup lemon juice
- ⅓ cup mayonnaise *or* salad dressing
- 1 cup cream-style cottage cheese, drained
- ¼ cup celery, finely chopped

Cook spinach according to package directions. Press against sides of a sieve to drain very thoroughly. Cool. In small saucepan soften gelatin in ½ cup cold water. Heat and stir until gelatin dissolves. Add sugar, salt, remaining water and lemon juice. Mix well. Place mayonnaise in a small bowl. Gradually stir in gelatin mixture. Chill until mixture begins to set. Beat gelatin mixture until fluffy. Fold in spinach, cottage cheese and celery. Turn into a 5-cup mold. Chill 4 hours or overnight.

PASTA AND VEGETABLE SALAD

Makes 5 quarts

- 1 pound mostaccioli noodles *or* other large pasta
- 2 tablespoons chicken soup mix
- 1 or 2 cucumbers, diced
- 1 large tomato, diced
- 1 small onion, finely chopped
- 1 green pepper, finely diced
  Sweet Herb Dressing (recipe follows)

Cook mostaccioli according to package directions, except substitute chicken soup mix for salt; drain and cool. Add cucumbers, tomato, onion and green pepper. Pour enough Sweet Herb Dressing over salad to moisten. Refrigerate several hours.

Sweet Herb Dressing:
Makes 2 cups

- 1 cup salad oil (or less)
- 1 cup vinegar
- ½ cup sugar
- 1 tablespoon parsley
- 2 teaspoons seasoning salt
- 2 teaspoons sweet 'n hot mustard
- 2 teaspoons minced green onion
- 1 teaspoon garlic powder
- ¾ teaspoon black pepper
- ½ teaspoon celery seed

Combine all ingredients in covered jar; shake well.

PASTA SALAD

- 1 pound medium shell macaroni
- 1/2 pound Provolene cheese
- 1/4 pound salami
- 1/2 pound pepperoni
- 1 can black olives
- 1 small bottle green olives
- 1 green pepper
- 3 stalks celery
- 1 small onion
- 1-1/2 teaspoons salt
- 1 teaspoon pepper
- 1 teaspoon oregano
- 3/4 cup oil
- 1/2 cup cider vinegar
- 3 tomatoes, chopped

Cook macaroni and drain. Cool. Cut cheese, salami, and pepperoni in bite-size pieces. Slice olives. Dice pepper, celery, and onions. Add salt, pepper, oregano, oil, and vinegar. Combine dressing with other ingredients, except tomatoes; chill overnight. Add tomatoes just before serving.

TOMATO CHEESE SALAD

Serves 8

- 1½ cups hot condensed tomato soup, undiluted
- ½ cup cream cheese
- 1 tablespoon butter
- ¼ teaspoon salt
- 1 tablespoon onion juice
- 1 tablespoon unflavored gelatin
- ¼ cup cold water
- ½ cup mayonnaise
- ½ cup heavy cream *or* evaporated milk
- ¼ cup stuffed olives, chopped

Heat soup, cheese, butter, salt and onion juice until cheese has softened. Soften gelatin in cold water and dissolve in hot mixture; cool until mixture starts to thicken. Whip cream and add with mayonnaise and stuffed olives. Turn into mold and chill. When firm, unmold on lettuce and garnish with stuffed olives, sliced. Serve with mayonnaise sprinkled with paprika.

ARTICHOKE GRAPEFRUIT SALAD
Serves 4
(Pastel and picture pretty)

- 1 (15-ounce) can artichoke hearts
- ¼ cup salad oil
- 2 tablespoons vinegar
- 1 teaspoon Worcestershire sauce
- ½ teaspoon salt
- ⅛ teaspoon pepper
- 1 tablespoon chopped parsley
  Lettuce, romaine, endive
- 2 pink grapefruit, sectioned

Drain artichoke hearts and cut in halves. Combine oil, vinegar, salt, Worcestershire sauce, pepper and parsley, mixing well. Pour over artichokes in bowl and chill for several hours. Combine greens; add artichoke mixture and grapefruit; toss and serve.

ARTICHOKE RICE SALAD

- 1 package chicken rice combination mix (cooked as directed)
- 3 green onions, chopped
- ½ green pepper, chopped
- 8 to 10 pimiento green olives, chopped
- 2 jars marinated artichoke hearts in oil (dice and reserve liquid)
- ¼ teaspoon curry powder
- ⅓ cup mayonnaise
  Oil from 1 jar artichokes
  Salt and pepper to taste

Mix onion, pepper, olives and artichokes with cooled rice combination mix. In separate bowl, mix mayonnaise, oil and curry powder. Pour this dressing over rice mixture. Add salt and pepper. Mix and refrigerate overnight.

BROCCOLI SALAD

- 1 large bunch broccoli, finely cut (may use frozen)
- 2 cups grated mozzarella cheese
- ½ pound bacon, fried and crumbled
- 1 small red onion, finely cut

Mix together and add dressing (recipe follows).

Dressing:
- 1 cup mayonnaise
- 2 tablespoons vinegar
- ¼ cup sugar

Refrigerate several hours.

LETTUCE STUFFED SALAD

- 1 medium head iceberg lettuce, washed and well-drained
- 1 (1¼-ounce) package blue cheese
- 2 (3-ounce) packages cream cheese
- 2 tablespoons mayonnaise
- 2 tablespoons minced green onion
- 6 sliced pimiento-stuffed olives
- 2 teaspoons sweet relish
  Salt and pepper to taste
- ½ teaspoon Worcestershire sauce
  Dash hot pepper sauce
- 2 slices crisp-fried bacon, well-drained
  Sliced apples for bed

Hollow out the heart of lettuce, leaving a 1½-inch shell. Beat cheeses and mayonnaise together until smooth. Add remaining ingredients and mix well. Fill lettuce shell; wrap well in a clean towel and chill 1–2 hours, or until cheese is firm. Cut into crosswise slices ¾-inch thick. To serve,

layer a platter with sliced apples. Set the sliced lettuce over apples and serve.

BAKED MACARONI SALAD
Serves 4

- 2 pounds macaroni salad
- ½ pound baked *or* boiled ham, diced
- ¼ pound sliced cheddar cheese, cut up
- 1 tablespoon melted margarine
- ¼ cup seasoned bread crumbs

Preheat oven to 350 degrees. In greased 1¼-quart casserole, combine macaroni salad, ham and cheese. In cup combine melted margarine and bread crumbs. Sprinkle over top of macaroni salad. Bake for 20–25 minutes.

SANTA FE SALAD
Serves 4–6

- 1 head iceberg lettuce
- 2 cups cooked pinto beans
- ¼ pound grated longhorn cheese
- 2 tablespoons chopped green chili
- 6½ ounces tortilla chips, crushed
- 4 ounces prepared herb oil and vinegar salad dressing
- 1 avocado, sliced
- 2 tomatoes, cut in wedges
  Ripe pitted olives

Tear crisp lettuce into bite-size pieces. Toss with beans, grated cheese, green chili and tortilla chips. Toss salad lightly with dressing. Garnish with avocado slices, tomato wedges and ripe olives. Serve chilled.

RED AND GREEN HOLIDAY SALAD
Serves 4

- 2 cups torn lettuce leaves, rinsed and patted dry
- 2 cups fresh broccoli florets
- ½ pint cherry tomatoes
- ⅓ cup olive oil
- 2 tablespoons lemon juice
- ¼ teaspoon mustard
- ¼ teaspoon salt
  Pinch of pepper
- ½ cup croutons, seasoned with herbs and cheese

Line salad bowl with lettuce. Arrange broccoli and tomatoes on top. Combine oil, lemon juice, mustard, salt and pepper in a small bowl. Mix well; pour over salad. Sprinkle with croutons.

FRENCH-POTATO AND CUCUMBER SALAD
Serves 6

- 2 pounds medium-size red-skinned potatoes (about 12), cut in quarters
- ¼ cup vegetable oil
- 2 tablespoons red-wine vinegar
- 2 tablespoons coarse-grain prepared mustard
- 1 teaspoon salt
- 1 large cucumber, peeled or not peeled

Cook potatoes in boiling water to cover for 15–20 minutes until fork-tender. Meanwhile, whisk oil, vinegar, mustard and salt in a large serving bowl. Drain potatoes and add while hot to the dressing. Gently stir to coat. When cool, cover and marinate at least 2 hours, turning occasionally. Just before serving, cut cucumber in half lengthwise, then cut crosswise in thin slices. Add to potatoes and toss to mix.

BROCCOLI AND MUSHROOMS ELEGANT SALAD

- 2 bunches (stalks) fresh broccoli
- 1 pound fresh mushrooms
- 1 bottle Zesty Italian dressing

Cut broccoli into flowerets. Add thickly sliced mushrooms. Pour Italian dressing over broccoli and mushrooms. Add tight-fitting cover. Refrigerate several hours or overnight, turning occasionally. This is very good and is really elegant-looking when served in a pretty dish. Perfect for potluck dinners and church suppers. Only you will know how easy it is!

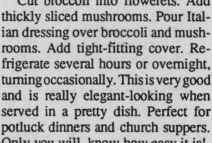

CHICK-PEA AND SPINACH SALAD

- 6 ounces dried chick-peas
- 1 pound fresh spinach
- 6 tablespoons olive oil
- 2 tablespoons wine vinegar
  Salt and pepper
- ½ cup plain yogurt
- 2 tablespoons chopped parsley

Soak chick-peas in cold water overnight. Strain. Put in large saucepan and add about 4 cups fresh water. Bring to a boil; cover; simmer gently for 1½ hours, or until peas are tender but not mushy. Let peas cool in the cooking liquid, then drain.

Wash spinach; discard any coarse or damaged leaves, and pull off all stems. Cut large leaves into pieces; leave small leaves whole. Combine chick-peas and spinach in a salad bowl. Pour in oil and vinegar; add salt and

pepper to taste. Toss ingredients together, but gently, so as not to break up peas. Chill salad until ready to serve. At serving time, arrange the mixture in a shallow bowl and top with yogurt. Sprinkle parsley over all.

BEST PEA SALAD

- 1 (14-ounce) can small-kernel white corn
- 1 can small-size peas
- 1 can French green beans
- 1 cup diced celery
- 1/4 cup fresh onion
- 1 green pepper, chopped
  Sliced olives as desired for taste

Dressing:
- 1 cup sugar
- 3/4 cup white vinegar
- 1/2 cup oil
- 1/2 teaspoon salt
- 1/4 teaspoon pepper

Boil together dressing ingrredients for about 3 minutes—then cool.

Put vegetables in bowl. Pour dressing over vegetables and marinate in refrigerator for about 24 hours before serving.

CUCUMBERS WITH YOGURT
Serves 8

- 2 medium cucumbers, peeled, seeded and diced
  Salt
- 1 garlic clove, mashed *or* minced
- 2 cups yogurt
- 2 tablespoons fresh lemon juice
- 1 teaspoon chopped dill
- 2 tablespoons olive oil
- 1 tablespoon chopped fresh mint *or* 1 teaspoon dried mint

Sprinkle cucumbers with salt; let stand 15 minutes and pour off liquid. Mash garlic in bowl with lemon juice; add yogurt, dill and cucumbers; mix well and chill. When serving, sprinkle with oil and mint.

GAZPACHO SALAD MOLD

- 1 envelope unflavored gelatin
- ¼ cup chicken broth
- 1¾ cups tomato juice
- ¼ cup minced green pepper
- ¼ cup chopped celery
- ¼ cup sliced green onion
- ¼ cup chopped cucumber
- 1 tablespoon Worcestershire sauce
- ¾ teaspoon lemon juice
  Dash celery salt
- 2 small tomatoes, chopped
  Lettuce

In small bowl sprinkle gelatin over chicken broth. Soften for 10 minutes. In medium saucepan combine tomato juice, green pepper, celery, green onion, cucumber, Worcestershire sauce, lemon juice and celery salt. Simmer 5 minutes. Remove from heat and stir in gelatin. Stir until dissolved. Set saucepan in cold water and stir until cool. Fold in tomatoes. Pour mixture into a small, shallow rectangular-shaped pan. Chill, covered, for 4 hours or overnight. Cut in squares or rectangles and serve on lettuce leaves.

BROCCOLI-RAISIN SALAD

- 3 heads broccoli, cut in small pieces
- ½ cup chopped onion
- 4 slices bacon, cooked and crumbled
- ¾ cup raisins

Toss ingredients together.

Dressing:
- 1 cup mayonnaise
- 2 tablespoons sugar
- 2 tablespoons white vinegar

Dressing should be tangy in flavor. Pour over salad. Again, toss lightly.

LEMON-LIME VEGETABLE SALAD
Serves 5–6

- 2 medium carrots, grated
- 1 stalk celery, thinly sliced
- 1 medium green pepper, seeded and finely chopped
- ½ small onion, finely chopped
- 2 tablespoons lemon juice
  Dash paprika
- 1 tablespoon water
- 1 envelope gelatin
- 1½ cups lemon-lime–flavor soda

Prepare vegetables and set aside. In small saucepan, mix lemon juice, paprika and water; heat almost to boiling point. Remove from heat and add gelatin, stirring until thoroughly dissolved. Add soda and stir until well-mixed. Add vegetables and pour into small, rectangular dish. Chill for several hours or overnight until set. Cut into squares and serve. Top with a dollop of mayonnaise, if desired.

BURGUNDY BEET SALAD
Serves 7

- 1 pound cooked beets, skinned and diced
- ½ cup walnuts, finely chopped
- 1 tablespoon prepared horseradish
- ⅓ cup unflavored yogurt
- 1¼ teaspoons mayonnaise
- ¼ cup half-and-half or cream
- ⅓ cup orange juice
- ¼ teaspoon salt
- ⅛ teaspoon pepper
- 2 tablespoons parsley, chopped

Place beets and walnuts in a salad or serving bowl; stir in horseradish, yogurt, mayonnaise, half-and-half and orange juice. Mix thoroughly; season with salt and pepper. When serving, sprinkle each serving with the chopped parsley.

CHINESE COLD PLATE
Serves 6

- 4 cups shredded lettuce
- ⅔ cup cooked rice, chilled
- 1 cup frozen peas, thawed
- ¾ cup lean pork, cooked and diced
- ½ cup water chestnuts, sliced
- ¼ cup Miracle Whip salad dressing
- ¼ cup sour cream
- ½ teaspoon celery seed
  Salt to taste

Toss first 5 ingredients together. Combine next 4 ingredients for dressing. Pour over vegetable-meat mixture and toss.

Chill until served. Garnish with pineapple slices and fresh strawberries.

FRESH SPINACH SALAD

- 1 package fresh spinach
- 1 (No. 2) can bean sprouts, rinsed and drained
- 1 (8-ounce) can water chestnuts, drained and sliced
- 4 hardcooked eggs, sliced
- 1 medium onion
- ½ package bacon, fried and crumbled

Dressing:
- ¾ cup sugar
- ¾ cup vinegar
- ¼ cup oil
- ⅓ cup ketchup
- 2 teaspoons salt
- 1 teaspoon Worcestershire sauce

Tear clean, crisp, well-drained spinach leaves in a large bowl. Add other ingredients. Mix dressing ingredients and pour over salad. Toss well and serve immediately.

QUICK MACARONI SALAD
Serves 10

1 box macaroni and cheese dinner
1 can tuna, drained
4 eggs, hard cooked
5 tablespoons mayonnaise
1/4 cup chopped pickles

Cook macaroni and cheese dinner as directed on package. Then add and mix all additional ingredients; refrigerate.

FROZEN SEAFOOD SALAD MOLD
Serves 4–6

2 teaspoons unflavored gelatin
1/3 cup cold water
2 cups flaked cooked seafood (crab, shrimp *or* lobster)
2/3 cup tomato ketchup
2 tablespoons lemon juice
3 tablespoons vinegar
1 teaspoon prepared horseradish
1/4 teaspoon salt
1/2 cup mayonnaise
Tomatoes *or* lettuce

Soften gelatin in cold water and dissolve over hot water. Combine with seafood, ketchup, lemon juice, vinegar, horseradish and salt. Fold in mayonnaise. Freeze in refrigerator tray until firm, about 2 hours. Cut into cubes and arrange on slices of tomatoes or lettuce.

Note: Serve Frozen Seafood Salad in hollowed-out tomatoes or in cucumber boats ... or serve as a loaf on watercress with border of overlapping cucumber and tomato slices.

FROZEN WALDORF SALAD

1/2 cup sugar
1/2 cup pineapple juice
1/8 teaspoon salt
1/4 cup lemon juice
1/2 cup diced celery
1/2 cup crushed pineapple, drained
2 medium apples, diced with skins left on
1/2 cup walnuts *or* pecans, broken in small pieces
1 cup heavy cream, whipped

Combine sugar, pineapple juice, salt and lemon juice in saucepan. Cook over medium heat, stirring until thick. Let cool. Stir in celery, pineapple, apples and nuts. Fold in whipped cream.

Spoon into an 8-inch square pan or individual molds. Freeze. Garnish with maraschino cherries. Allow salad to be at room temperature for about 20 minutes before serving.

CUCUMBER DELIGHT

1 (3-ounce) package lime gelatin
3/4 cup boiling water
1 package unflavored gelatin
1/4 cup cold water
1 cup salad dressing
1 tablespoon finely minced onion
1 cup cottage cheese
1 cucumber, peeled and chopped
1/8 to 1/4 teaspoon Tabasco sauce
1 clove garlic, minced
1/2 cup slivered almonds
Green food coloring

Dissolve lime gelatin in boiling water, then unflavored gelatin in cold water. Put salad dressing, onion, cottage cheese, cucumber, Tabasco sauce, garlic and almonds in blender; blend well. Then add lime and unflavored gelatins; blend again. Add green food coloring for a more vivid color. Mold and chill overnight.

This is so creamy and good!

ORANGE CHICKEN SALAD
Serves 2

2 cups cooked, cubed chicken
1 cup sliced celery
1/4 cup chopped walnuts
1 teaspoon grated onion
1/2 teaspoon salt
1/3 cup orange juice
1/4 cup mayonnaise
2 oranges, peeled and sectioned
1/4 cup dry bread crumbs
1/4 cup grated Parmesan cheese

Combine chicken, celery, walnuts, onion, salt, orange juice and mayonnaise in mixing bowl; mix well. Cover and refrigerate for 1 hour. Stir in orange sections. Spoon mixture into casserole; sprinkle with bread crumbs and Parmesan cheese. Bake in a preheated 350-degree oven for 25 minutes, or until mixture is heated through and cheese is lightly browned. Serve with rolls.

CHRISTMAS TREE SALAD

1 1/2 cups canned fruit cocktail
1 package lime gelatin
2 tablespoons lemon juice
Whipped cream

Drain fruit cocktail, reserving syrup. Add enough hot water to syrup to make 2 cups liquid. Dissolve gelatin in hot liquid; stir in lemon juice. Cool until slightly thickened; fold in 1 cup fruit cocktail. Set cone-shaped paper cups lined with waxed paper into small glasses. Fill with thickened gelatin mixture. Chill until firm. Unmold onto individual dessert plates, gently pulling off paper. Trim trees with whipped cream festoons piped on with cake decorating tube; decorate base of tree with remaining fruit cocktail.

This is bound to get raves and compliments from your guests!

SANTA'S RED RASPBERRY RING
Serves 8–10

1 (10-ounce) package frozen red raspberries, thawed
2 (3-ounce) packages raspberry-flavored gelatin
2 cups boiling water
1 pint vanilla ice cream
1 (6-ounce) can (¾ cup) frozen pink lemonade concentrate, thawed
¼ cup pecans

Drain raspberries, reserving syrup. Dissolve gelatin in boiling water. Add ice cream by spoonfuls, stirring until melted. Stir in lemonade concentrate and reserved syrup. Chill until partially set. Add raspberries and pecans. Turn into a 6-cup ring mold. Chill until firm.

PEPPERONI SALAD
Serves 6–8

1 medium onion, thinly sliced
8 ounces pepperoni, thinly sliced
¼ cup crumbled bleu cheese
⅔ cup salad oil
⅓ cup cider vinegar
Salt and freshly ground pepper to taste
10 ounces fresh spinach, washed thoroughly, dried and chopped
½ head iceberg lettuce, chopped

One day before serving, separate onion slices into rings and place in large bowl; add pepperoni slices and bleu cheese. Add oil, vinegar, salt and pepper. Toss in the spinach and lettuce. Chill salad overnight in covered bowl.

ORANGE-CREAM SALAD
Serves 10

1 (20-ounce) can pineapple chunks, drained
1 (16-ounce) can peach slices, drained
1 (11-ounce) can mandarin orange sections, drained
3 medium bananas, sliced
2 medium apples, cored and chopped
1 (3-1/3 to 3-3/4 ounce) package vanilla instant pudding mix
1-1/2 cups milk
1/2 of a 6-ounce can (1/3 cup) frozen orange juice concentrate, thawed
3/4 cup dairy sour cream
Lettuce

In a large bowl combine pineapple chunks, peaches, orange sections, bananas, and apples; set aside. In small bowl combine dry pudding mix, milk, and orange juice concentrate. Beat with rotary beater 1 to 2 minutes or until well blended. Beat in sour cream. Fold into fruit mixture. Cover and refrigerate several hours. Serve salad on lettuce leaves.

RASPBERRY-WINE MOLD
Serves 4–6

1 (16-ounce) can raspberries
½ cup red wine
Water
2 (3-ounce) packages raspberry-flavored gelatin

Drain raspberries into 2-cup measure; add ½ cup red wine and water to make 2 cups. Prepare raspberry gelatin, using berry-wine-water mixture. Pour into individual molds. Add raspberries to molds when gelatin has cooled. When firm, invert onto serving plates.

THREE-FRUIT MOLDED SALAD

2 envelopes unflavored gelatin
½ cup grapefruit juice
½ cup sugar syrup*
¼ cup orange juice
1 teaspoon lemon juice
2 cups ginger ale
Pinch of salt
½ cup cherries, drained
1 cup grapefruit sections
1 cup orange sections
Lettuce

In top of double boiler over medium heat, combine gelatin with the grapefruit juice and stir to dissolve the gelatin. Remove from heat. Add sugar syrup, orange and lemon juices, ginger ale and salt. Stir well. Chill until slightly thickened. Add cherries, grapefruit and orange sections. Pour and spoon into a lightly oiled 6-cup mold or 6 individual (1-cup) molds. Chill until firm, about 1–2 hours. Unmold and serve on a bed of lettuce. Top each serving with a dollop of mayonnaise.

*To make sugar syrup, combine ½ cup sugar and ½ cup boiling water.

YOGI BERRY SALAD

1 Red Delicious apple, cored and chopped
1 cup halved, seedless green grapes
1 cup sliced strawberries
½ cup sliced celery
¼ cup raisins
½ cup lemon yogurt
2 tablespoons sunflower seeds
Lettuce

In a bowl, combine apple, grapes, strawberries, celery and raisins. Toss gently. Fold in yogurt. Cover and chill. Just before serving, stir in sunflower seeds. Serve on lettuce leaves.

OLIVE WREATH MOLD

- 1 (20-ounce) can crushed pineapple
- 1 (3-ounce) package lime gelatin
- ¼ teaspoon salt
- ½ cup grated cheddar *or* American cheese
- ½ cup chopped pimientos, drained
- ½ cup chopped celery
- ⅔ cup chopped pecans
- 1 cup whipping cream
  Stuffed green olives

Drain pineapple into saucepan. Reserve pineapple. Heat juice; add gelatin and dissolve thoroughly. Let cool in refrigerator until it starts to thicken. Stir in salt. Add cheese, pimientos, celery, pecans and reserved pineapple. Whip cream and fold into gelatin mixture. Line bottom of a 4-cup mold with sliced green olives. Carefully spoon mixture into mold. Chill until firm. Unmold and serve.

HOLIDAY DELIGHT
Serves 10–12

- 2 large packages lime gelatin
- ½ pint whipping cream, whipped
- 1 small can crushed pineapple, drained
- 1 small jar maraschino cherries, drained and sliced
- 1 cup miniature marshmallows

Prepare gelatin in large bowl according to package directions. Place gelatin bowl on ice. Beat with rotary beater until fluffy and firm. Fold in whipped cream. Combine pineapple, cherries and marshmallows with gelatin. Pour into lightly greased mold. Refrigerate overnight.

24-HOUR SALAD

- 1 can Eagle Brand sweetened condensed milk (not evaporated)
- 1 cup large grapes, seeded and halved
- 1 cup nuts, coarsely broken
- 1 (8-ounce) can crushed pineapple, including juice
- ½ pound small marshmallows
- 1 package Dream Whip (whipped) *or* equal amount of Cool Whip
- ¼ cup vinegar
- 1 teaspoon prepared mustard

Mix milk, vinegar and mustard together, then add all other ingredients. Make the day before, if needed.

CRANBERRY MALLOW SALAD
Serves 10–12

- 2 cups raw cranberries, ground
- 4 cups miniature marshmallows
- ½ cup sugar
- 1 (8-ounce) can crushed pineapple, drained
- ½ cup chopped nuts
- ¼ cup unpared, chopped apple
- 1 cup whipping cream, whipped

Add marshmallows, sugar and pineapple to ground cranberries. Chill overnight. Add apple and nuts. Fold in whipped cream. Chill.

BING CHERRY SALAD

- 1 (3-ounce) package cherry gelatin
- 1 cup boiling water
- 1 large can black bing cherries

- ½ pint sour cream
- ½ cup chopped pecans

Dissolve gelatin in bowl with boiling water. Drain cherry juice and add to water. Refrigerate until gelatin begins to form, about 70 minutes. Beat sour cream into gelatin; add cherries and pecans. Pour mixture into a 9 x 9 x 2-inch square pan and refrigerate until firm.

THANKSGIVING MINCEMEAT MOLD
Serves 10–12

- 2 large packages cherry gelatin
- 3½ cups hot water
- ½ cup walnuts, finely chopped
- 2 cups moist mincemeat

Dissolve cherry gelatin in hot water. Pour ¾ cup mixture into 1½-quart mold; chill until firm. Chill remaining gelatin until slightly thickened; fold in nuts and mincemeat. Turn into mold over firm gelatin; chill again until firm; unmold. Garnish with sweetened whipped cream, maraschino cherry halves and mint leaves.

CRANBERRY-PLUS RELISH
Makes 7½ cups

- 4 cups (1 pound) fresh *or* frozen cranberries
- 4 oranges, peeled, sectioned and seeded
- 2 cups sugar (add less for tart taste)
- 1 apple, unpeeled and cut up
- ½ teaspoon almond flavoring
- 1 (8½-ounce) can crushed pineapple, undrained

Chop cranberries in a food processor, then add oranges and chop. Add remaining ingredients; pulse for several seconds to blend. Chill several hours before serving.

FRUIT AND COTTAGE CHEESE MOLD
Serves 4

2 teaspoons unflavored gelatin
3 tablespoons canned pineapple juice
2½ cups cottage cheese
   Lettuce *or* other greens
   Sliced pineapple
   Strawberries
   French dressing

Soften gelatin in pineapple juice and dissolve over hot water. Stir into cottage cheese. Pour into 1 large or 6 individual oiled molds and chill until firm. Unmold on lettuce or other greens and garnish with sliced pineapple and halved strawberries. Serve with French dressing.

LOW-CALORIE PINEAPPLE SALAD
Serves 8

2 (8-ounce) packages lemon gelatin
2 cups boiling water
1 (1-pound) can grapefruit sections, drained
1 (8-ounce) can crushed pineapple, drained
2 cups (1 pint) plain low-fat yogurt

In bowl, combine the gelatin and boiling water. Stir until dissolved. Add drained fruits; mix until blended. Chill until mixture is syrupy. Add the yogurt and mix well. Turn into a 1½-quart mold and chill until firm.

CONGEALED FRUIT SALAD

2 (3-ounce) packages strawberry gelatin
2 cups boiling water

---

1 (10-ounce) package frozen strawberries, thawed
2 ripe bananas
1 (8-ounce) can crushed pineapple, not drained
1 cup sour cream

Mix strawberry gelatin with boiling water; add strawberries, mashed bananas and pineapple. Chill until set. Top with sour cream.

CELERY AND ORANGE SALAD
Serves 6

3 medium oranges
2 ribs celery
2 shallots, chopped
4 tablespoons oil
1 tablespoon lemon juice
   Salt and pepper
   Chopped parsley

Peel oranges, cutting just beneath the pith. Hold the fruit in one hand and cut out each segment, freeing it from its protective membranes as you cut. Cut the celery into 1½-inch julienne strips. Put the shallots, oranges and celery into a bowl; add the remaining ingredients and toss. Allow salad to rest for 1–6 hours before serving.

SALAD BY CANDLELIGHT
Serves 2

2 lettuce leaves
1 banana, cut in half crosswise
2 pineapple rings
1 cherry *or* red grape, cut in half

On two small plates, place lettuce leaves. Place pineapple in center of leaf. Stand ½ banana in hole of each pineapple ring. Attach cherry half on top of each banana to represent a flame. Now doesn't that look like a candle?

ORANGE DELIGHT

2 cups small-curd cottage cheese
2 cups crushed pineapple, drained
2 small *or* 1 large package orange-flavored gelatin
2 cups whipped topping

Fold all ingredients together; chill before serving. For fewer calories, use low-fat cottage cheese, unsweetened pineapple and sugar-free gelatin.

FRUIT WALDORF
Serves 4

2 cups diced apples (small)
1 cup diced pineapple
2 tablespoons (*or* less) honey
½ cup chopped walnuts
½ cup coconut

Combine and mix all ingredients together well. Chill thoroughly before serving on a bed of lettuce.

FRUIT SALAD

1 can fruit cocktail, drained
1 can tidbit pineapple, drained
3 apples
1 orange
2 or 3 bananas
1 bottle maraschino cherries
1 cup miniature marshmallows
1 cup Cool Whip
   Sauce (recipe follows)

Sauce for Fruit Salad:
2 tablespoons vinegar
2 eggs
2 tablespoons sugar

Beat eggs. Add sugar and beat well. Add vinegar. Cook mixture in double boiler until thick; cool. Add cooled sauce to salad; fold in Cool Whip.

FRUIT COCKTAIL SALAD

1 (5-5/8 ounce) package vanilla flavored Jello instant pudding mix
1-1/3 cups buttermilk
1 (8-ounce) container Cool Whip
1 (30-ounce) can fruit cocktail, well-drained
2 cans mandarin oranges, well-drained
1 cup miniature rainbow-colored - marshmallows (optional)

Blend buttermilk into pudding mix using medium speed of mixer. When smooth, blend in Cool Whip. If consistency of mixture seems too thick, add a little more buttermilk. Fold in fruit cocktail and mandarin oranges, reserving half a can of oranges for garnish. Swirl a design on top of salad with a tablespoon. Gently arrange balance of mandarin orange slices in swirled design on top of salad.

Add colored marshmallows to mixture before garnishing, if desired.

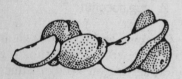

GOLDEN FRUIT SALAD

2 large Golden Delicious apples, diced
2 large Red Delicious apples, diced
4 large bananas, sliced
2 (20 ounce) cans pineapple chunks, drained (reserve juice)
2 (16 ounce) cans Mandarin oranges, drained
Whole green grapes, optional

Mix Together:
1 cup sugar
4 tablespoons corn starch
Reserved pineapple juice
2 tablespoons lemon juice
2/3 cup orange juice

Stir and boil 1 minute. Pour hot mixture over fruit. Leave uncovered until cool.

SHORTCUT FROZEN SALAD

1 small package *instant* lemon pudding
1 pint whipped topping, thawed
1/2 cup mayonnaise
2 tablespoons lemon juice
1 (1-pound) can fruit cocktail, drained
1 cup miniature marshmallows
1/4 cup chopped pecans

Prepare pudding according to package directions; blend in whipped topping, mayonnaise, and lemon juice. Fold in remaining ingredients. Turn into a 9x5x3-inch loaf pan and freeze until firm. Slice to serve.

GUM DROP FRUIT SALAD

Serves 8

1 (#2 can) pineapple tidbits
1/4 cup sugar
2 tablespoons flour
1/4 teaspoon salt
3 tablespoons lemon juice
1-1/2 teaspoons vinegar
2 cups seedless grapes, halved
2 cups miniature white marshmallows
2/3 cup gumdrops, halved (do not use black drops)
1 (4-ounce) bottle maraschino cherries, drained and halved
1/4 cup chopped pecans
1 cup whipping cream, whipped

Drain pineapple, reserving 1/3 cup of syrup. Combine sugar, flour, and salt. Add reserved pineapple syrup, lemon juice, and vinegar. Cook over medium heat, stirring constantly until thick and boiling. Continue cooking 1 minute. Set aside and cool. Combine pineapple and remaining ingredients, except the whipped cream. Fold the cooked dressing into the whipped cream. Cover and refrigerate for 12-24 hours.

BANANA BAVARIAN CREAM

1 (6-ounce) package lemon-flavored gelatin
2 cups hot water
1/4 teaspoon salt
2/3 cup sugar
1/2 cup heavy cream
5 bananas

Dissolve gelatin in hot water. Add salt and sugar. Chill until cold and syrupy. Fold in cream, whipped only until thick and shiny, but not stiff. Crush bananas to pulp with fork, and fold at once into mixture. Chill until slightly thickened. Turn into mold. Chill until firm. Unmold. Serve with Strawberry Sauce. (Recipe below)

Strawberry Sauce:
1/3 cup butter
1 cup powdered sugar
1 egg white
2/3 cup strawberries

Cream butter and sugar, gradually add crushed strawberries and egg whites. Beat well.

BUNNY SALAD

Serves 6-8

1 (3-ounce) package orange gelatin
1 cup boiling water
1 cup pineapple juice and water
1 teaspoon grated orange rind
1-1/3 cups crushed pineapple, drained
1 cup grated raw carrots

Dissolve gelatin in boiling water. Add pineapple juice/water mixture and orange rind. Chill until slightly thickened. Then fold in pineapple and carrots. Pour into 6-8 individual round molds. Chill until firm. Unmold on crisp lettuce. Add carrot strips to form ears, a large marshmallow for the head, and half a marshmallow for the tail. Serve plain or with mayonnaise, if desired.

SLICED CUCUMBERS IN SOUR CREAM
Serves 4

2 cups thinly sliced cucumbers
1/4 cup sliced Spanish onions
1/4 cup seasoned vinegar
1/4 cup sour cream

Pour vinegar over cucumbers and onions, let stand 15 minutes. Drain in a strainer and discard liquid. Combine sour cream with cucumbers. Serve icy cold.

CUCUMBER-YOGURT SALAD
Serves 6

5 cups thinly sliced cucumbers (2 large)
3/4 cup thinly sliced red onion (1 small)
1 (8-ounce) carton plain low-fat yogurt
3 tablespoons wine vinegar
1 tablespoon lemon juice
1 tablespoon minced fresh basil
1 clove garlic, crushed
1 teaspoon Dijon mustard
1/8 teaspoon salt
1/8 teaspoon pepper

Combine cucumber and onion in large bowl; cover and chill. Combine yogurt and remaining ingredients in a small bowl; stir to blend. Cover and chill. Pour mixture over vegetables and toss. Serve immediately. (45 calories per serving)

CELERY SLAW
Serves 6

3 cups celery, thinly sliced
1/2 cup carrots, grated
1 apple, unpeeled, cored, and diced
1/2 cup mayonnaise
2 tablespoons sugar
1/2 teaspoon salt

2 tablespoons vinegar
1/2 cup walnuts, coarsely chopped (optional)

Combine celery, carrots, and apples. Thoroughly blend remaining ingredients and fold into celery mixture. If desired, fold in walnuts or sprinkle over top as a garnish. Chill at least 30 minutes before serving in lettuce-lined bowl. Delightfully crunchy!

SWEET-SOUR CABBAGE SLAW
Serves 6-8

3 cups finely-shredded cabbage
1 tablespoon grated onion
1/2 teaspoon celery salt
1 tablespoon sugar
1 tablespoon vinegar
1/4 teaspoon salt
1/8 teaspoon cayenne pepper
1/2 cup heavy cream, whipped or sour cream

Combine cabbage, onion, and celery salt. Blend together sugar, vinegar, salt, pepper, and cream. Pour over cabbage and toss.

YOGURT COLESLAW
Serves 10-12

1 cup unflavored yogurt
1/4 cup mayonnaise
1/2 teaspoon dry mustard
1 teaspoon seasoned salt
1/2 teaspoon salt
1/2 teaspoon celery salt
1/8 teaspoon pepper
1/4 cup chopped onion
2 tablespoons sugar
8 cups shredded cabbage
1 medium carrot, grated
1/2 cup grated green pepper

Combine yogurt, mayonnaise, dry mustard, seasoned salt, salt, celery salt, pepper, onion, and sugar in a medium bowl. Cover and chill.

Combine cabbage, carrots, and green peppers in large bowl. Pour chilled dressing over vegetables, tossing lightly. Serve immediately.

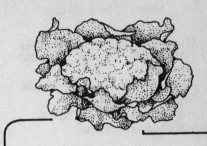

FRUITED COLE SLAW

1 medium head cabbage, shredded
1 medium carrot, grated
1/2 cup crushed pineapple, drained
1 teaspoon salt

Mix salt with cabbage and let stand about half an hour. Squeeze out excess moisture and add carrot and pineapple.

1 cup vinegar
1/2 cup water
1-1/2 cups sugar
1 teaspoon dry mustard
1 teaspoon celery seed

Combine and boil these ingredients 1 minute. Cool. Pour over cabbage, carrot and pineapple mixture; toss to blend. Serve as a chilled salad, if desired. (This slaw can be frozen.)

SPINACH SALAD

2 to 3 packages fresh spinach
1 pound cooked bacon, chopped
1 can water chestnuts, chopped
1 can bean sprouts
2 hard-cooked eggs, chopped

Wash spinach thoroughly and break into bite-size pieces. Add remaining ingredients.
Dressing:
1 cup salad oil (Mazola)
1/4 cup ketchup
1/2 cup vinegar
1/2 cup sugar

Stir dressing into salad and toss well.

115

CHERRY FROZEN SALAD

Makes 32-34 small cups

1 (16-ounce) can cherry pie filling
1 large can crushed pineapple, drained
1 can sweetened condensed milk
1 large carton Cool Whip
2 cups miniature marshmallows
1 cup chopped pecans

Mix all together in order given. Spoon into paper cups. Freeze.

This is delicious and can also be used as a dessert.

SPRINGTIME SALAD

Serves 6

1 (1-pound) can grapefruit sections
4 green onions, thinly sliced
1/2 cup sliced radishes
1/2 cup cucumber, sliced or greens of your choice

Drain grapefruit. Wash and dry greens (of your choice) and tear into bite-size pieces. Add grapefruit sections, onions, radishes, and cucumber. Toss and serve with a Roquefort dressing, before serving.

MOUNTAIN DEW SALAD

1 large package lemon gelatin
1-2/3 cups boiling water
1 cup small marshmallows
1 cup Mountain Dew soda
1 (#303 can) crushed pineapple, drain
1 can lemon pudding or pie filling
1 medium container Cool Whip

Mix gelatin in boiling water with marshmallows until dissolved. Add Mountain Dew and drained pineapple. Chill until set. Mix pudding and Cool Whip. Spread on top of gelatin which has set.

SILHOUETTE SALAD

Serves 4

1 envelope Knox unflavored gelatin
1 cup water, divided
1 (10-1/2 ounce) can condensed cream of chicken soup
1 tablespoon lemon juice
1/8 teaspoon pepper
1 (5-ounce) can boned chicken, diced
1/2 cup diced celery
1/4 cup chopped green pepper
2 tablespoons chopped pimiento
2 teaspoons grated onion

Sprinkle gelatin on 1/2 cup water to soften. Place over low heat and stir until gelatin is dissolved. Remove from heat; stir in soup until well-blended. Add other 1/2 cup water, lemon juice, and pepper. Chill until the consistency of unbeaten egg white. Fold in chicken, onion, green pepper, and pimiento. Turn into a 3-cup mold and chill until firm.

MOUNTAIN DEW SALAD

1 (6-ounce) package lemon gelatin
1 cup boiling water
1 can cold Mountain Dew beverage
1 (15-ounce) can pineapple chunks or tidbits, drained and juice reserved
1 package lemon pudding (cooked type)
1 cup whipping cream (whipped) or Cool Whip
1 cup colored mini marshmallows

Dissolve gelatin in boiling water; add Mountain Dew and juice drained from pineapple; chill until it begins to thicken. Cook pudding according to package instructions; cool.

Mix gelatin, lemon pudding, and whipped cream, beating together. Add drained pineapple and marshmallows. Pour into a large bowl and chill.

COTTAGE CHEESE DELIGHT

1 quart cottage cheese
1 can crushed pineapple, drained
1 (6-ounce) box orange gelatin
1 small package miniature marshmallows
1 large container Cool Whip

Mix cottage cheese, pineapple, and gelatin powder together. Blend in marshmallows and Cool Whip; chill before serving.

SHAMROCK SALAD

First Layer:
1 (3-ounce) package lime gelatin
1 small can undrained crushed pineapple

Dissolve gelatin in one cup hot water, then cool. Add pineapple. Pour mixture into large mold and chill until set.

Second Layer:
1 (3-ounce) package lemon gelatin
2 (3-ounce) packages cream cheese
10 marshmallows
2 cups whipping cream

Dissolve lemon gelatin in one cup hot water. Mix one package cream cheese with one cup whipping cream. Pour mixture on top of set lime gelatin. Chill until set. Mix remaining cream cheese with one cup whipped cream and the marshmallows cut into small pieces. Turn out mold on lettuce green and top with this mixture. You may decide to serve this creation as a dessert.—Whip 1/2 cup cream; add drained maraschino cherries and drained pineapple slices, arranged, to form an attractive circle on top.

St. Patrick's Day is a special one, not only because it is the beginning of spring, but because of the teasing, elfish nature of this man who makes "everything come up green" on this day. Special foods are your way of contributing to a genial atmosphere for both children and adults. On this day, we are all the same age—Happy St. Patrick's Day!

BANANA YOGURT SALAD

2 large bananas
2 cups yogurt
1/4 cup nuts, chopped
Orange sections
Lettuce

Peel and split bananas; place in serving dishes. Spoon one cup of yogurt onto each banana. Sprinkle with nuts; surround with orange sections and shredded lettuce.

APRICOT SALAD

Serves 10-12

2 (16-ounce) cans apricots in syrup, drained. (Reserve juice)
1 (8-ounce) package cream cheese, diced
1 (3-ounce) package lemon gelatin
1 (3-ounce) package lime gelatin
1 (12-ounce) package Cool Whip

Put both gelatins in large bowl and add 2 cups boiling apricot juice, adding enough water to make 2 cups, if not enough juice. Mix until dissolved. Add diced cream cheese. Mix until smooth. Mash apricots slightly and add to gelatin mixture. Fold Cool Whip into mixture.

Pour into 13x9-inch pan. Chill overnight. May be kept in refrigerator for 2 weeks. Spoon serve, or cut into squares. This is a delicious, refreshing, simple-to-prepare salad.

BLUEBERRY SALAD

2 (3-ounce) packages grape gelatin
2 cups boiling water
1 (No. 2) can undrained crushed pineapple
1 (16-ounce) can blueberry pie filling
1 cup sour cream
1 (8-ounce) package cream cheese
1/2 cup granulated sugar
1 teaspoon vanilla

In a 9x13-inch pan, mix the gelatin and boiling water until dissolved. Add undrained pineapple and blueberry pie filling. Stir and let set in refrigerator. Mix sour cream with the softened cream cheese, sugar, and vanilla. Do not overbeat. Spread on top of the set gelatin mixture. Chill again in refrigerator. This is a great potluck dish. It can be served as salad or dessert.

TASTY APPLE SALAD

1 (20-ounce) can pineapple tidbits, drain and save juice
2 cups miniature marshmallows
1/2 cup sugar
1 tablespoon flour
1 egg, beaten
1-1/2 tablespoons vinegar
1 (8-ounce) container Cool Whip
2 cups chopped apples with skins (Red Delicious)
1-1/2 cups dry roasted peanuts, chopped

Mix pineapple juice, sugar, flour, egg, and vinegar in pan. Cook until thick. Refrigerate overnight. Next day, or 8 hours, mix together apples, nuts, Cool Whip, pineapple, marshmallows and pineapple juice; mix and refrigerate until ready to serve.

SPICY PEACH SALAD

6 large canned peach halves
1/2 stick whole cinnamon
1 teaspoon whole cloves
1/2 cup white vinegar
1/2 cup sugar

1 (3-ounce) package cream cheese
1/4 cup fresh lime juice
1/4 cup pecans, chopped

Place cinnamon stick and cloves in a small cheesecloth bag; tie firmly; cook with sugar and vinegar for 3 minutes. Remove spice bag; pour over peaches; chill. Fill center of each peach with cream cheese seasoned with lime juice and chopped pecans. To serve: Arrange each peach half on a chilled, crisp lettuce leaf.

PEACH PARTY SALAD

Serves 12

1 (6-ounce) package orange flavored gelatin
2 cups boiling water
1 (15-1/4 ounce) can crushed pineapple, undrained
2 cups canned or fresh sliced peaches, drained
1 egg, beaten
1/4 cup sugar
1-1/2 tablespoons all-purpose flour
1-1/2 tablespoons butter or margarine, softened
1/2 cup whipping cream, whipped
1/2 cup miniature marshmallows
1/2 cup (2 ounces) shredded Cheddar cheese

Dissolve gelatin in boiling water; set aside. Drain pineapple, reserving juice; set pineapple aside. Add enough water to juice to make 1 cup. Add 3/4 cup of juice mixture to gelatin mixture; chill until consistency of unbeaten egg white. Set remaining 1/4 cup of juice mixture aside. Arrange peach slices in a lightly-oiled 12 x 8 x 2 inch dish. Pour gelatin mixture over peaches. Chill until almost firm. Combine egg, sugar, flour, butter, and remaining 1/4 cup juice mixture in a small saucepan. Cook over low heat, stirring constantly until smooth and thickened; cool. Combine pineapple, whipped cream, marshmallows, and cheese; fold in egg mixture. Spread evenly over salad. Cover; chill overnight.

SPINACH-ORANGE TOSS
Serves 6

1 small onion, thinly sliced
Boiling water
6 cups (8 ounces) fresh spinach, torn
1 (11-ounce) can mandarin oranges, drained
1 cup fresh mushrooms, sliced
3 tablespoons salad oil
1 tablespoon lemon juice
1/4 teaspoon salt
Dash pepper
3/4 cup almonds, slivered

Place onions in bowl and cover with boiling water; allow to stand 10 minutes; drain; and dry on paper towels. Place spinach, which has been torn into pieces, in large salad bowl. Add onions, mandarin orange slices, and mushrooms. Toss lightly with hands; cover with plastic wrap and chill thoroughly.

For dressing, place salad oil, lemon juice, salt and pepper in a screw-top jar and shake well. Chill. Before serving, shake again and pour over spinach-orange mixture. Toss lightly until ingredients are coated. Sprinkle almonds over top and serve immediately. This is a very good side dish with Chinese food.

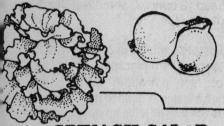

SPINACH SALAD
Serves 6

1/2 pound spinach
1/2 head iceberg lettuce
1 small red onion, thinly sliced and separated into rings
1 slivered hard-cooked egg white (yolk saved for vinaigrette)
Vinaigrette (recipe follows)

Tear spinach and lettuce into bite-size pieces and layer with onion and slivered hard-cooked egg white in a salad bowl. Add vinaigrette and toss well.

Vinaigrette:

In a small bowl mash saved hard-cooked egg yolk; add 1 teaspoon salt, 1/4 teaspoon pepper, 1/4 teaspoon paprika, 1/4 teaspoon dry mustard, 1/4 cup red wine vinegar,

1/2 cup vegetable oil, and 2 tablespoons finely chopped parsley; whisk well.

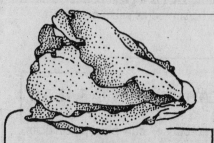

GREEN VEGETABLE SALAD

1 small can English peas, drained
1 can French style green beans, drained
1 can shoe peg corn, drained
1 cup chopped celery
1 cup chopped green pepper
1 cup chopped onion
1 small jar pimientos, chopped

Mix together 1/2 teaspoon salt, 1/2 cup vinegar, 1/2 cup salad oil and 1/3 cup sugar; stir until dissolved. Pour over vegetables; mix well and chill 4-5 hours before serving. Will keep for several days in refrigerator.

FRESH VEGETABLE SALAD

1 bunch broccoli, broken into flowerettes
1 head cauliflower, broken or sliced
1 bunch celery, sliced
1 box mushrooms, sliced
1 box cherry tomatoes, halved
1 can ripe olives, pitted and drained
1 bag radishes, sliced
3 or 4 carrots, sliced

Toss with one large bottle Italian dressing mixed with one package dry Italian dressing mix. Can prepare several hours ahead of time before serving.

GREEN VEGETABLE SALAD

1 can English peas, drained
1 can French-style green beans, drained
1 can shoe peg corn, drained
1 cup diced celery
1 cup diced green peppers
1 cup chopped green onions or regular onions
1 small can pimientos, diced

Mix together:
1/2 teaspoon salt
1/2 cup sugar
1/2 cup vinegar
1/2 cup salad oil

Stir until sugar is dissolved. Pour over vegetables. Chill overnight. Will keep for several days.

MUSHROOM SALAD
Serves 4

1 tablespoon butter
1/2 pound mushrooms, cleaned and stems trimmed
3 ounces champagne
1 teaspoon clear Karo syrup
2 tablespoons catsup
2 tablespoons raisins
1 teaspoon pine nuts (pignoli)
Coarsely shredded lettuce

Soak raisins in 1 tablespoon of champagne for 5 minutes. Drain well and set aside. Melt butter in a saucepan. Add mushrooms, and gently sauté for 2 minutes over medium heat, stirring constantly. Add the Karo syrup; mix well a few seconds. To this add champagne, catsup, pignoli, and raisins. Simmer only 1 minute. Pour mixture into a bowl and chill thoroughly. When ready to serve, be sure to serve on a bed of shredded lettuce.

EASTER CROWN SALAD

3 (3-ounce) packages cream
   cheese
1/2 teaspoon salt
2 cups grated cucumber, drained
1 cup mayonnaise
1/4 cup minced onion
1/4 cup minced parsley
1 clove garlic
1 tablespoon unflavored gelatin
1/4 cup cold water
1 head lettuce
2 hard-cooked egg yolks, sieved

Mix first 6 ingredients in a bowl that has been rubbed with garlic. Soften gelatin in cold water and dissolve over hot water. Cool to lukewarm and combine with cheese mixture. Beat thoroughly and pack into a deep spring-form pan. Chill until mixture is firm. Remove from mold onto a bed of lettuce and sprinkle sieved egg yolks over top. Garnish with radish roses, if desired.

BEAN AND TOMATO SALAD

1 (15-1/2 ounce) can garbanzo beans
3 tablespoons vegetable oil
1 tablespoon wine vinegar
Salt and pepper
1 pound tomatoes, peeled and sliced
1 medium-size onion, sliced into thin
   rings
2 teaspoons fresh chopped basil or 1
   teaspoon dried basil

Drain beans; rinse under cold water. Beat oil and vinegar together; season with salt and pepper. Add the beans and mix until well coated, being careful not to break up the beans. Arrange tomato and onion slices in a shallow dish; sprinkle with basil, salt, and pepper. Spoon beans on top. Serve chilled.

ZESTY MEXICAN BEAN SALAD

2 medium limes
1/2 of a 12-ounce jar chunky salsa
   (about 3/4 cup)
1/3 cup salad oil
1-1/2 teaspoons chili powder
1 teaspoon salt
1 (16-ounce) can black beans,
   drained
1 (15 to 19-ounce) can red kidney
   beans, drained
1 (15 to 19-ounce) can garbanzo
   beans, drained
2 celery stalks, thinly sliced
1 onion, sliced
1 medium tomato, diced

Squeeze lime juice into bowl; stir in salsa, oil, chili powder, and salt. Add beans, celery, onion and tomato. Toss to mix well. Serve at room temperature or cover and refrigerate, to serve chilled later. Many ingredients may be purchased in the Ethnic Department of your food store.

CARROT SALAD
Serves 6

1 pound carrots
1 bunch chives, chopped
1 cup mayonnaise (homemade or
   commercial variety)
2 tablespoons vinegar
Salt and pepper

Peel and finely grate carrots. Combine chives, mayonnaise, and vinegar; season with salt and pepper; blend with a whisk. Pour over carrots and let stand 15 minutes. Serve.

RAISIN-CARROT SALAD
Serves 8

1 cup seedless raisins
1-1/2 cups shredded carrots
1/2 cup celery, finely chopped
1/2 cup chopped walnuts
Pinch of salt
Dash cayenne
4 tablespoons mayonnaise

Rinse raisins in hot water; drain; cool and combine with remaining ingredients. Chill and serve on crisp lettuce.

CARROT-RAISIN SALAD

1/2 cup shredded carrots
1/2 cup seedless (or seeded) raisins
4 tablespoons lemon juice
1/4 cup mayonnaise
6-12 lettuce leaves or 1-1/2 cups
   shredded cabbage

Shred carrots. Soak raisins in lemon juice. Combine ingredients; mix with dressing. Serve in lettuce cups.

PICNIC SALAD BOWL
Serves 6

1 (No. 2) can asparagus tips
Mustard French Dressing (recipe follows)
3 hard-cooked eggs
1/3 cup deviled ham
Hearts of lettuce
2 strips pimiento
6 wedges Swiss cheese

Marinate asparagus in dressing; chill. Cut eggs lengthwise and remove yolks. Stuff with deviled ham and mashed egg yolks which have been moistened with dressing. Toss lettuce hearts in salad bowl with dressing. Arrange asparagus tips in center (held together with pimiento strips); surround with cheese; border with stuffed egg halves. May substitute cooked green beans for asparagus tips.

Mustard French Dressing:
1 cup olive or salad oil
1/4 cup vinegar
1/2 teaspoon salt
Few grains cayenne
1/4 teaspoon white pepper
2 tablespoons chopped parsley
2 teaspoons prepared mustard

Combine; beat or shake thoroughly before using. Makes 1-1/4 cups dressing.

SEAFOOD SALAD
Serves 6-8

1/2 small cabbage (about 1 pound) washed and pulled apart
1 small onion, peeled and sliced
4 tablespoons sweet pickles, finely chopped
1 cup mayonnaise
3 tablespoons sugar
12 fish sticks
12 popcorn shrimp

Combine cabbage, onion, and pickles, and chop until fine, using a hand chopper. Mix mayonnaise and sugar, and add to cabbage salad. Fry fish sticks and shrimp until golden brown; drain on paper towels. Cut six fish sticks and six shrimp into chunks. Mix into cabbage salad. Place in serving bowl. Place remaining fish sticks

SHRIMPLY GREAT MOLD
Serves 8

1-1/2 tablespoons unflavored gelatin
1/4 cup cold water
1 (10-ounce) can tomato soup
1 (8-ounce) package cream cheese, softened
20 salad shrimp, cooked, peeled and coarsely chopped
1 cup mayonnaise
1 small onion, grated
3/4 cup celery, diced finely
1 tablespoon prepared horseradish

Dissolve gelatin in cold water; set aside. In a saucepan, heat soup; add gelatin mixture; stir until dissolved. Add cream cheese; remove from heat; beat until well blended. Add remaining ingredients. Pour into a well-oiled 1-quart mold; chill until firm. Serve portion on a crisp lettuce leaf; garnish with a lemon twist.

SKILLET HAM SALAD
Serves 4

1/4 cup chopped green onions
1/4 cup chopped green pepper
2 cups diced cooked ham
1 tablespoon fat
3 cups potatoes, cooked and diced
1/4 teaspoon salt
Dash pepper
1/4 cup mayonnaise
1/2 pound sharp, processed American cheese, diced (1-1/2 cups)

Cook onions, green pepper, and meat in hot fat, stirring occasionally until meat is lightly browned. Add potatoes, salt, pepper, and mayonnaise. Heat, mixing lightly. Stir in cheese; heat just until it begins to melt. Garnish with green onions, if desired.

SUPER SUPPER SALAD
Makes 6-1/2 cups

1 (8-ounce) package chicken-flavored rice mix
2 (5-ounce) cans Swanson Mixin' Chicken
1-1/2 cups (about 2 medium) diced tomatoes
1/2 cup chopped fresh parsley
1/2 cup chopped green onion
2 tablespoons vinegar
3/4 cup undiluted evaporated milk
1/2 cup mayonnaise
1/2 teaspoon Italian seasoning

Cook rice mix according to package directions. Cool. Mix rice with chicken, tomatoes, parsley, and onion. Stir vinegar into evaporated milk until milk thickens. Add mayonnaise and Italian seasoning. Stir into rice mixture. Chill thoroughly.

CRANBERRY TURKEY SALAD
Serves 4-6

1 can whole cranberry sauce
2 cups cooked diced turkey
1 cup finely diced celery
1/2 cup chopped walnuts
1/4 cup mayonnaise
2 tablespoons lemon juice
Lettuce leaves

Combine all ingredients except lettuce leaves and mix well. Arrange salad on lettuce leaf. Garnish with additional reserved walnut pieces, if desired.

CHUNKY CHICKEN SALAD

1 cup raw carrot, shredded
1/2 cup Miracle Whip, thinned slightly with cream
1 cup chicken, cooked and diced
1/4 cup minced onion
1 cup diced celery
1 tablespoon pickle relish
1 small can shoestring potatoes or 2 cups sesame sticks

Combine vegetables with dressing and relish. Add chicken and potato sticks or sesame sticks just before serving.

POPCORN SALAD
Serves 6-8

6 cups popped popcorn
1/2 cup green onion, sliced
1 cup celery, diced
3/4 - 1 cup mayonnaise
3/4 cup chopped cooked bacon (reserve some for top)
1 cup grated cheese (reserve some for top)
1/2 cup sliced water chestnuts

In bowl, combine popcorn, sliced onion, diced celery, mayonnaise, bacon, cheese, and water chestnuts. Chill. Top with reserved bacon and grated cheese. Best when used within 3-4 hours.

ARTICHOKE RICE SALAD

6-ounce package long grain and wild rice mix
14-ounce can artichoke hearts, drained and chopped
2-ounce jar chopped pimentos, drained'
3 green onions with tops, chopped
1 cup chopped celery
1/2 cup mayonnaise
1 teaspoon curry powder

Cook rice according to package directions, omitting butter; cool. Add remaining ingredients; mix well. Cover and chill thoroughly.

TASTY MACARONI SALAD

3 cups macaroni
12-ounce can corned beef
2 medium cucumbers, diced
2 medium tomatoes, diced
1 medium carrot, diced
1 cup plus 4 tablespoons mayonnaise
Salt to taste
Celery seed and boiled egg to garnish

Cook macroni; drain. Rinse with hot water. Turn macaroni into mixing bowl. While macaroni is still hot, add corned beef, which has been broken apart and shredded; mix together until corned beef has been thoroughly worked through macaroni. (Macaroni must be hot or corned beef will not mix through properly). Set aside to cool.

Add cucumbers, tomatoes and onion. Add mayonnaise; mix all ingredients together thoroughly. Add salt to taste. Garnish with celery seed and sliced boiled egg.

CHICKEN SALAD

Serves 8-10

4 cups large chunks cooked chicken (white meat)
1 cup drained pineapple chunks
3/4 cup raisins
1 cup mayonnaise
1/4 cup plain, low-fat yogurt
1/2 cup chopped walnuts

In large bowl, mix chicken, pineapple, and raisins. In small bowl, mix mayonnaise and yogurt. Combine the two mixtures and sprinkle walnuts on top. Chill thoroughly before serving.

Could be served in half of pineapple shell, cut lengthwise, for an attractive display.

CHICKEN SALAD HAWAII

1 cup cooked, cubed chicken
1/4 cup diced celery
1/4 cup blanched slivered almonds
1/4 cup chunk pineapple
1/2 teaspoon onion juice
1/2 teaspoon salt
Salad greens

Toss all ingredients together except salad greens. Serve over greens.

Dressing:

2 tablespoons finely chopped candied ginger
1/4 cup chopped nuts
1 teaspoon honey
1 cup sour cream

Mix together and serve over chicken salad.

CRABMEAT SALAD

2 cups cooked shell macaroni
1/2 small jar pimiento peppers, cut up
1 tablespoon diced onion
1/2 cup diced celery
3 hard-cooked eggs, diced
2 sweet pickles, diced
1 cup mayonnaise
1 can crabmeat, cut up

Mix all ingredients together in bowl and chill before serving.

Mrs. W. Gergen, Phoenix, AZ

PICNIC TUNA SALAD

2 pounds potatoes
1 cup tuna fish
1-1/2 cups diced celery
1 teaspoon onion juice
1 clove of garlic
1/2 cup French dressing
1/2 cup mayonnaise
2 tablespoons chopped sweet pickle
1 tablespoon minced parsley
1/2 teaspoon salt

Boil potatoes in their skins. When cool, peel and dice into a large bowl that has been rubbed with a cut clove of garlic. Sprinkle with salt. Add onion juice to French dressing; mix lightly, and let stand in refrigerator for 1 hour. Drain fish and flake into tiny pieces. Combine potatoes, tuna, celery, sweet pickle, and mayonnaise. Sprinkle with minced parsley. Serve very cold. The longer this stands, the better the flavor.

Makes a good main supper dish on a hot summer night.

TURKEY CRANBERRY SALAD

Serves 4-6

1 cup cubed cranberry jelly
1 cup diced turkey
1 cup diced celery
3 tablespoons French dressing
Several lettuce cups
1/4 cup walnut meats.

Lightly toss cranberry jelly, turkey, celery, and French dressing. Place in lettuce cups and sprinkle with walnuts.

Salad DRESSINGS

FRUIT SALAD DRESSING

1/4 cup Karo light corn syrup
1/2 cup sour cream
1/2 cup mayonnaise

Mix sour cream with mayonnaise until smooth. Add Karo syrup and blend well. Spoon over a salad of assorted fresh fruits or canned fruits.

FRENCH DRESSING
Makes 2 cups

1 cup vegetable oil
½ cup sugar
½ cup ketchup
¼ cup vinegar
¼ cup chopped onion
1 teaspoon celery seed
½ teaspoon salt

Combine all ingredients in an electric blender; process until smooth. Cover and chill thoroughly.

FABULOUS ROQUEFORT DRESSING
Makes 1 quart

1 (3-ounce) package Roquefort cheese
2 cups mayonnaise
3 teaspoons chives *or* green onion, finely chopped

1 teaspoon black pepper
1 teaspoon garlic powder
½ teaspoon Worcestershire sauce
1 cup sour cream
½ cup buttermilk

Blend all ingredients, mixing in sour cream and buttermilk last. Chill. If dressing is too thick, thin with additional buttermilk at serving time. We use this recipe as a dip with corn chips and potato chips, as well as salad dressing.

MASON JAR DRESSING

1 can condensed tomato soup
3/4 cup herb salad vinegar
1 teaspoon salt
1/2 teaspoon paprika
1/2 teaspoon pepper
1 teaspoon onion juice
1 tablespoon mustard
1-1/2 cups oil, (salad or olive)
1/2 cup sugar

Combine dry ingredients separately. Combine liquid ingredients separately. Moisten dry ingredients with a little of the liquid, then pour all together into a quart fruit jar and *shake*.

Worcestershire sauce or a little liquid from dill pickles may be added for additional zest.

Always shake well before using.

SUPER SALAD SEASONING MIX

2 cups Parmesan cheese
2 teaspoons salt
1/2 cup sesame seeds
1/2 teaspoon garlic salt
3 tablespoons celery seed
1 tablespoon instant minced onion
2 tablespoons parsley
1/2 teaspoon dill seeds
1/8 cup poppy seeds
2 teaspoons paprika
1/2 teaspoon freshly grated black pepper

Mix all ingredients together well. Use as a sprinkle on salads, baked potatoes, buttered French bread, and rolls. Also good as a garnish for potato and egg salads.

FAMOUS FRUIT-SALAD DRESSING
Makes 2 cups

1 cup sweet cream
½ cup brown sugar
¼ cup vinegar
½ cup granulated sugar
Salt to taste

Beat cream until slightly thickened; add remaining ingredients and mix well. Refrigerate overnight to thicken. Delicious on spinach salad, too!

ONION SALAD DRESSING

Makes 1 cup

1/2 cup finely chopped onion
1/4 cup cider vinegar
1/4 cup sugar
1/2 teaspoon salt
1/2 teaspoon dry mustard
1/4 teaspoon celery seed
1/2 cup oil

Combine all ingredients, except oil, in blender; mix well, stopping as necessary to scrape down sides of container. With blender running, gradually pour in oil, blending until dressing is creamy. Transfer to container with tight-fitting lid and refrigerate before using. Whisk or shake, if dressing separates on standing.

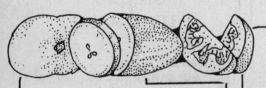

ITALIAN DRESSING MIX POWDER

(One envelope of commercial dressing mix equals this entire recipe)

2 teaspoons onion powder
1 tablespoon white sugar or sugar substitute
1/8 teaspoon black pepper
1/8 teaspoon powdered allspice
1 teaspoon dry minced onions
1 teaspoon dry celery flakes
1/8 teaspoon crushed marjoram leaves
1/4 teaspoon dry oregano, crushed
1 clove garlic peeled, sliced fine or 2 teaspoons bottled minced garlic
1/8 teaspoon paprika
2 squares of soda crackers (1-1/2" x 1-1/2")

Mix all ingredients in blender. Keep covered. Will keep up to 3 months.

To Use: Combine all the above with 1/2 cup vinegar, 2/3 cup cold water and 1/3 cup corn oil. Mix well. Keeps in refrigerator up to 1 month. Shake well before using. Makes 1-1/2 cup prepared dressing.

TANGY LOUIS DRESSING

Makes 4 cups

2 cups mayonnaise
1-1/2 cups chili sauce
1/3 cup minced celery
1/3 cup minced sour pickles
2 tablespoons lemon juice
1 tablespoon Worcestershire sauce
1 teaspoon prepared horseradish

Combine all ingredients, stirring well; chill. Store covered, in refrigerator. Serve over seafood, ham, or salad greens.

NOTE: This recipe may be halved very successfully for smaller quantity.

DILLED YOGURT DRESSING

1 cup non-fat plain yogurt
2 tablespoons vinegar
1/2 small onion
1/2 teaspoon dill seeds
1/4 teaspoon dry mustard
1/4 to 1/2 teaspoon fresh garlic

Combine all the ingredients in blender until smooth. Great topping for salads, vegetables, or dip for crackers or chips.

LOW CALORIE SALAD DRESSING

Makes 1-1/2 cups

1/2 cup cottage cheese
1/2 cup low fat milk
1 teaspoon salt
1 teaspoon paprika
2 tablespoons lemon juice
1 sliver garlic
1/2 green pepper, cut into strips
4 radishes
2 green onions, coarsely cut

Put all ingredients into blender container. Cover; blend on high speed for 10 seconds or until

vegetables are finely chopped. Refrigerate dressing for proper storage.

CREAMY LOW-CAL DRESSING

2 cups of dressing

1/2 cup skim milk
2 tablespoons lemon juice
1 tablespoon vegetable oil
1-1/2 cup low-fat cottage cheese (12 ounce)
1 small onion, chopped
1 cloves garlic, crushed
1/2 teaspoon salt
1/4 teaspoon pepper
1/4 teaspoon paprika

Place all ingredients in blender container in order listed above. Cover and blend on medium speed until smooth, about 1 minute. Cover and refrigerate.

CHILI FLAVORED DRESSING

1/2 teaspoon chili powder
1 tablespoon wine vinegar
2 tablespoons orange juice
3 tablespoons mashed green chilies
1-1/4 cups mayonnaise

Blend chili powder with wine vinegar and orange juice. Then add green chilies and stir into mayonnaise.

VINAIGRETTE DRESSING

Makes 1-1/2 cups

1 cup oil and vinegar dressing
2 tablespoons chopped parsley
1/4 cup finely chopped pickle
2 teaspoons chopped onion
2 teaspoons capers (optional)

Blend above ingredients thoroughly.

CREAMY SALAD DRESSING
Makes 1 pint

1/4 cup sugar
3/4 teaspoon dry mustard
1/2 teaspoon salt
2 tablespoons flour
2 egg yolks or 1 whole egg
1/2 cup vinegar
1/3 cup hot water
1/2 cup cream, whipped

Mix dry ingredients in saucepan. Add beaten egg; stir to blend well. Add vinegar and hot water. Cook on low heat; stir until mixture is thickened. Remove from heat; cool. Fold in whipped cream. Store in covered jar; refrigerate.

THOUSAND ISLAND DRESSING

3 large dill pickles
3 medium onions
3 large green peppers, seeded
1 small can pimientos
5 hard-cooked eggs
1 quart mayonnaise
1 bottle chili sauce

Grind ingredients together and drain well. Clean grinder and grind 5 hard-cooked eggs. Combine all ingredients with 1 quart mayonnaise and one bottle chili sauce. Store in refrigerator until ready to serve.

RANCH SALAD DRESSING
Makes 2-1/4 cups

2 cups plain lowfat yogurt
1/4 cup mayonnaise
1/2 teaspoon garlic powder
1/4 teaspoon monosodium glutamate
1 teaspoon dried minced onion
1/4 teaspoon pepper
1/4 teaspoon paprika
1/2 teaspoon onion powder
1 teaspoon dried parsley flakes
1/4 teaspoon dried dill weed
1/2 teaspoon celery salt

Mix all ingredients together. Refrigerate for 1 hour to blend flavors. Use as dip for raw vegetables or salad dressing.

POPPY SEED SALAD DRESSING

1 small onion, grated
1-1/2 cups sugar
2/3 cup cider vinegar
2 teaspoons dry mustard
1-1/2 teaspoons salt
2 tablespoons poppy seeds
2 cups oil

Blend first six ingredients. With blender still running, pour in oil in a slow but steady stream. Continue to blend until thick and creamy.

An old, but delicious family favorite.

TARRAGON DRESSING
Makes 3/4 cup

1/2 cup vegetable oil
1/4 cup cider vinegar
1-1/2 teaspoons sugar
1 teaspoon tarragon
1/2 teaspoon salt
1/4 teaspoon freshly ground black pepper
Dash liquid hot pepper sauce

Whisk together oil, vinegar, sugar, tarragon, salt, pepper, and hot sauce, until slightly creamy.
Note: Dressing can be made in advance. Shake or whisk before serving.

GARLIC DRESSING

3 cups Miracle Whip
1-1/2 cups salad oil 1/2 cup vinegar (scant) white or wine
2-1/2 tablespoons sugar
1-1/2 teaspoons salt
1-1/2 teaspoons Accent
1 or more cloves garlic
1/3 cup onion
Parsley

Mix all together in blender. Store in covered container in refrigerator. Add blue cheese, if desired. Shake well before serving.

LOW-CAL DRESSING
Makes 1/2 cup

1/2 cup skim milk
1 teaspoon onion juice
1 tablespoon lemon juice
1 tablespoon minced parsley
1 tablespoon minced pimiento

Combine milk with lemon juice and flavoring agents; shake thoroughly in a small jar with tightly fitting lid. More or less lemon juice may be used according to taste.

Use at once; serve immediately. Great dressing for all types of salads.

TRUE RUSSIAN DRESSING
Makes 3 cups

2 cups mayonnaise
2/3 cup chili sauce
2/3 cup chopped dill pickles
1/2 teaspoon seasoned salt
1 tablespoon minced onion
2 tablespoons sugar

Blend all ingredients in a bowl and chill.

CREAMY BLUE CHEESE DRESSING
Makes 2 cups

6 ounces crumbled blue cheese
1 cup real mayonnaise
3/4 cup buttermilk
1/4 teaspoon onion powder
1/4 teaspoon garlic powder

Combine all ingredients; mix until well blended and creamy. Serve over tossed green salad.

Savory Cooking
INDEX

INDEX

INDEX